IMAGES
of America

INTERCOURSE, LEACOCK, PARADISE, AND SALISBURY

BarbieDoll,
You are one of the
most amazing women I
know. Thank you for your
friendship - in the past,
present & future.
You've always been
there for me & always
make me laugh -
Heres to the
future!!
Michele

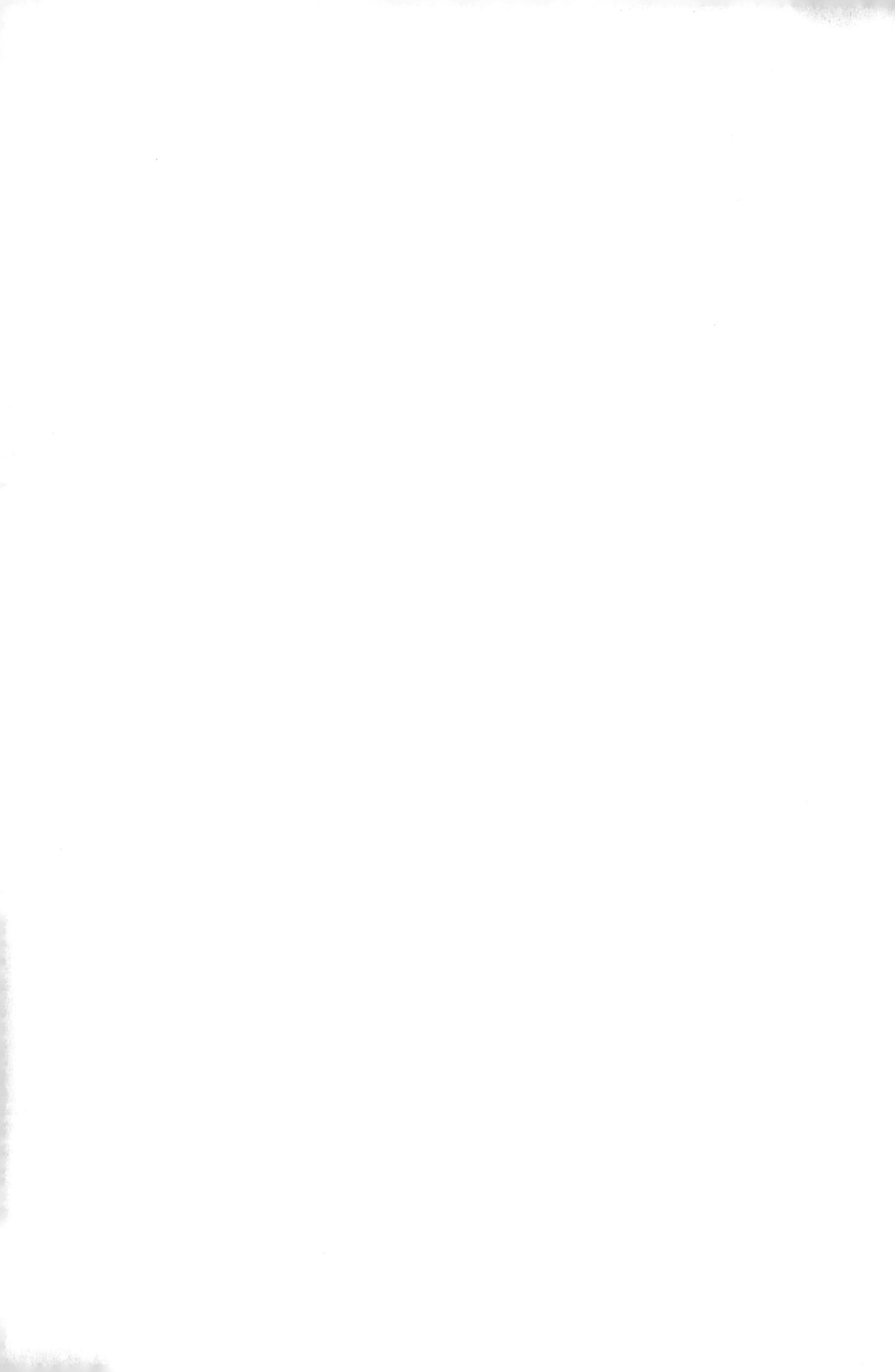

IMAGES
of America

INTERCOURSE, LEACOCK, PARADISE, AND SALISBURY

Michele Maria Paiva

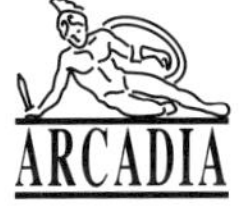

Copyright © 2005 by Michele Maria Paiva
ISBN 0-7385-3837-X

Published by Arcadia Publishing
Charleston SC, Chicago IL, Portsmouth NH, San Francisco CA

Printed in Great Britain

Library of Congress Catalog Card Number: 2005924552

For all general information contact Arcadia Publishing at:
Telephone 843-853-2070
Fax 843-853-0044
E-mail sales@arcadiapublishing.com
For customer service and orders:
Toll-Free 1-888-313-2665

Visit us on the Internet at http://www.arcadiapublishing.com

CONTENTS

ACKNOWLEDGMENTS

Since my childhood, living locally in Chester County, I have visited the Lancaster area often, with many stops in the towns of Intercourse, Leacock, Paradise, and Salisbury through the years. Although I do not reside here, I feel the area is a part of my own culture since it was so prevalent in my youth. My parents put much importance upon visiting their friends in the area, as well as frequenting shops and businesses along the way. They held much esteem for the people and places of the region, and they instilled this respect within my own ideals as well. Time went on. My sisters moved to Intercourse and opened a shop there—Artisan Village. My sister Karen also found her soul touched, and she tapped into her talents and skills, turning out numerous folk paintings and prints celebrating the area and its people.

During this time, I developed a new sense of admiration for the area. Many dusk evenings were spent in my sister's farmhouse kitchen around a table made by a local artisan, sipping coffee and talking about the buzz of the area, the new friendships made, and the new culture that they were learning and living.

I owe much of this inspiration to my sisters, Karen A. Paiva and Martha M. Montes, and to all of the local people who touched their lives directly (and my life indirectly) through their stories.

Many of the photographs you see in this book were borrowed from the Cocalico Historical Society. These fine people were not only helpful in this endeavor to preserve history, but they went beyond the call of duty to do so. Readers are encouraged to look into the Cocalico Historical Society for even more information on the area.

Thanks go the countless businesses that spent time talking to me about the area. Their stories helped me to gain a better understanding of their own plight from the beginning to the present.

I owe a lot to my friends Kathy and Jim Makris, Barbie Doll Todd, Karen Mortzfield, and Pat Bria. They all kept me from becoming a hermit during this project and got me out to see the sun once in a while—and also kept the laugh quotient quite high with phone calls and e-mails.

It goes without saying that my family was invaluable during the composition of this book. My husband exercised undying support throughout this entire endeavor. My children, Alexandria and Nicholas, have been amazing. Always my sidekicks when I visited the area for research, they have been instrumental in allowing me to see sights through their eyes with newfound wonder.

I extend my sincere thanks to Erin Loftus, my editor, for all that she did. She always remained cool and collected (at least in front of me) with deadlines, some upheavals, and my endless questions and e-mails to her.

Author and historian Bruce Mowday, my mentor from long ago and now a dear friend, has helped tremendously by providing encouragement and support throughout every stage of this book—and life!

I would like to pay homage to the Pequea Valley Public Library staff for their support of this project and to the director of the Pequea Valley Public Library, Margaret Perella, who has been an integral component of the library since 1975. I extend a very heartfelt thank-you for guiding me and supporting my efforts. A portion of the proceeds of the sale of this book (ongoing) will be donated to the library as a continual thank-you.

INTRODUCTION

Sometimes called Amish Country, parts of Lancaster County and surrounding counties are home to a region that is rich in culture, religion, business, and industry. The area is also an integral part of the nation's history. Although the region does boast one of the largest Amish populations in the entire country, there are many cultures that embrace the land. Early immigrants include the Swiss, Mennonites, English, German, and Dutch, just to name a few. Ethnic and religious cultures coexist in the region peacefully and respectfully—Quakers among the Mennonites, and the Amish among the Baptist and Catholics.

In researching the area, I did not want to focus on only prominent families, individuals, cultural groups, collections, or businesses, as is often the case in some preservation. By spotlighting only a select few, a shadow can easily be cast upon many. Instead, I wanted to portray to the reader a wider breadth of what the region holds historically.

It is more important historically to embrace where the roots of the communities originated, why they found local foundation so ideal, and how they planted themselves and flourished through the years. Through research, one of the most interesting documents I found is one that would not reproduce well, per its age and general frail condition. It was first printed in 1868 as a governmental booklet. The unique fact is that the obvious stress of government in the past in this region was not solely about laws and policies, but ethics. Written on the first page of the book is "Principles of Moral Philosophy Illustrated & Manual of Useful Knowledge." Under this, in italics, appears *"Law of Nature, National law, Municipal Law, Criminal Law, Moral Law, Government, The Making of Laws, The Ten Commandments, Religion, Manners, Notices, Facts and Opinions, Connected with the Acquisition of Knowledge."*

The paragraph in the book under the heading of civil government reads, "The name of the Commonwealth (of Pennsylvania) should be pronounced with reverence. In its ordinary acceptation and definition it means union of forces for the public good." Another excerpt explains what a law is: "It requires that man should live honestly, should hurt nobody, and render every man his due."

These are just but a few of the high moral and ethical principles that this region has been built upon, and these are the principles upon which the area still rests its foundation.

For tourists, Paradise, Intercourse, Bird in Hand, Blue Ball, and surrounding towns usually strike a humorous chord because of their distinctive names. One of the most popular towns (or villages) that is wildly popular for its name, Intercourse, has a mysterious and refuted beginning. It is said that the word came from the early races that were held on Old Philadelphia Pike; folks would say that they were entering the race course, which became "enter course," which evolved into Intercourse. Another version states that it is simply the old way of saying "to mix, to commune."

A few of the towns and villages in the region are rumored to have been given their names from the taverns that were found along the old roads. Other towns may have been named for what the area looked like or, as is the case with many older towns, for the people involved in the underpinning of the towns.

Regardless of the origin of their names, Intercourse and the surrounding towns of Leacock, Paradise, Salisbury, and the entire Pequea Valley demonstrate an unyielding connection to Lancaster County, and they are extremely rich and quite influential in history.

The entire area was actually once the combined area of Chester and Lancaster Counties, and it was referred to often as Conestoga Township. Cocalico Township was later established in the area. Cocalico is a unique Native American word that means "snake den." Today these areas have very strict boundaries. Long ago, however, land boundaries were a bit more liberal, and often land was still being staked by owners.

The Pequea Valley was an important area, as it housed the trading roads that ran south to New Castle, Delaware, through bustling Philadelphia. Additionally, those very places, those very roads, lead to and beyond the city of Lancaster, a thriving city even in that era.

Although I was in love with this area for years, visiting the region from my childhood to adulthood, and I now live close by in Chester County, I never really knew about the history until it was unfolded upon my research.

The photographs that I found and the people I met in researching the photographs all translated into a visual story that simply cannot be told with words. It is impossible to put on paper some of the emotions and action that are actually preserved within the photographs. As a writer by profession and passion, I would like to think I could convey the stories on paper, but after looking at them I know that I could never do them complete justice simply with pen and ink.

These preservations of history are simply too cavernous to simplify with just a few words. My captions help with the story, but the important elements are the photographs themselves. It is within the photographs that you will truly garner your own emotion and experience.

Enjoy this picturesque tour of the people and places found within the perimeters of this scenic nucleus of history. Known today for its beauty and tourism; may you glean admiration for one of William Penn's original territories, the birthplace of the Conestoga wagon, and the rich heritage that accompanies the region.

One

People and Cultures

Among some of the early immigrants to this area were the German, Dutch, English, and the Swiss. Most of the buildings were built in the theme of familiar European styles, such as many of the log structures.

Most visitors to this area are in awe of the Amish culture. It is documented that the first large groups of Amish immigrated to this region in the early 1700s. Although the Amish do not demand that their children stay within the church and culture, it is thought that at least 80 percent of the family is retained through their own will; thus, the Amish culture continues to grow, partially due to their large family sizes. Families often have more than six children per family.

All Amish families do not share the exact same beliefs, as there are many orders within the Amish culture. Two examples of this are the New Order and the Old Order. The churches within each culture or religion operate differently, as they each have regulations to which they are held in regard to their conduct. Although some are more conservative than others, the English consider all Amish cultures to be quite conservative in comparison.

The Mennonites are another prominent presence in the area. Tourists sometimes confuse Mennonites and the Amish. They often appear very similar in dress and in the way that they conservatively carry themselves. Though they have some similarities, they are not the same at all. Mennonites evolved from a group called the Anabaptists, who rebaptize adults. A Dutch priest by the name of Menno Simons led a group of believers and became quite prominent in Holland, which is where the name Mennonites is said to be derived from. Mennonites have a strong belief in the written scripture and focus on peace and fairness, embracing simplicity within life.

Quakers are also a prominent and important religious culture in the history of the area. William Penn, a Quaker himself, was a founding father in the region of Intercourse and the surrounding areas. Attempting to explain what it means to be Quaker can be challenging, as there are many varying orders of Quakers. While many religions or cultures have definite rules, policies, or beliefs to abide by, the Quakers as a whole prefer that each individual member search for their own beliefs within a liberal, but very connected, religious base.

As you can see, the cultures of the past were very religion-oriented, as they are today. It is partly this strong sense of spirituality that lends itself to steadfast community.

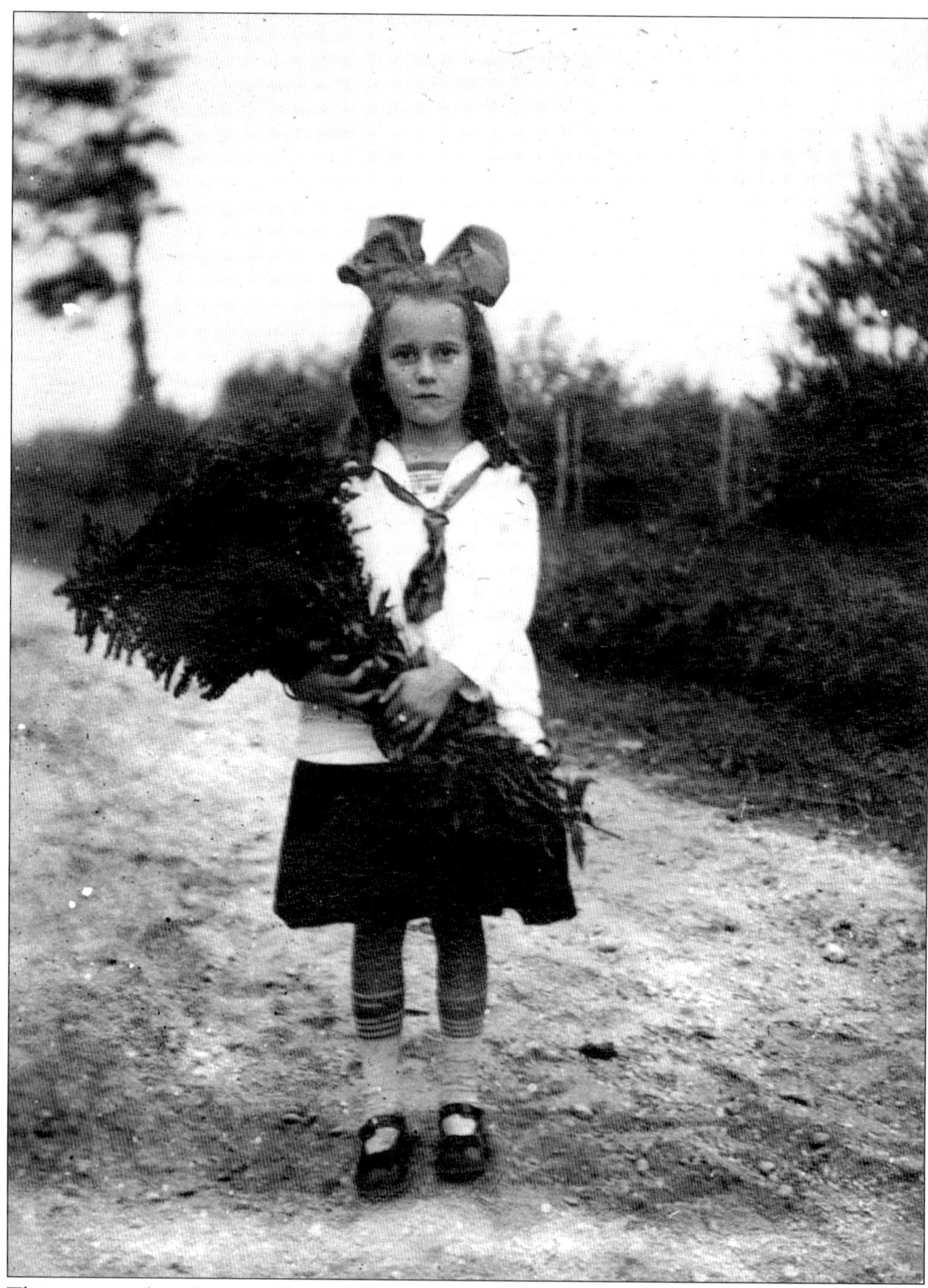

This young girl, perhaps age 9 or 10, walks with an armful of plants along a dirt road or down a long dirt driveway. Her fine clothes and ring lead one to believe she is from a wealthy family or is dressed in her Sunday best.

An unidentified child walks to or from what appears to be an outhouse to the right of the home. Outhouses were very common before there was running water in the area, and many homes today still use outhouses because they choose, per their religion, to not have running water.

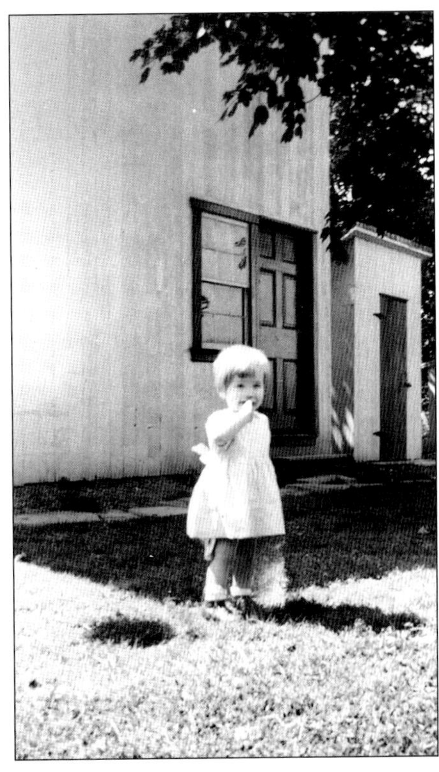

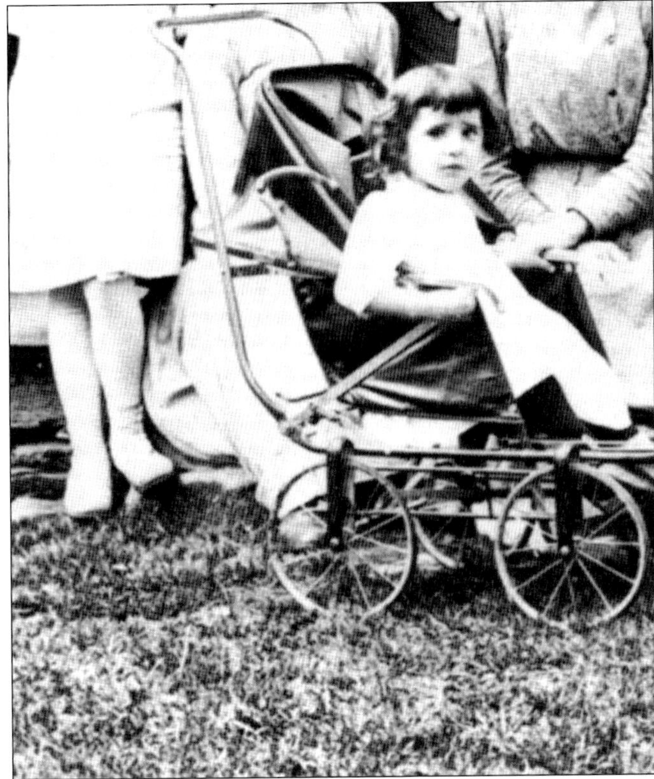

Though not very happy, but at least looking at the camera, this toddler sits in a carriage. Notice that the carriage seems to have metal wheels.

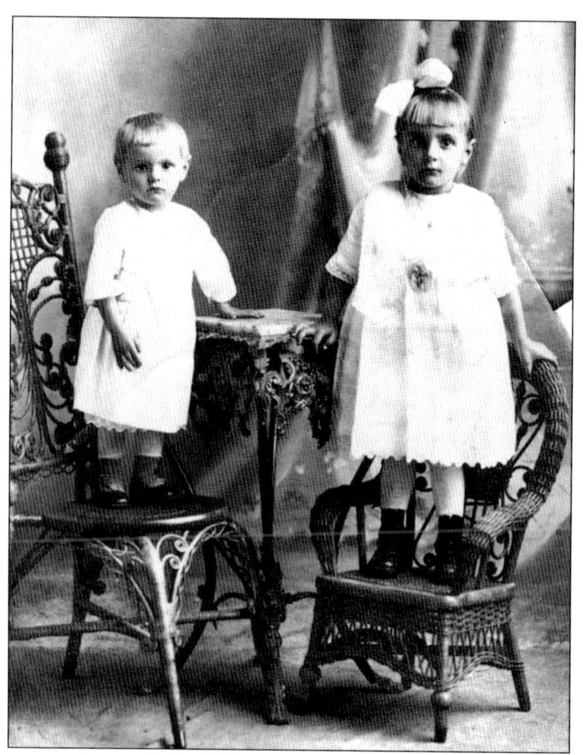

According to the back of the photograph, this picture was taken in 1907. It seems that it was customary for children to stand on chairs for photographs at this time. Both the boy and the young girl appear to be holding on to the table and chair for dear life.

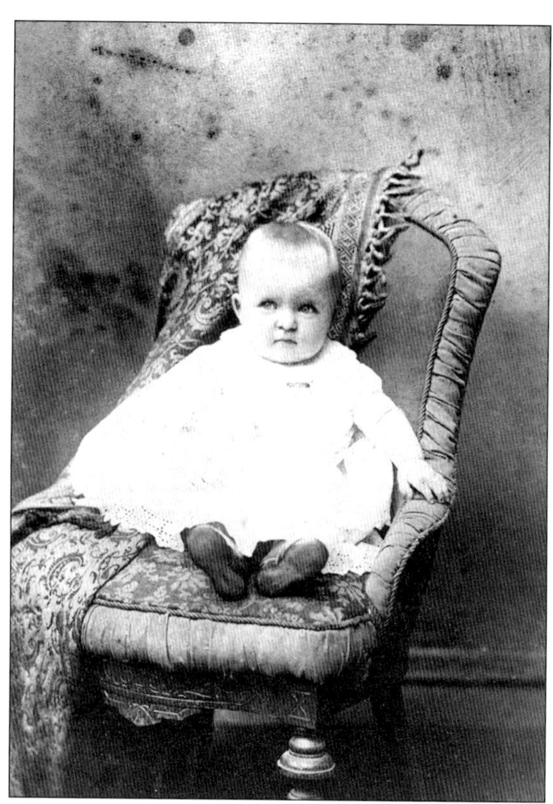

Martin Herr is shown here as a baby between 1905 and 1910. He does not look happy to be having his photograph taken.

This young man of about four years old is dressed to the nines. Notice his bow, very fine woven pants, and matching hat. His boots, however, give him away, as they are worn. Most of the wealthy individuals of the early 1900s had dress shoes for outings and photographs.

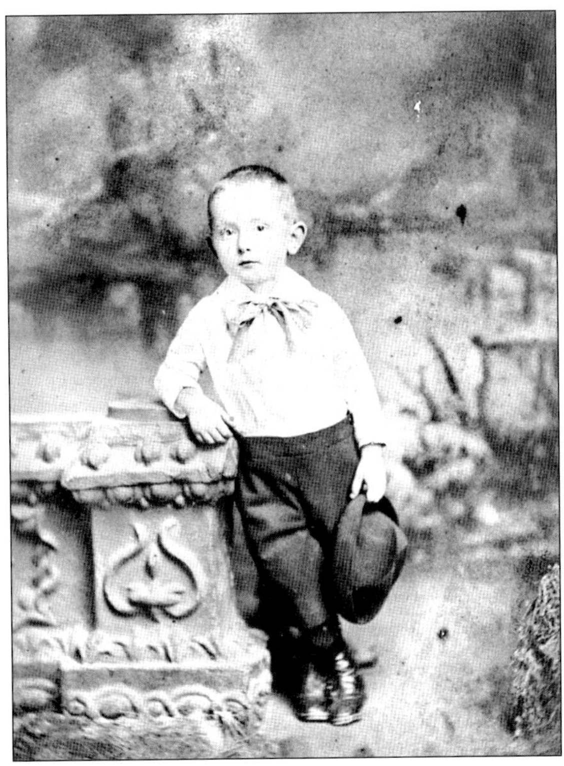

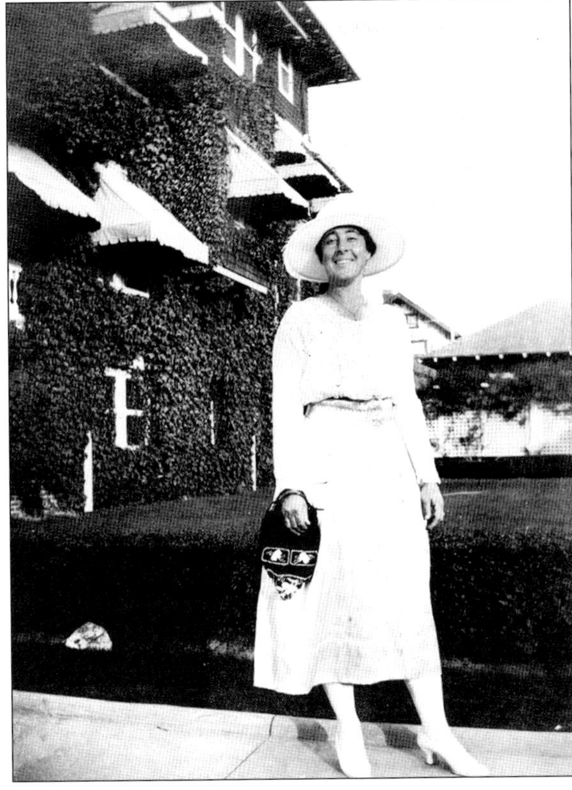

An unidentified woman poses with verve in August 1919. Notice the intricate beading on the purse she is holding.

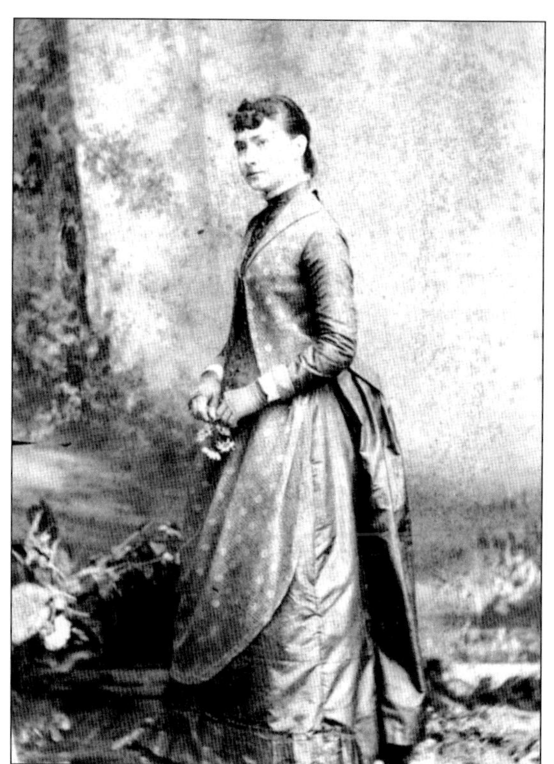

This woman is dressed in very elegant Victorian-style attire. The back of this 1888 photograph reads, "Compliments of Your Loving Sister." Given the formality of her writing in ink and the attire, one might assume that this is an educated or well-to-do woman of the era.

These folks seem to look at the camera as if to say, "Get this over with." More than likely, they are on their way to church or a family gathering, as the photograph is dated December 25, 1935. They may be farmers, as they are posing in front of a barn.

Notice the simplicity of this area couple, from their dress and shoes to their home. The religious photograph in the background was and still is typical for this region.

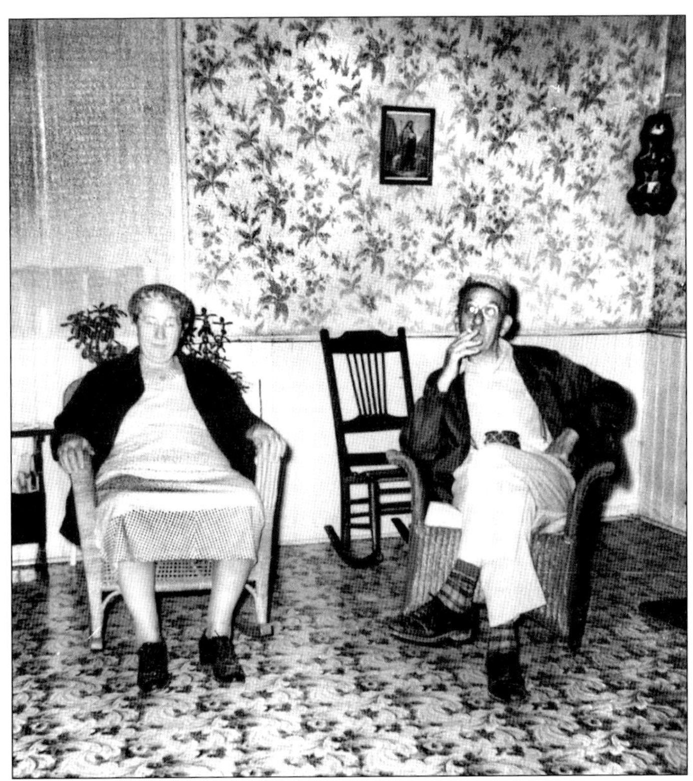

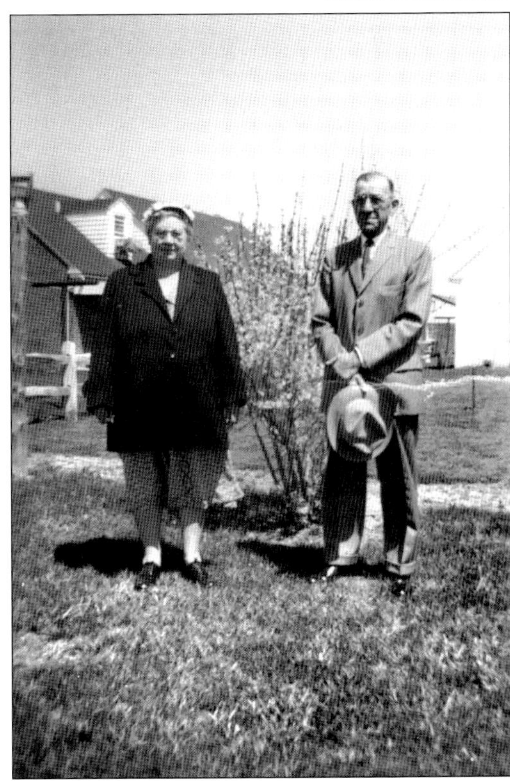

This photograph may have been taken on the way to church or a special event. Given the type of homes in the background as well as the couple's manner of dress, the picture probably dates from the late 1940s or early 1950s.

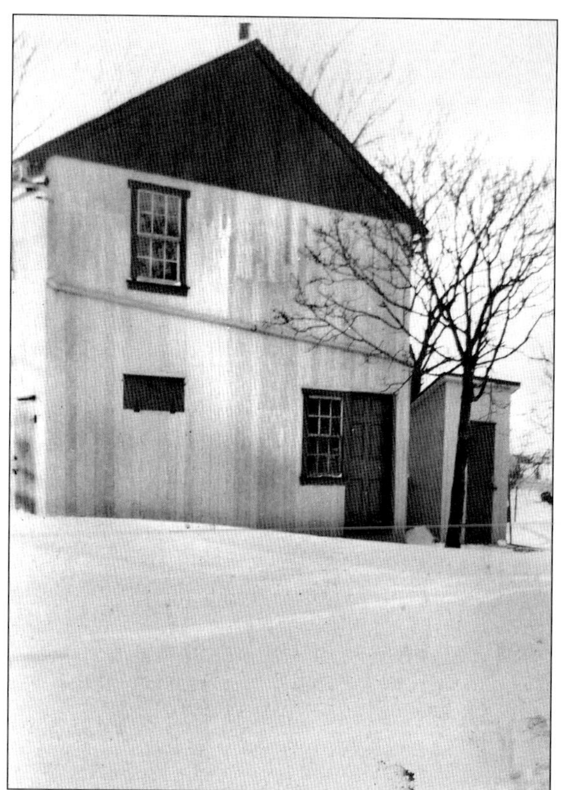

A snow-covered home, which also appears on page 11, is shown here with the outhouse.

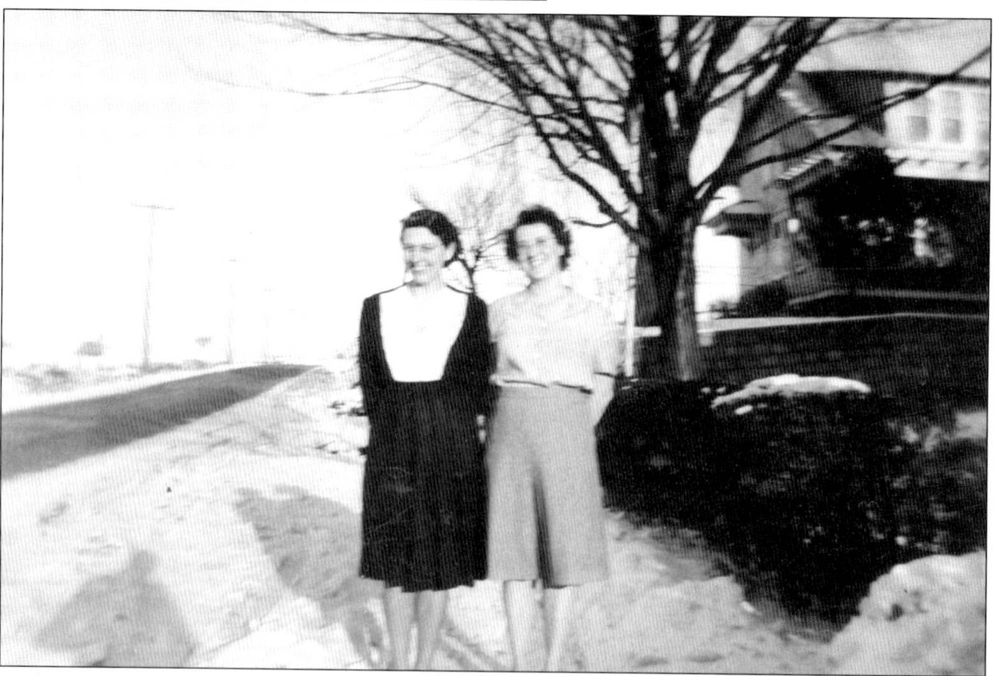

At first glance, this photograph seems to be a simple portrait of two women posing after a snowfall. A closer inspection reveals the shadow of the photographer to the lower left. Since the photographer seems to be using a standing camera, this image probably dates from the 1940s.

The formality of this photograph cannot hide that this man seems to be uneasy. His hands are clenched, and though it was common during this time not to smile in a photograph, he appears angry. The woman, who is also unidentified, seems to be hiding something behind her back.

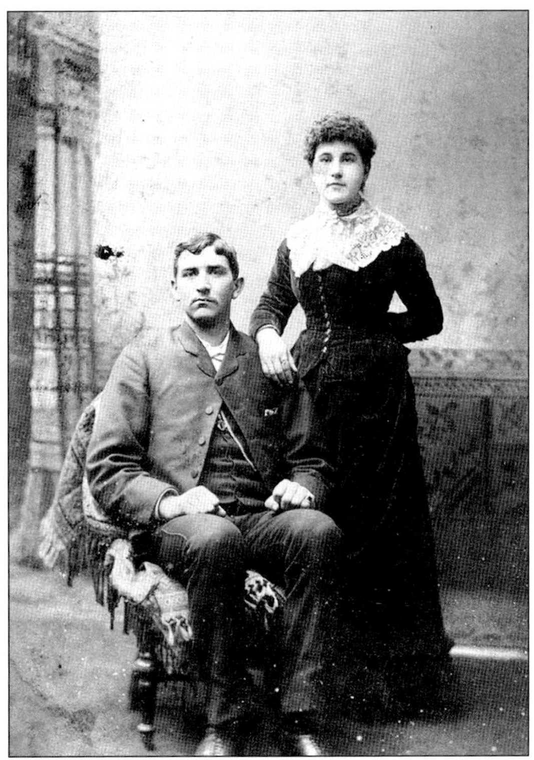

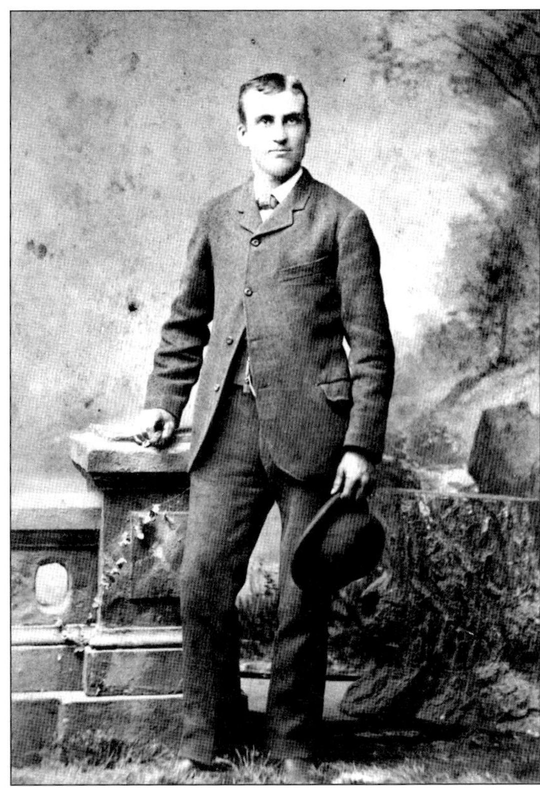

Although the men in both of these photographs have only the top buttons done on their jackets, this particular man seems a little bit sloppier, or perhaps, for the era, he was stylish. Notice that the entire outfit is woven of the same fabric and probably color, including the hat. His hands do not look smooth, indicating that Isaac Cosletter was a hardworking man who worked with his hands.

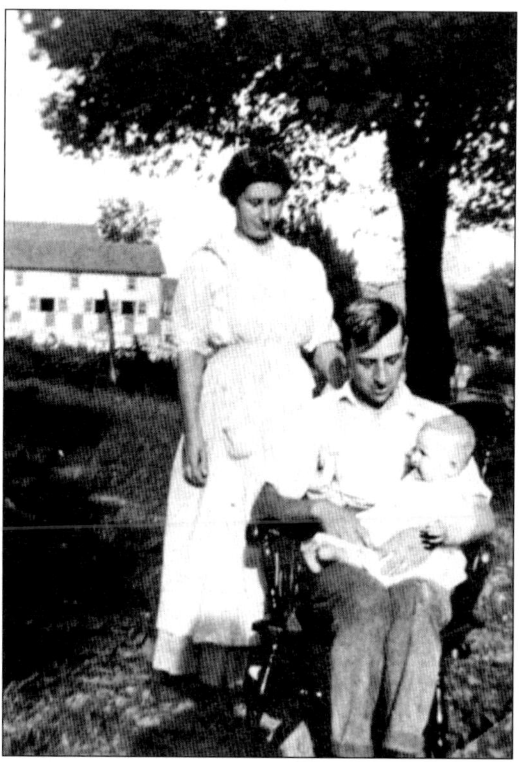

This farming family was photographed c. 1940. The chair that the man is sitting on appears to be a kitchen or living room chair that was brought outdoors for the photograph. The photographer's shadow can be seen toward the bottom of the woman's dress.

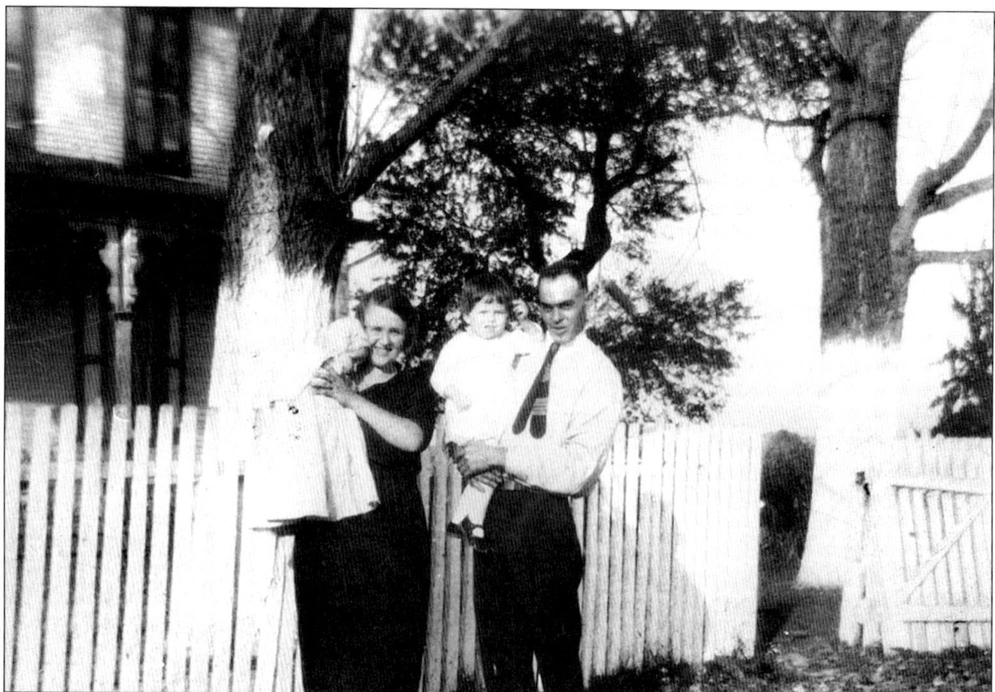

This family photograph was taken in the late 1930s. The white picket fence in the background is barely attached, and the home seen on the far left of the photograph looks as though it could also use some repair.

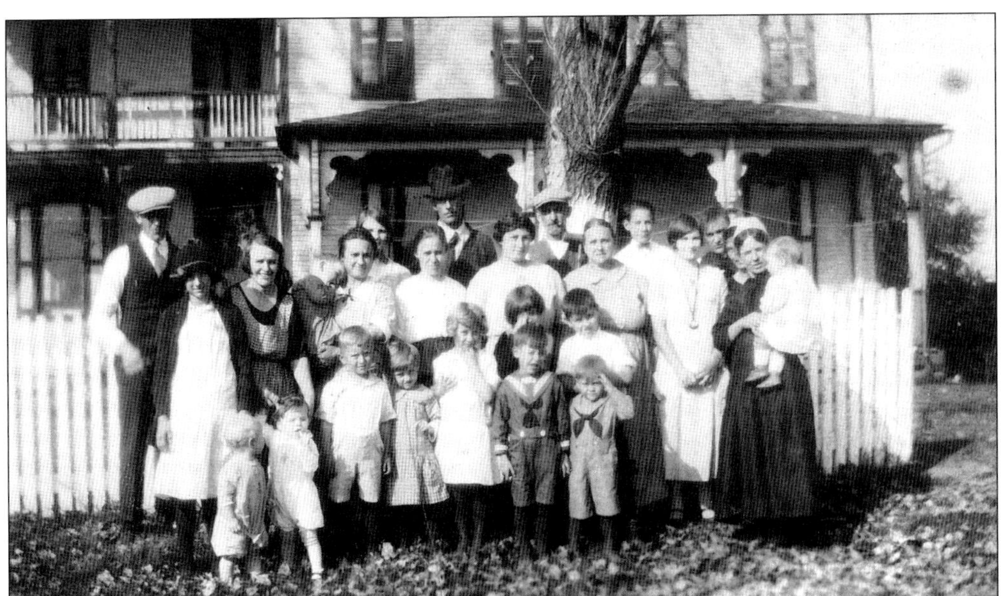

This is a photograph of an unidentified family gathering. The men have not taken off their hats, a faux pas even in those days. Some of the family looks as if they may be Mennonites.

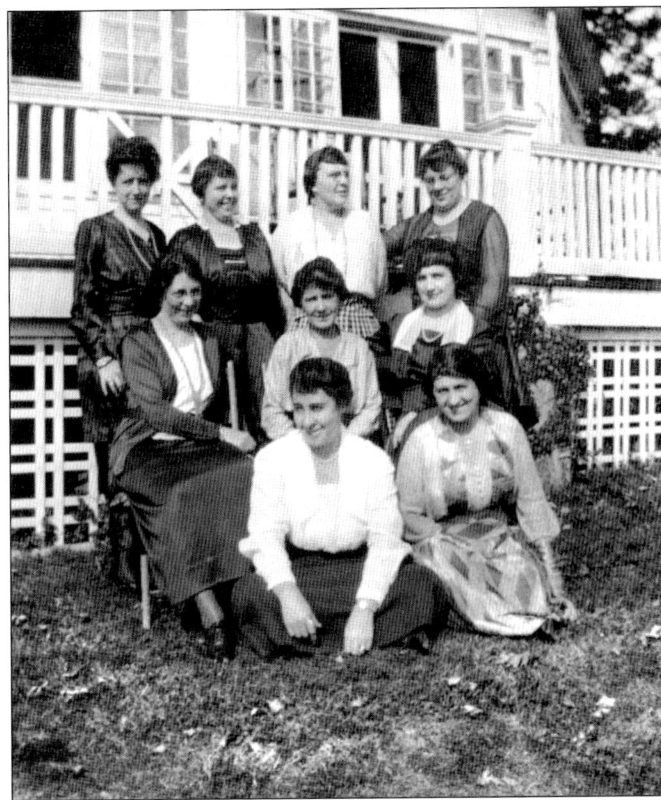

This photograph of a group of unidentified women was taken in 1919. They appear to be either middle or upper class, considering their hairstyles, clothing choices, and the very well appointed home in the background.

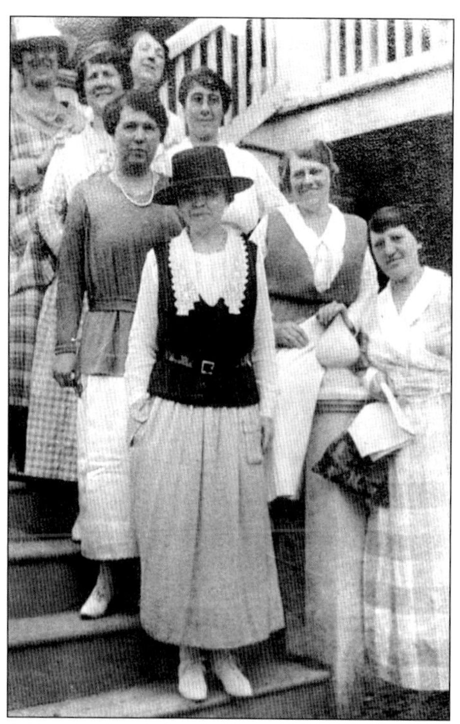

These eight women, photographed in 1917, seem to be on their way to somewhere important. From what is visible, all are wearing white lace-up shoes and white stockings.

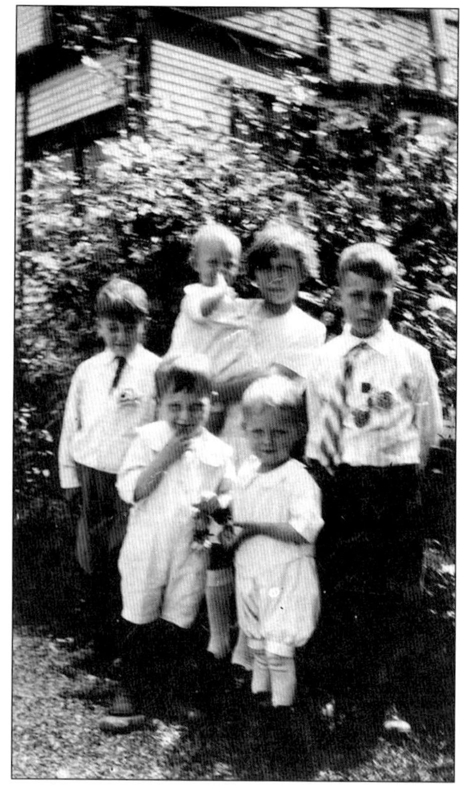

Pictured here is a group of unidentified children. Notice that the boy on the right in the back row has all but pulled off his tie.

This Mennonite girl is dressed in traditional historical garb. Today, many Mennonites dress very similarly, as styles need not change much when attempting to maintain the simplicity of life. Notice that her lap is wrinkled quite a bit, as if she was sitting on the side waiting for her turn to get photographed.

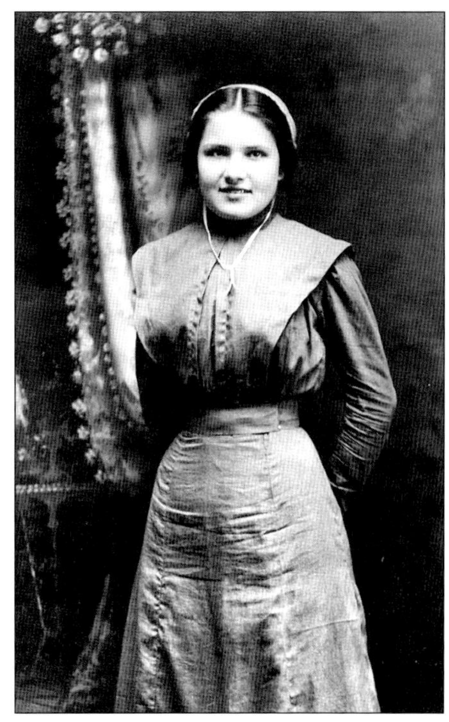

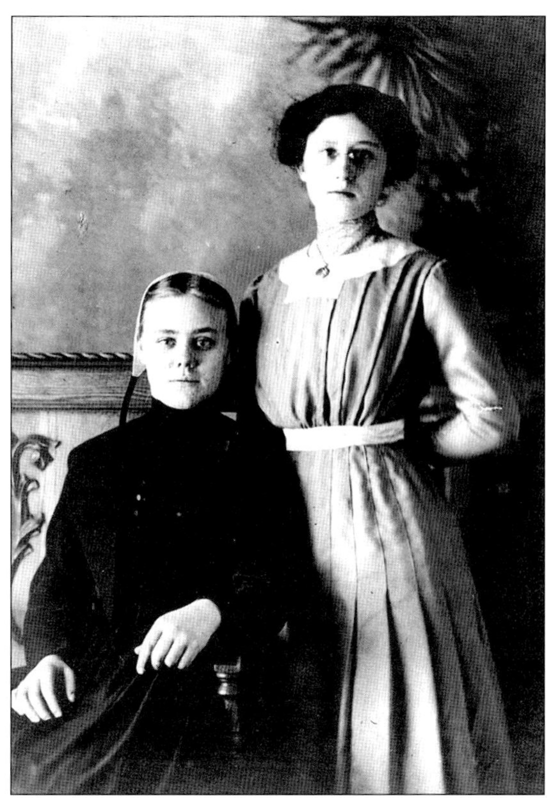

The women in this photograph appear to be Mennonite. The woman is dressed in Mennonite attire; however, the woman standing does not appear to be wearing strict Mennonite clothing for that era. The photograph was probably taken between 1905 and 1920.

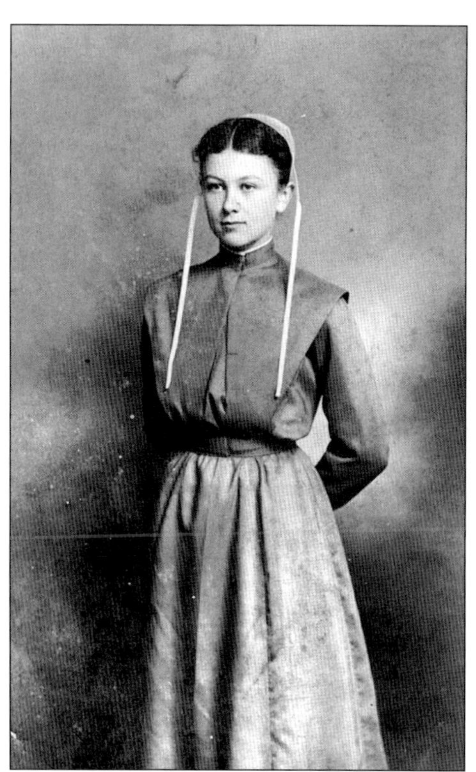

Pictured here is a Mennonite girl of about 17. In accordance with Mennonite traditions, she was likely married soon after this photograph was taken, if she was not already married.

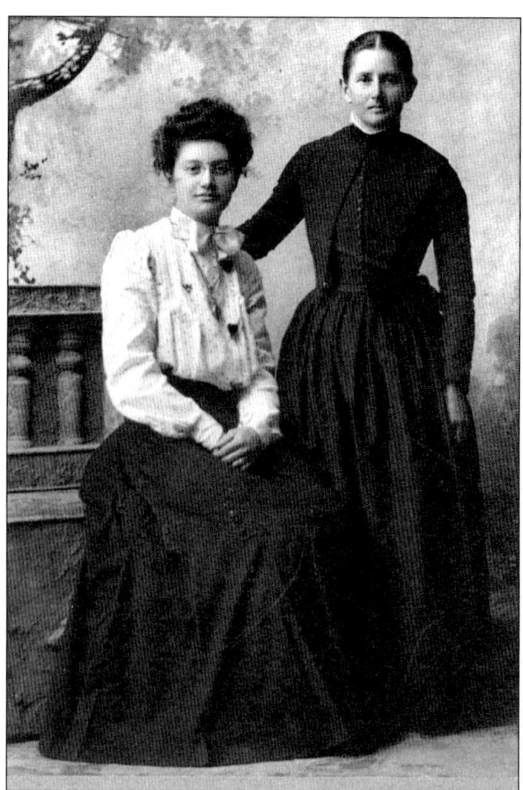

This photograph shows an unidentified Mennonite woman standing beside a woman who is perhaps her lady of the house, or boss.

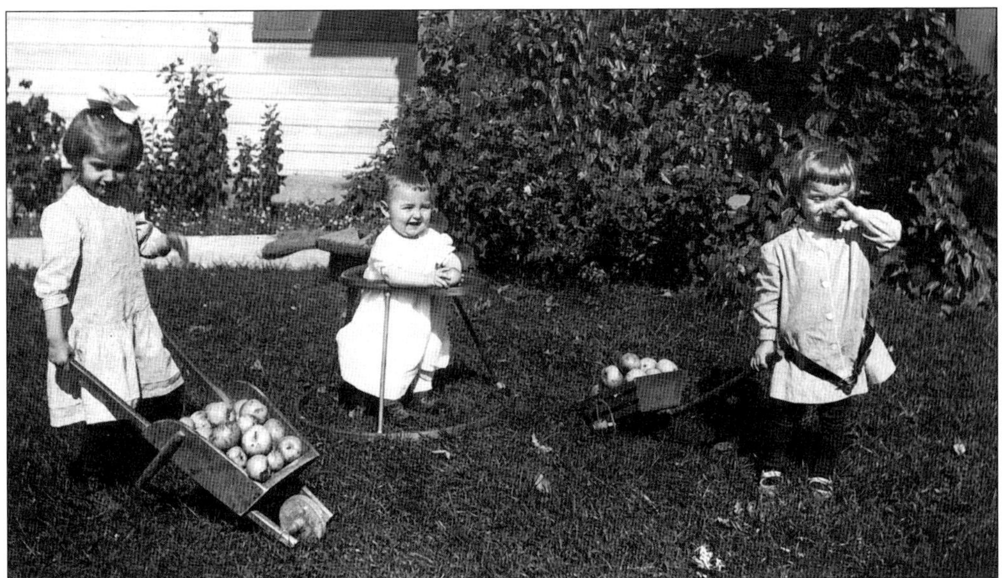

This interesting photograph is a rare spotlight of infants and toddlers in action. The unidentified children are outside enjoying a warm day. Notice that the walker has few safety features.

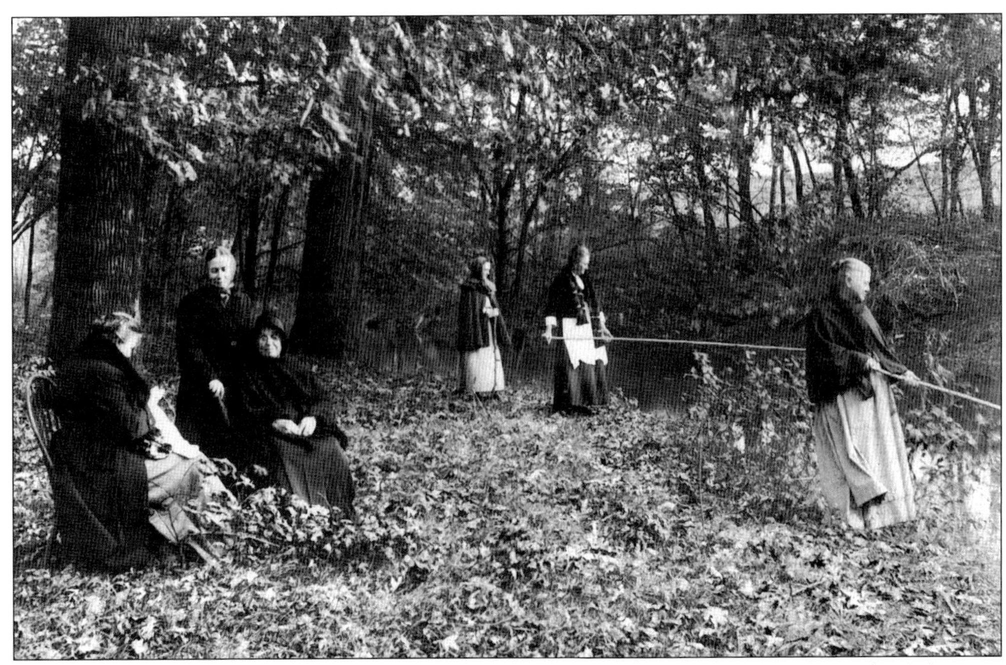

These women, likely Mennonites, are enjoying a late fall outing. They appear to be fishing or pulling something out of the water.

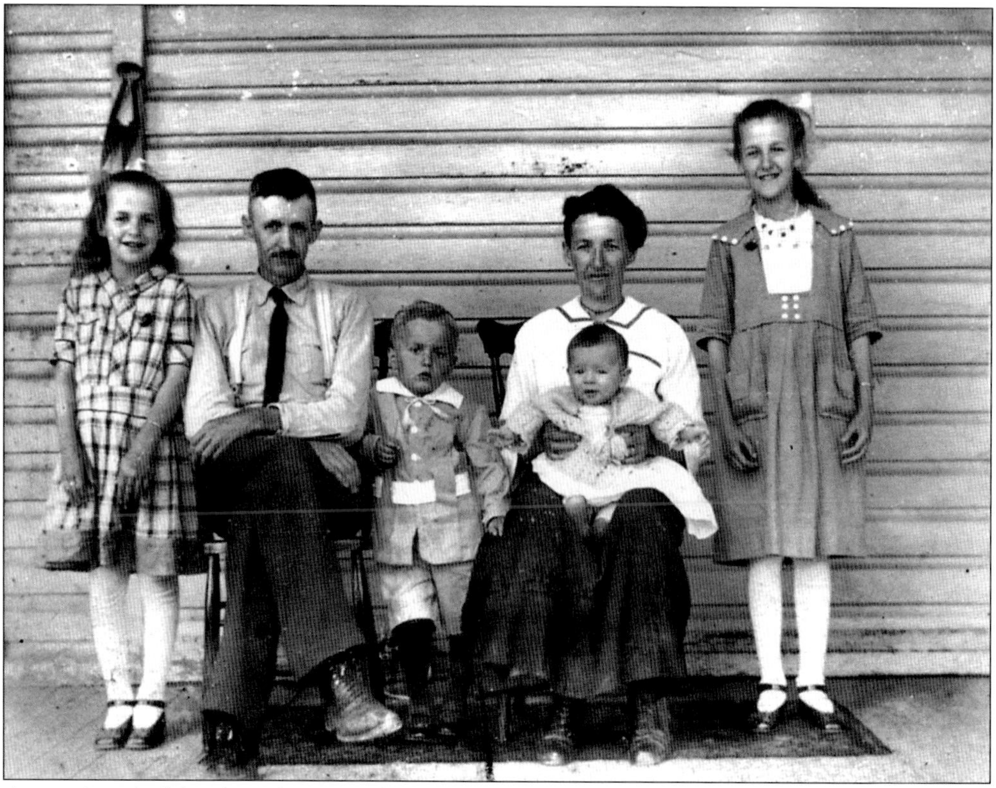

An unidentified family is shown in this photograph from the 1930s.

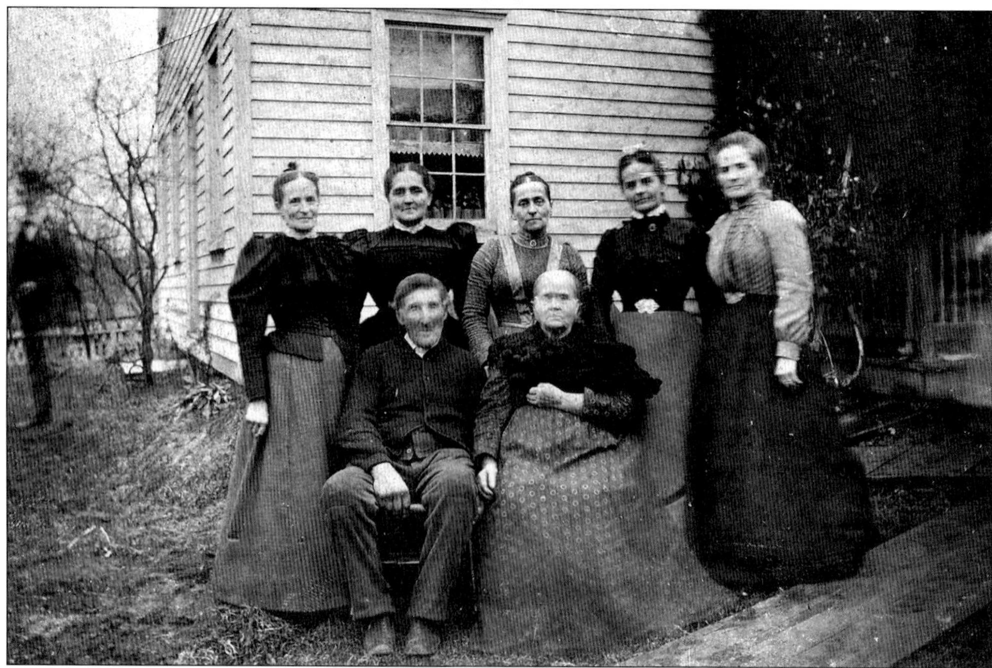

This photograph, taken between 1905 and 1920, very interestingly captures this family. The two seated individuals are likely parents or a close aunt and uncle.

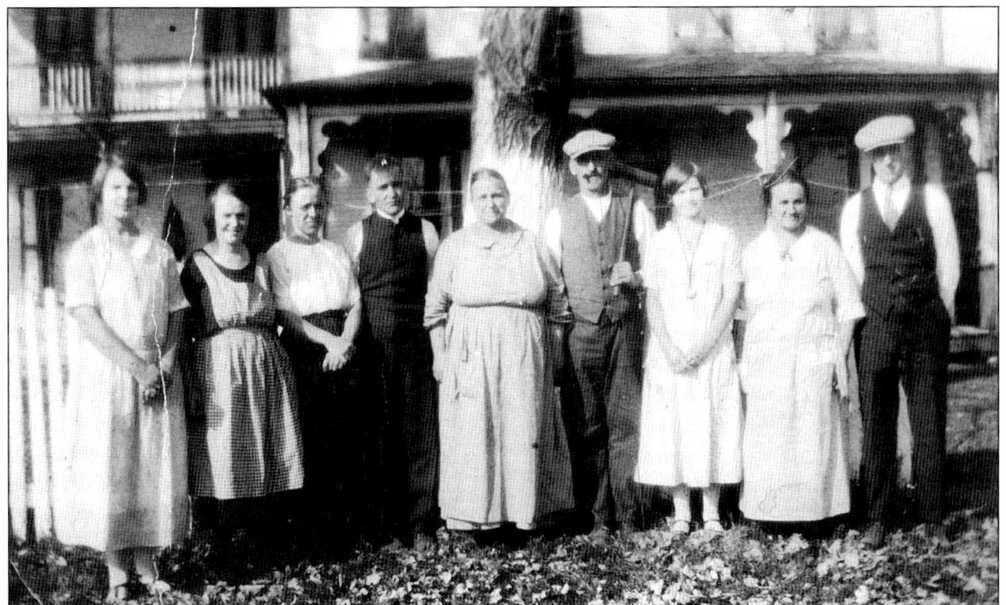

The people in this photograph appear to be the same unidentified family that appears on page 19. Photographs of family outings were quite popular. The men have again chosen to keep their hats on for the photograph, which was not common in this time.

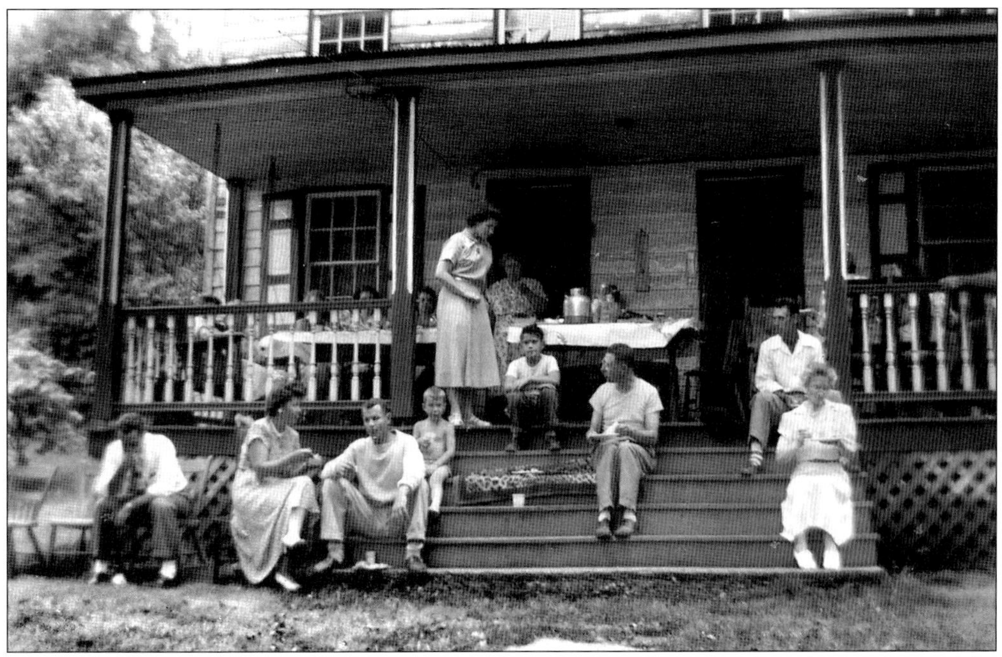

A common gathering place, the trusted front porch, was a popular spot for families in the past and present. This family seems to be in motion and half unaware that a photograph is being taken.

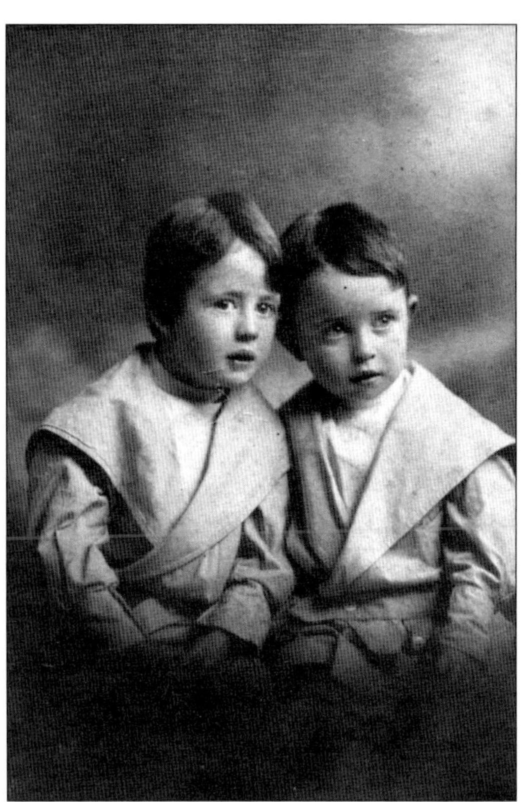

Two unidentified young boys sit for a formal portrait.

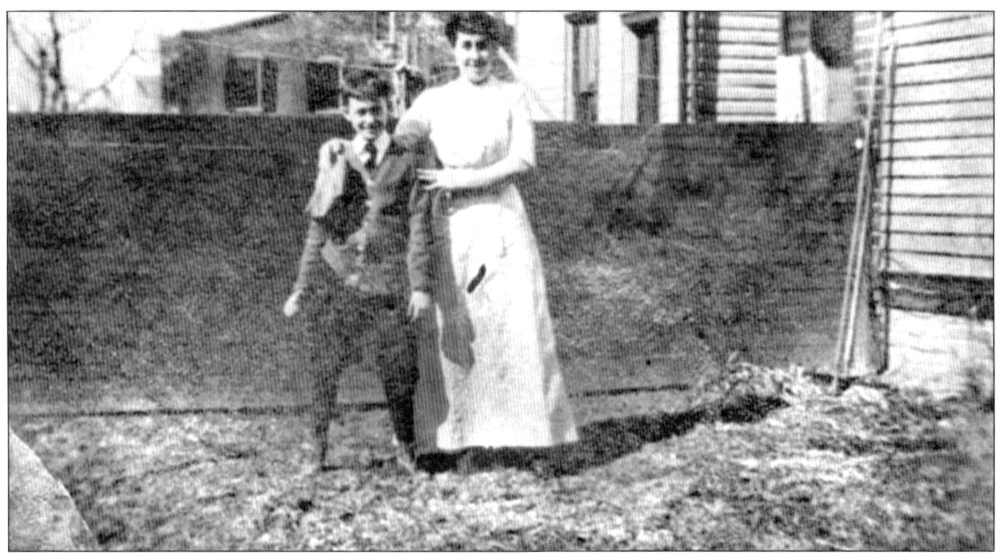

This is possibly a son and mother, or a nephew and aunt, or perhaps even a family friend with a neighbor boy. Both are unidentified, but the photograph is dated 1919.

This woman poses in front of a car, possibly her own, although during the 1940s and 1950s, most vehicles were owned by men. The cat, however, does appear to be hers!

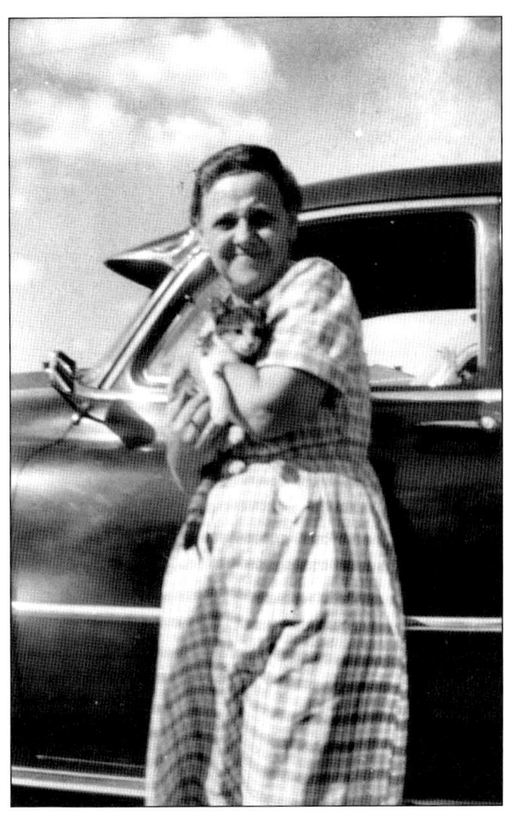

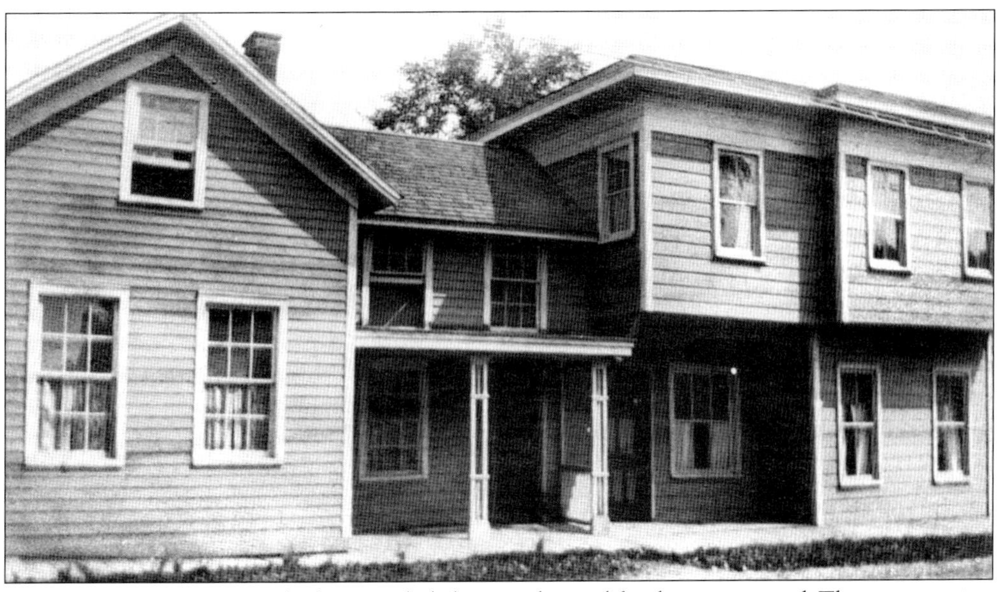

This home was built in a style that was slightly untraditional for this time period. The construction still fits in with the simplistic design popular in the outer Lancaster area during the foundation of the communities.

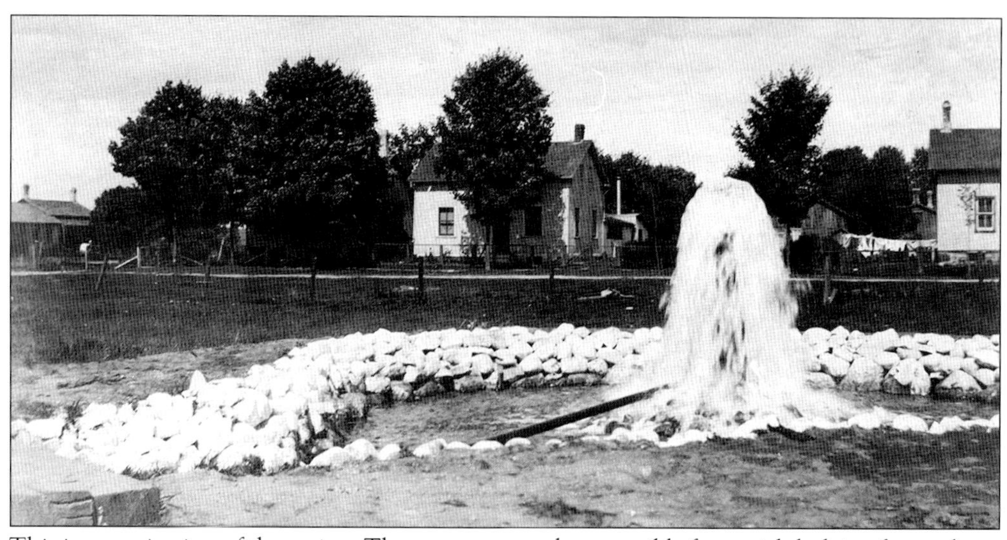

This is a scenic view of the region. The area seems to be a possible farm with lodging for workers, or simply a rustic road with very modest homes.

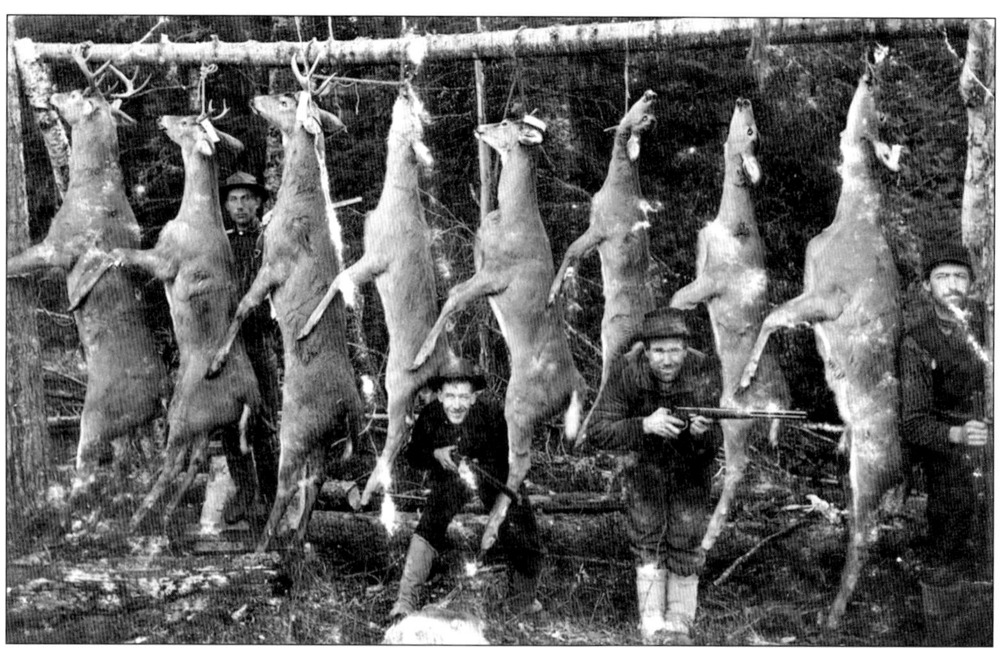

The four hunters seem to be yucking it up in this *c.* 1915 photograph. They may be in a grand mood because they have caught eight deer, a few with impressive racks.

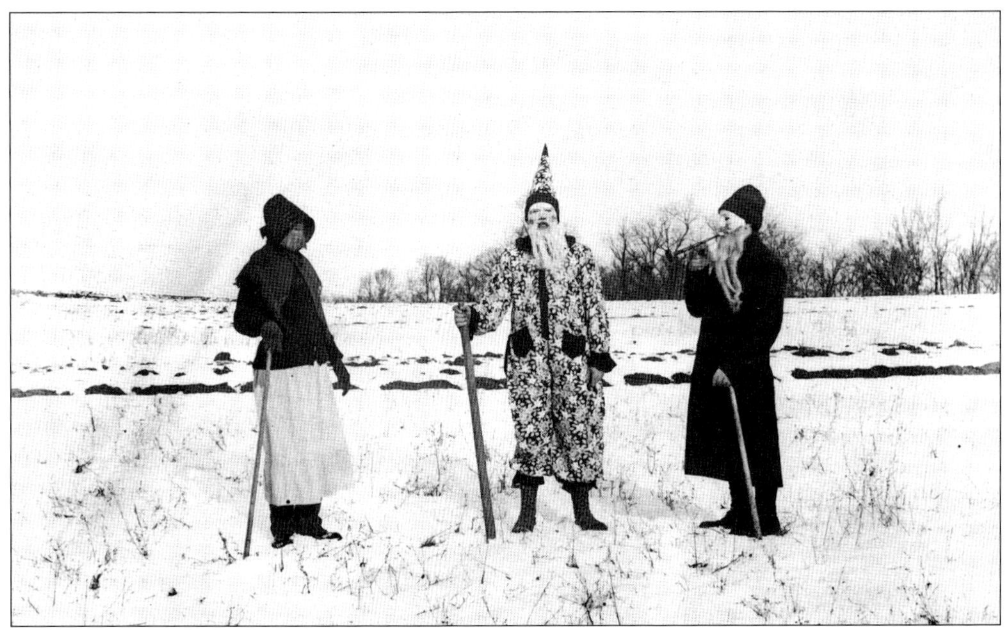

An unidentified Santa Claus and friends are the unique subjects of this photograph. In the area's humble beginnings, many of the German and Dutch still had their traditions of a long-bearded Santa who visited with helpers. This is a dramatization of that very tradition, captured on film c. 1910.

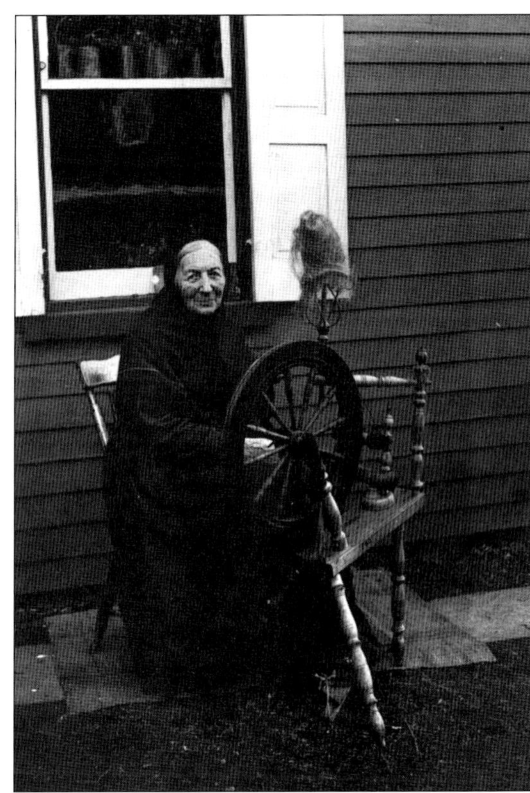

A typical sight for the region, a woman poses with a spinning wheel. She appears to be Mennonite, based upon her attire. Notice the fiber on the top of the wheel that she is spinning.

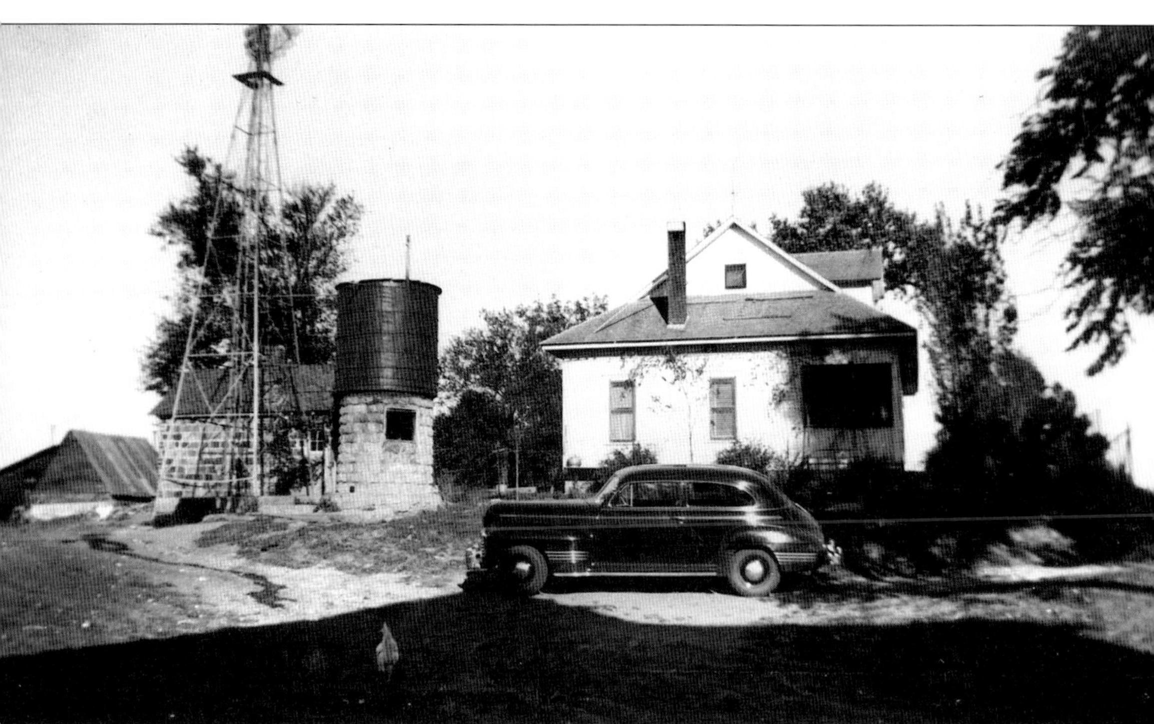

This is a typical small farmhouse in the region. Many homes like this are seen scattered throughout the outskirts of the towns of Intercourse, Leacock, Paradise, and Salisbury. Although many think of sprawling, large farmhouses as being in the area, the fact is that many of the common farms had modest homes. A windmill is to the left. While the car in the front may not have belonged to the farm owners, it was a feather in the cap of whoever owned it in that era.

Two

Community

To understand more about community life in the area, one has to have an understanding as to how the area was shaped. Most of the groundwork for the area was laid by the founder of Pennsylvania, William Penn.

Penn set out with the Holy Experiment to bring forth a community that was peace loving and godly. Because he was basically the proprietor of the entire state, he was able to chart out with much input how the land was to be used and who was to own it. It was through this power that he shaped his ideals of what Pennsylvania should be.

From just a few homes in the early years to a population that supports hundreds of thousands of tourists per year, this area has grown considerably. The region's modern community life is not that far removed from its humble beginnings. While many communities have lost the sense of belonging, this area has retained its tightly woven relationship of unity.

This is an area where everyone seems to know everyone else, and news of neighbors' trials and tribulations travels quickly through telephone communication and word of mouth. Though the Amish do not have telephones, they are still a valuable part of the community and are also very much an integral neighbor to all who reside here.

As transportation became more prominent in the community, more and more stagecoaches and wagons became a mainstay for bringing goods, services, and people to and from the area, which was conveniently located between the cities of Lancaster and Philadelphia.

Today, when large chain stores push out small business owners, this region seems immune to the retail conglomerates surrounding them. Small businesses in this area are plentiful, as they were years ago when general stores were the popular shop for locals to purchase much-needed items and luxuries like scented soaps. As in years past, one can still see locals riding scooters or bicycles as opposed to driving to and from shops and work. One can still see roadside produce stands with fresh vegetables, canned and baked items, and even homemade root beer.

Looking past the heavily prosperous tourism of the region, it is clear that although much has changed over the past 100 years, a great deal has also stayed very much the same. It seems that for this region the phrase "If it ain't broke, don't fix it" is very much a true statement. The preservation of history and community foundation is very much what has made this area not only a favorite of travelers, but a treasure for residents.

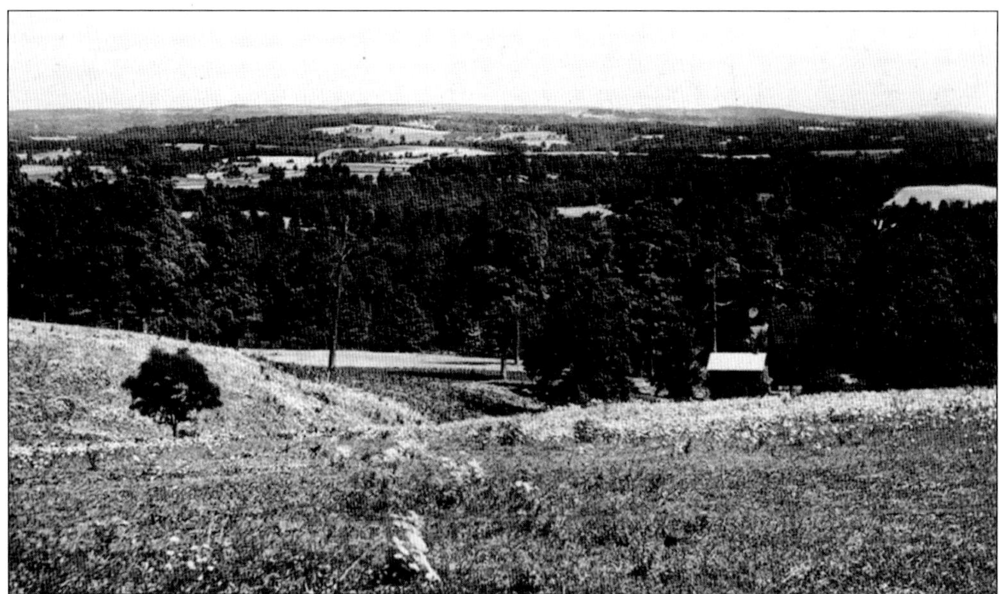

This fabulous postcard dated August 4, 1910, depicts what was called Old Negro Mountain, located near Elk Lick. The sender of the postcard does not state their name, but they do wish Sarah Blough hopes that she benefited from a day in the country. The landscape shows many farms and fields rather than homes at this time.

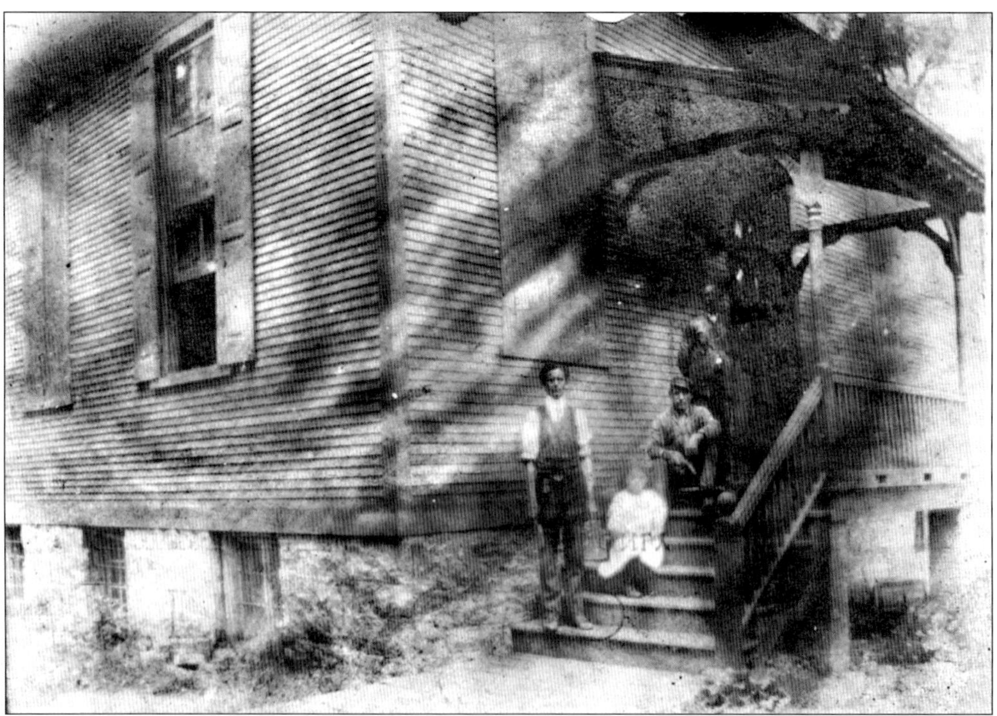

This postcard was sent by a person identified only as B. N. C. to Maude Morrette in Cumberland County. B. N. C seems to be a jokester, as the card reads, "Hello Maude, This is a Chinese Puzzle. Guess who the folks are in the picture."

This lucky man is flanked by two lovely women. It seems his hands are a little too high up for this era, which may explain his Cheshire cat grin.

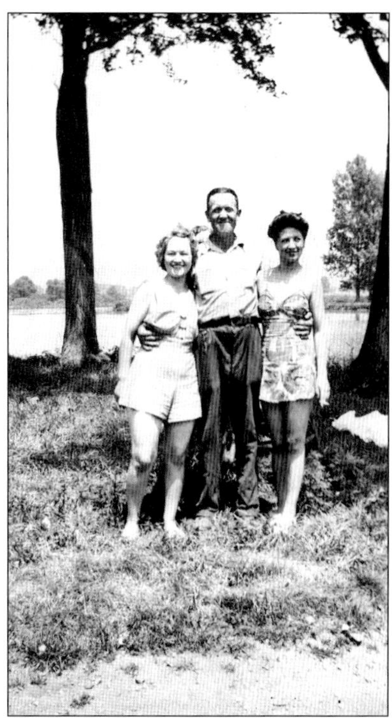

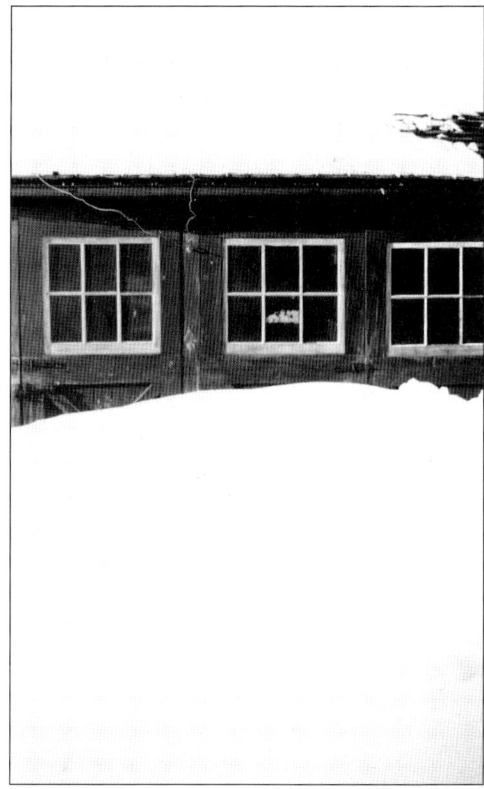

This image is a study of contrast from the above photograph, and it is a bit of chill to cool one off from the above photograph as well. The photograph was taken after a large snowstorm, and it depicts the frustration, or possibly the humor, for the farmer who cannot open the doors to his garage or barn.

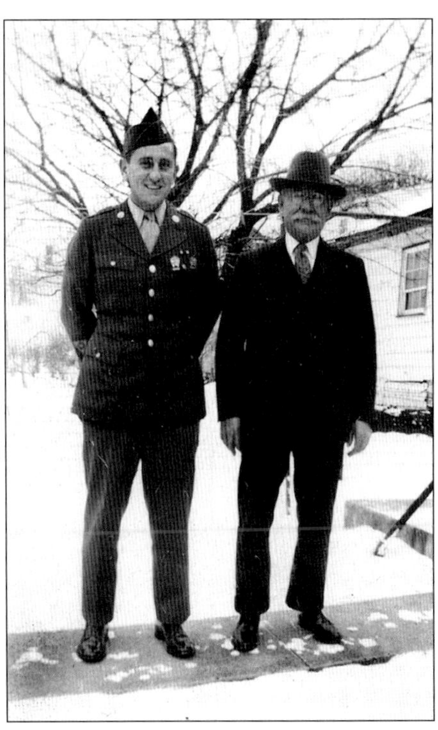

This photograph seems bland at first, but it contains a great deal of emotion, as this is a bittersweet wartime photograph. It is not known whether the fellow in uniform has just returned home or if he is on his way to war.

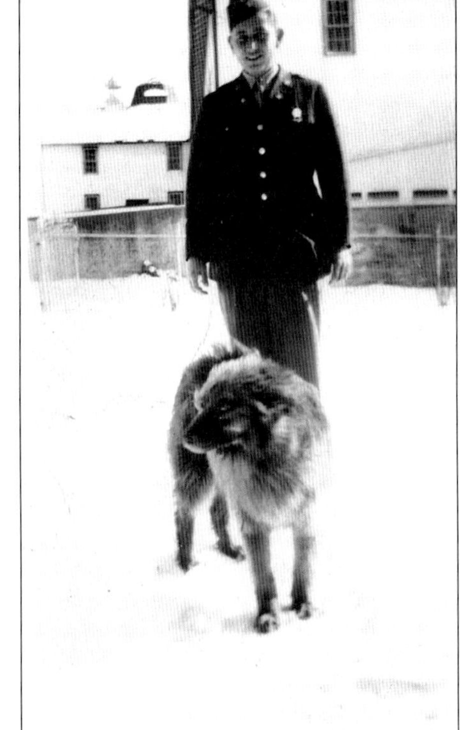

The same officer as seen in the previous photograph is seen here in what seems to be the backyard of the very same home shown above. Here he poses with a dog.

This unidentified man has apparently just caught something that he is quite proud of. It is difficult to tell if it is a rodent of some sort or a fish, but there is some type of licensure on his left hip.

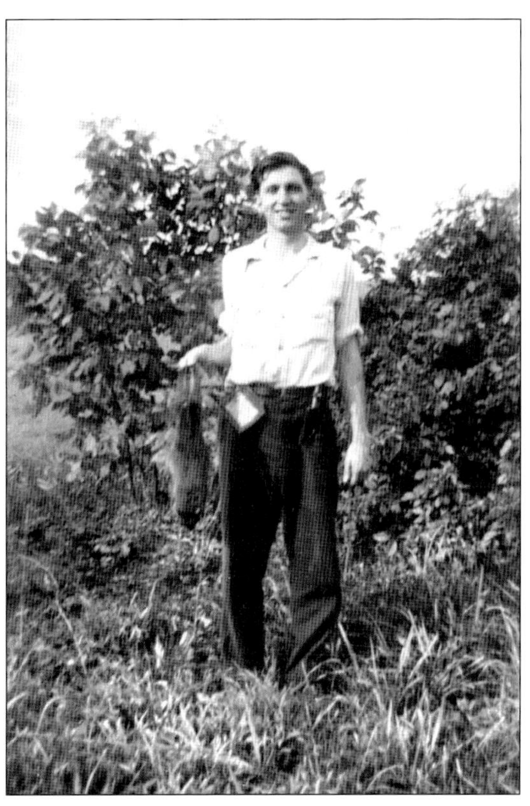

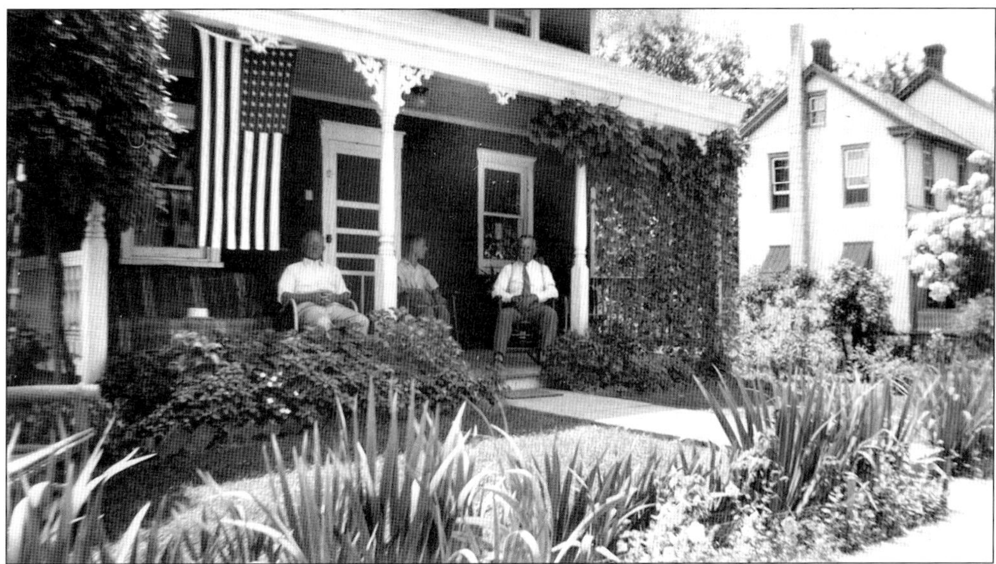

This photograph captures this region's patriotism and Americana at its best—a porch with people on rocking chairs and an American flag proudly swaying in the breeze. The photograph was likely taken in the 1920s or early 1930s.

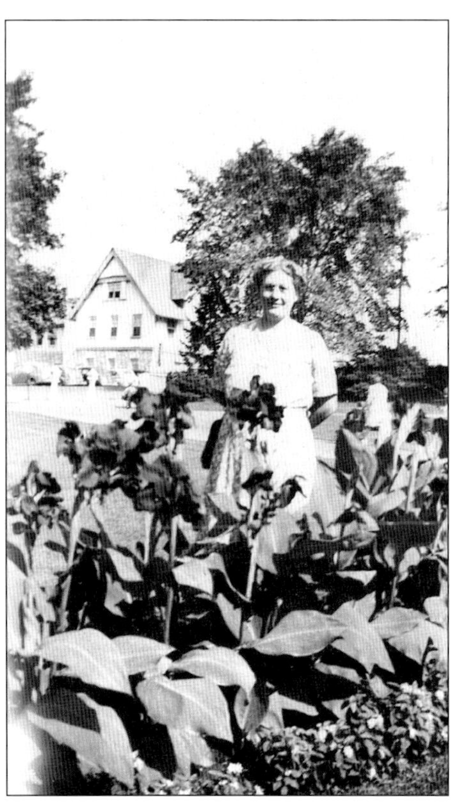

This proud woman is showing off flowers that she seems to have grown herself in her pride and joy of a garden. A farm is visible in the background.

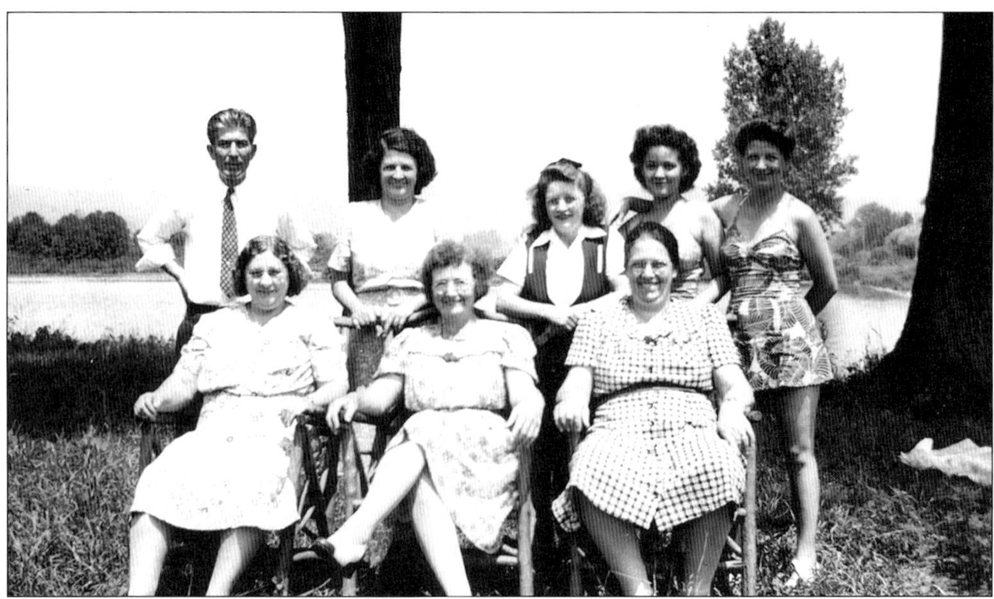

The bathing beauty on the right is the same woman seen in the photograph on page 33. She appears to be enjoying a day at the lake with her family.

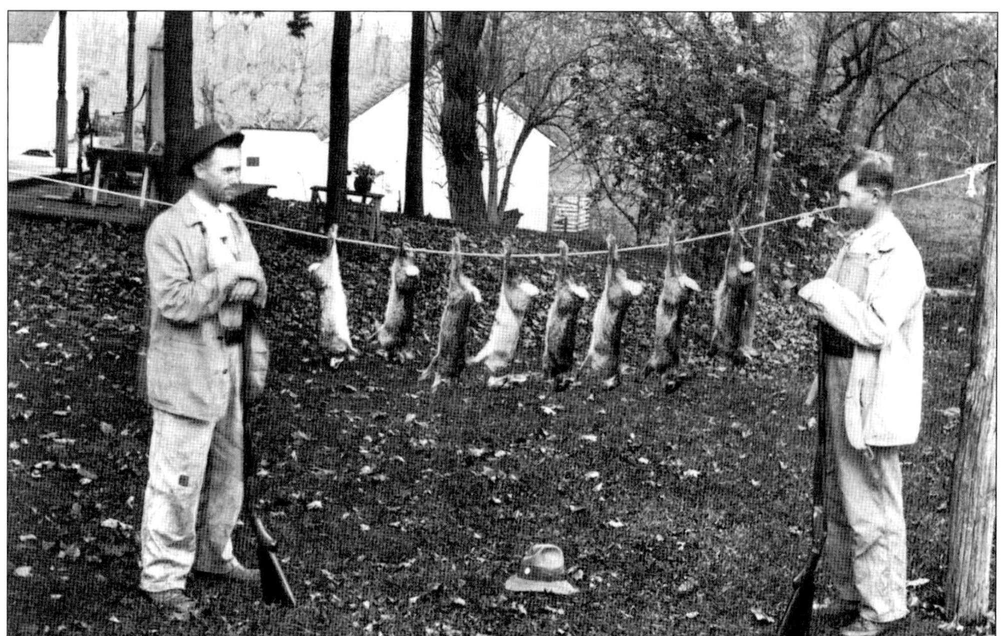

Levi Wissler and David Wissler pose for a photograph on November 1, 1915. Their rabbit hunting seems to have been a success.

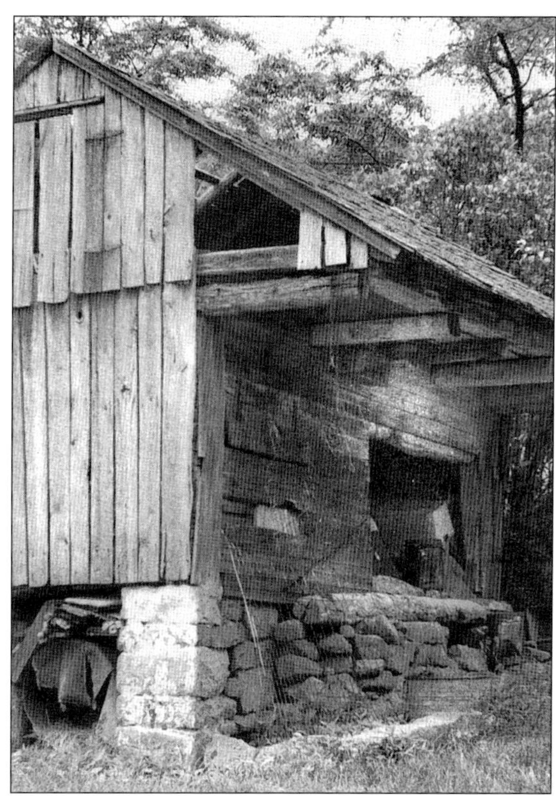

This building was located on Route 272, but it was torn down in the early 1980s.

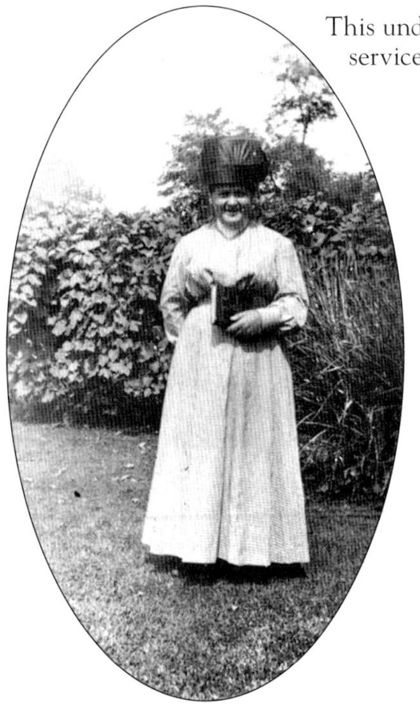

This undated postcard shows a woman on her way to a religious service in which she was apparently a key participant.

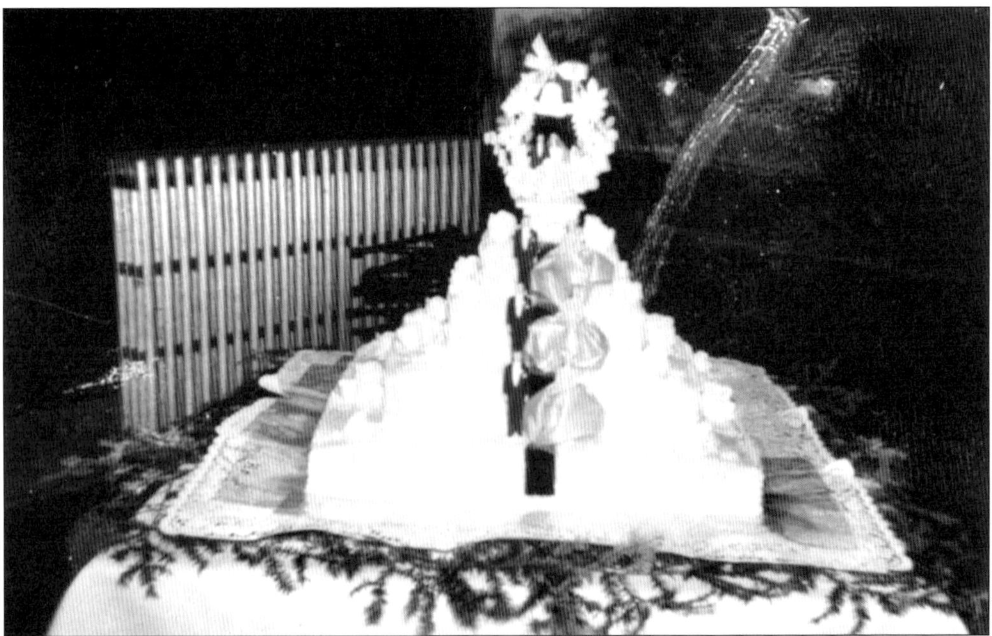

This is a wedding cake from a resident of the area. Though there is not a date associated with this photograph, it is obviously for a winter wedding, as the cake is decorated with evergreen.

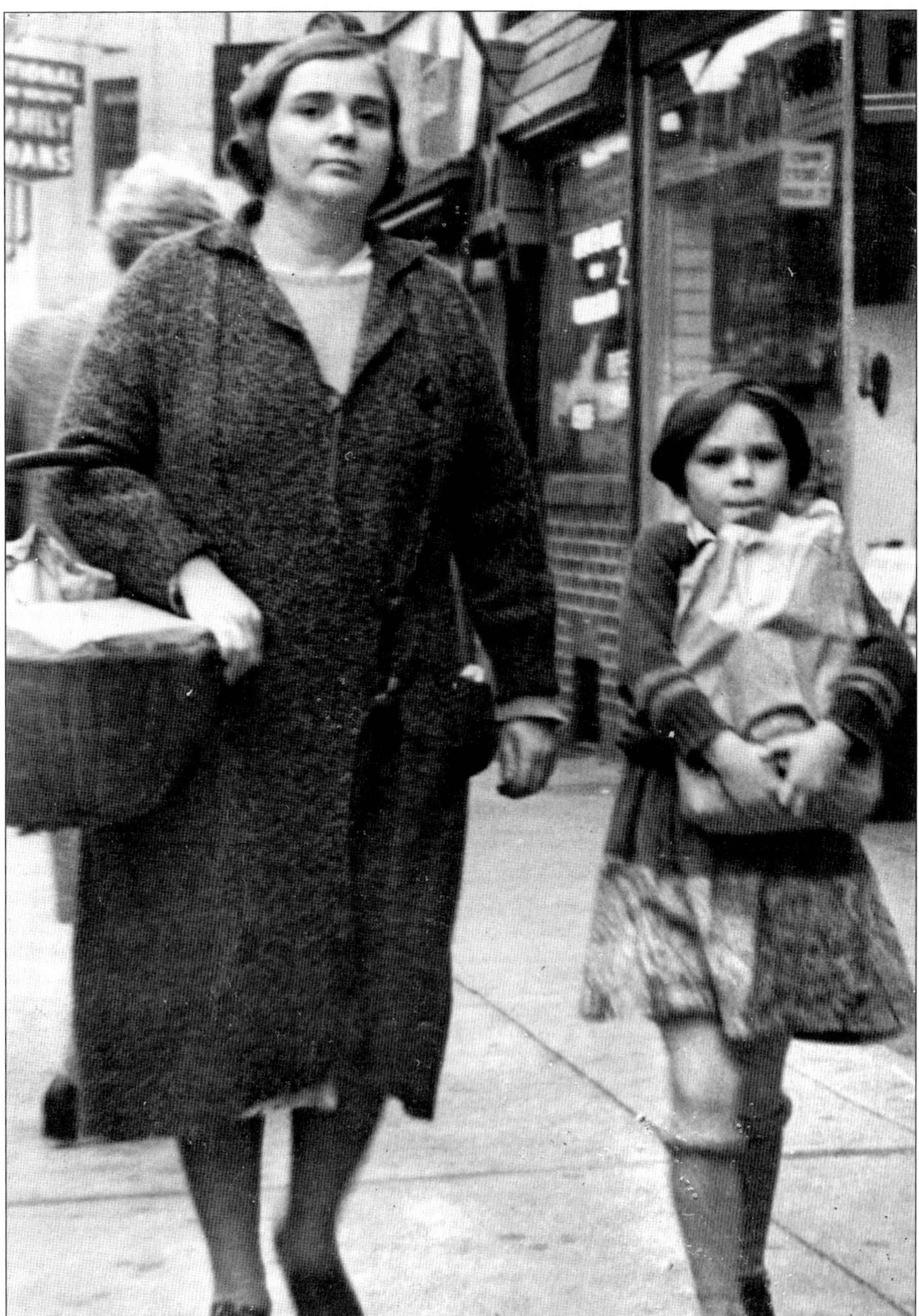

This photograph from *c.* 1925 is a true slice of time. We can almost see the busy sidewalk bustling with activity and almost can hear the child telling her mother that her load was too heavy. By the look of the casual expressions on their faces, they probably did not realize the photograph was being taken until the last minute.

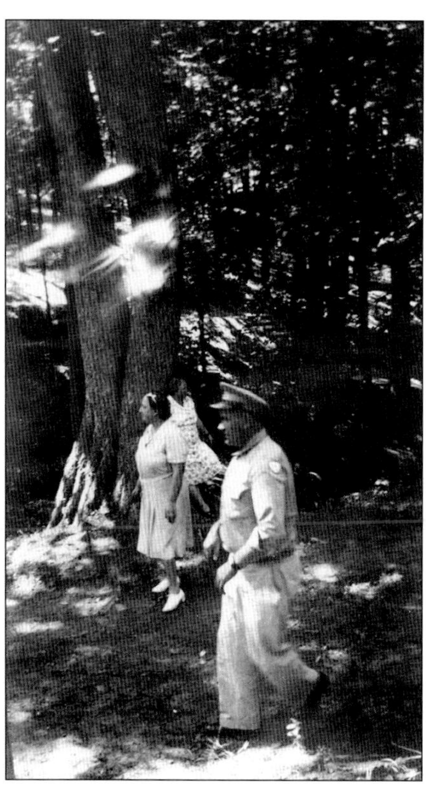

It is not often that you see a photograph of members of a family and the postal worker or milkman walking together, as is seen in this undated photograph.

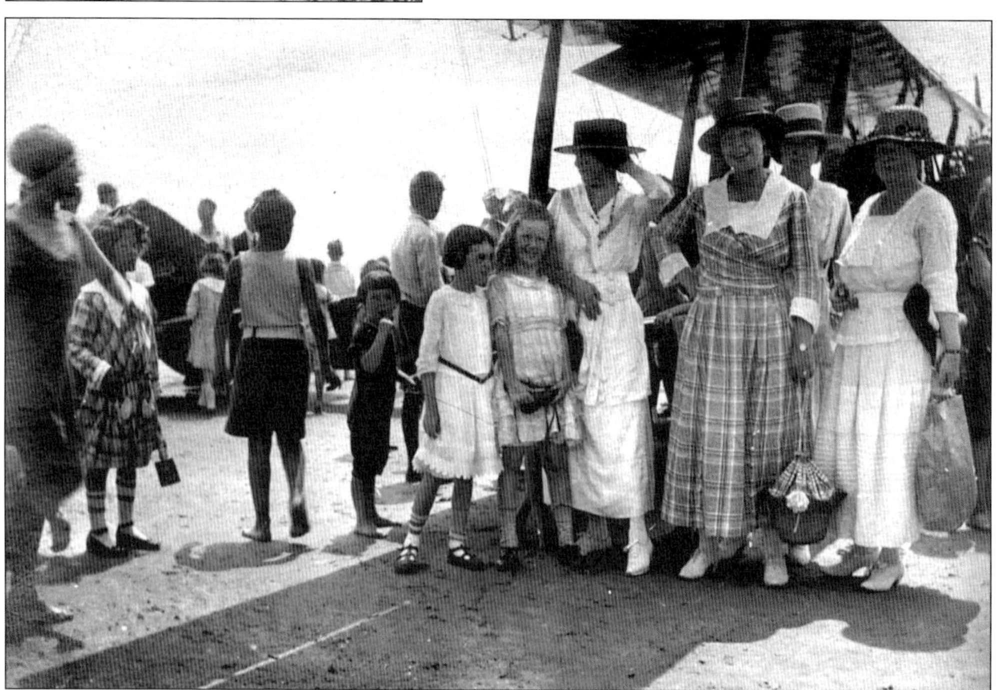

This photograph looks to be from the 1940s. The unidentified people seem to be either traveling (notice the airplane wing) or perhaps attending a county fair. Not all the individuals are wearing shoes, yet some are very well dressed. They all seem to be together yet apart from each other.

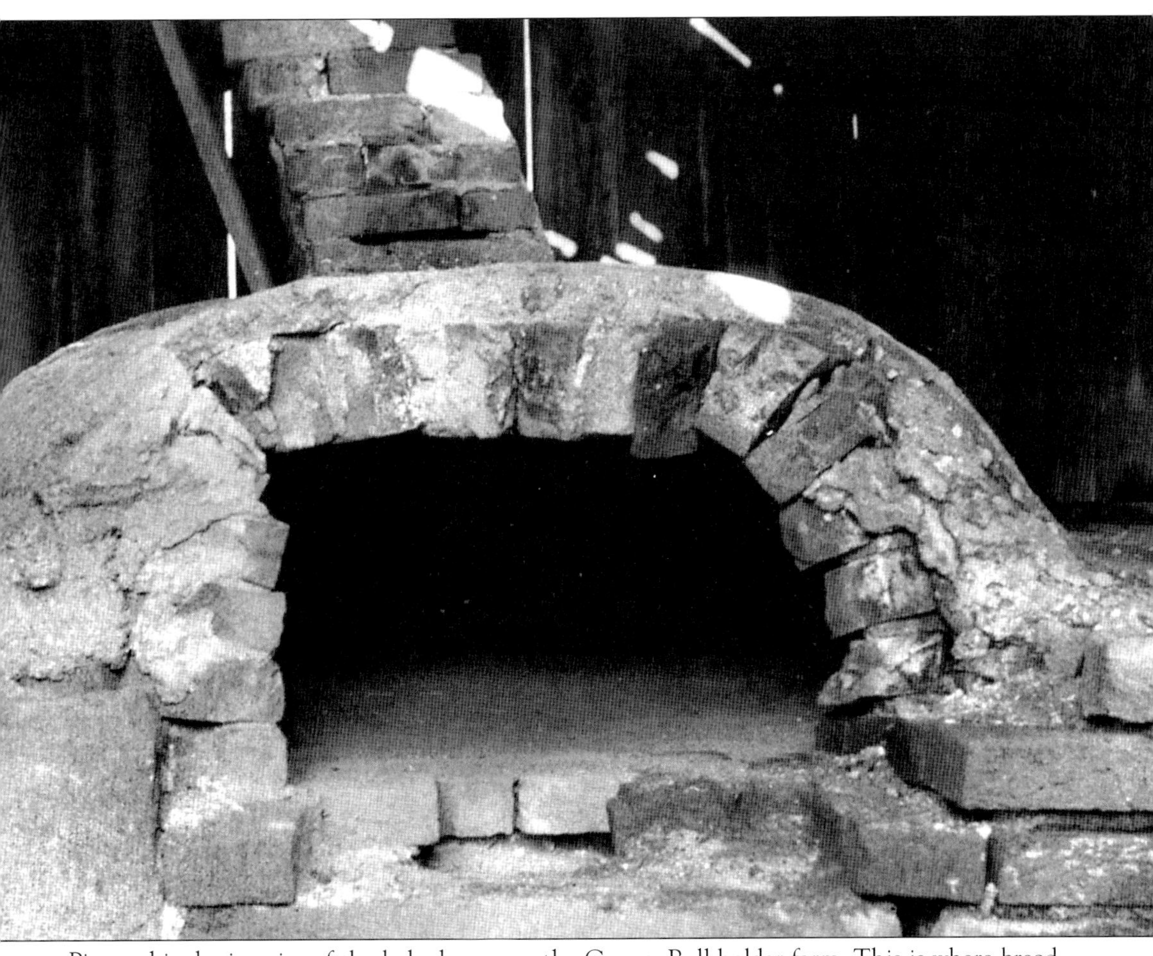

Pictured is the interior of the bake house on the George Bulkholder farm. This is where bread and other baked goods were cooked.

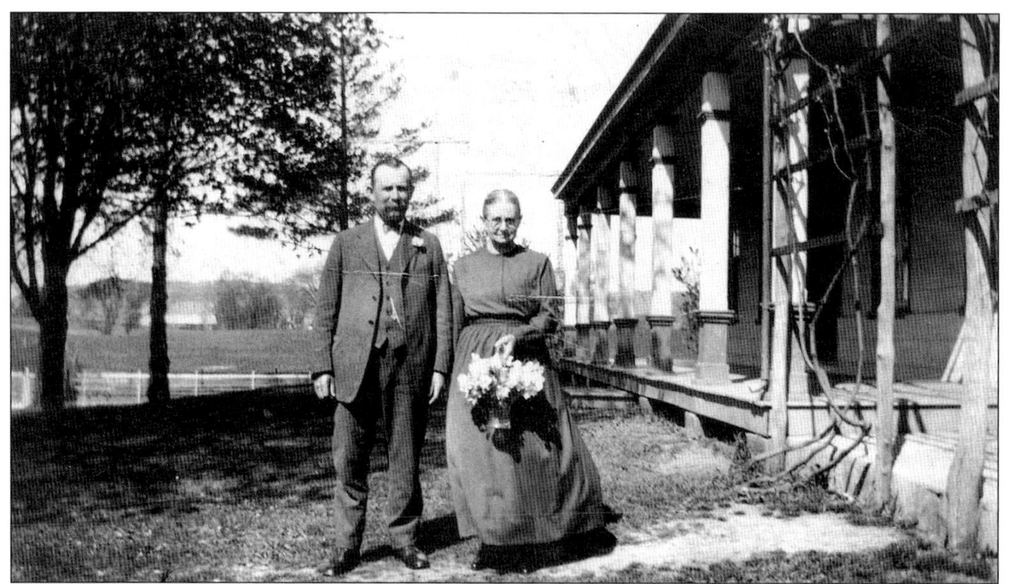

An unidentified man and woman strike a formal pose *c.* 1910. They are perhaps Mennonites, but the attire is a bit wayward for the traditional Mennonite of that era.

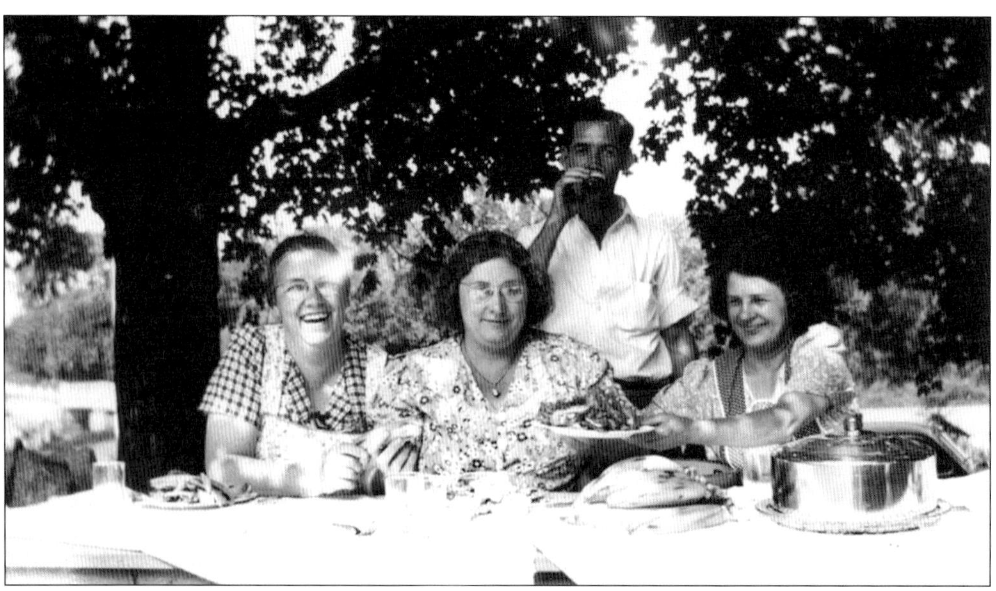

It appears that this outdoor meal was a great time for these unidentified individuals. As the aprons are still being worn, we get the feeling that they are not quite yet ready to sit down to eat.

This woman poses with a puppy that looks like the one from *Our Gang*. The photograph seems to have been taken *c.* 1920, and it appears to be summer, perhaps around the Fourth of July.

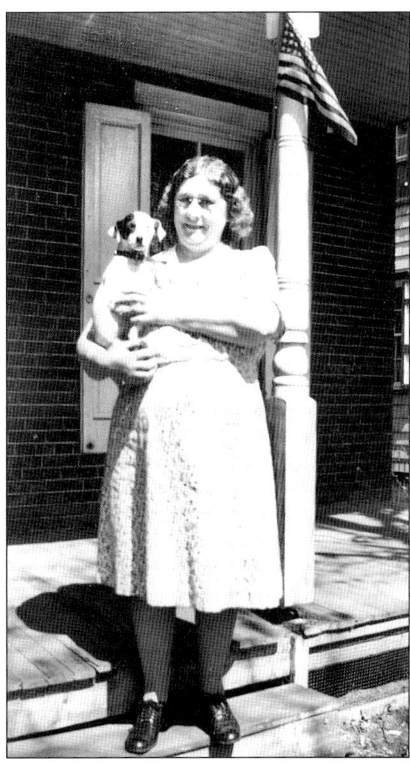

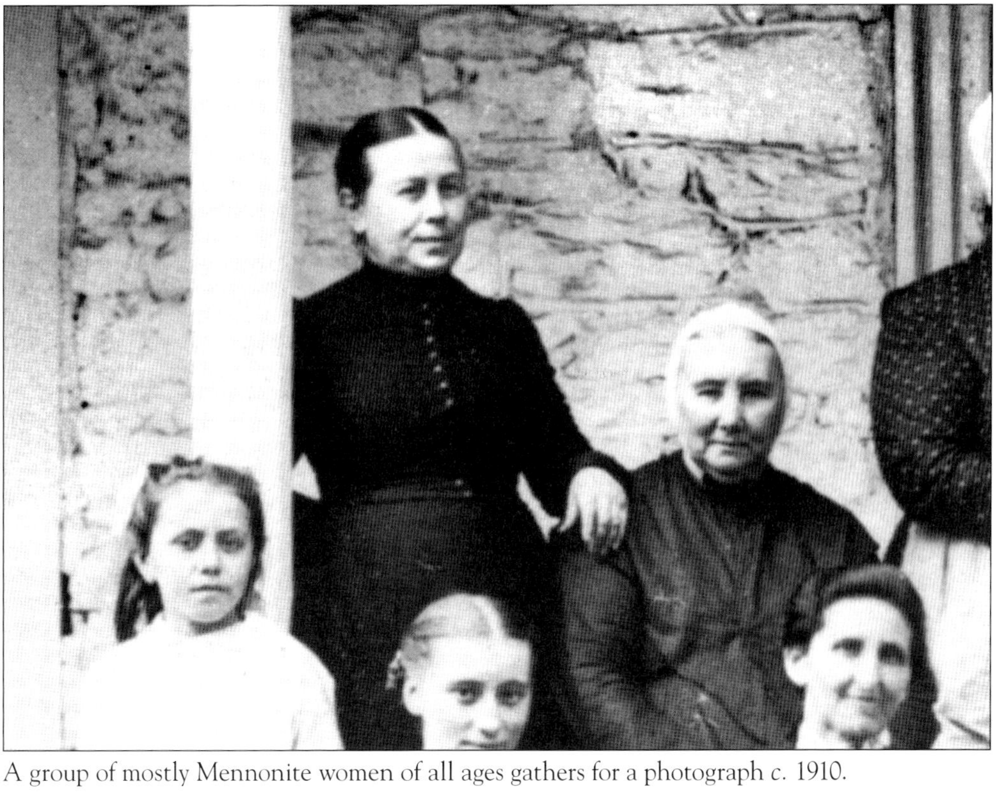

A group of mostly Mennonite women of all ages gathers for a photograph *c.* 1910.

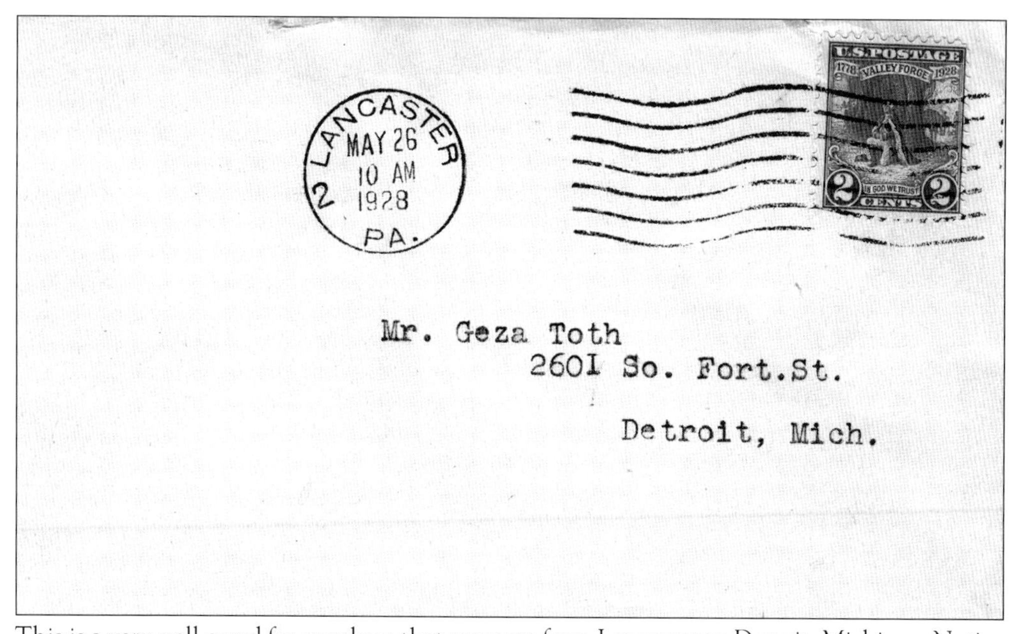

This is a very well cared for envelope that was sent from Lancaster to Detroit, Michigan. Notice that the envelope has a 2¢ stamp for postage. It is unusual to find an intact envelope in such good condition from the year 1928.

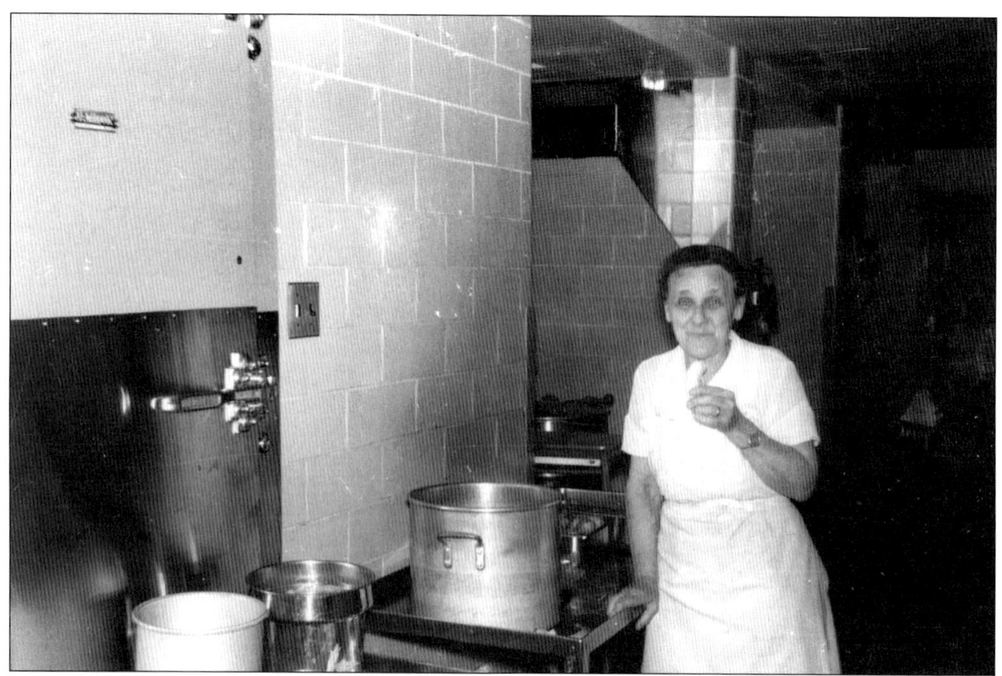

This undated photograph shows that this woman worked in a kitchen and seemed to enjoy eating bananas on the job.

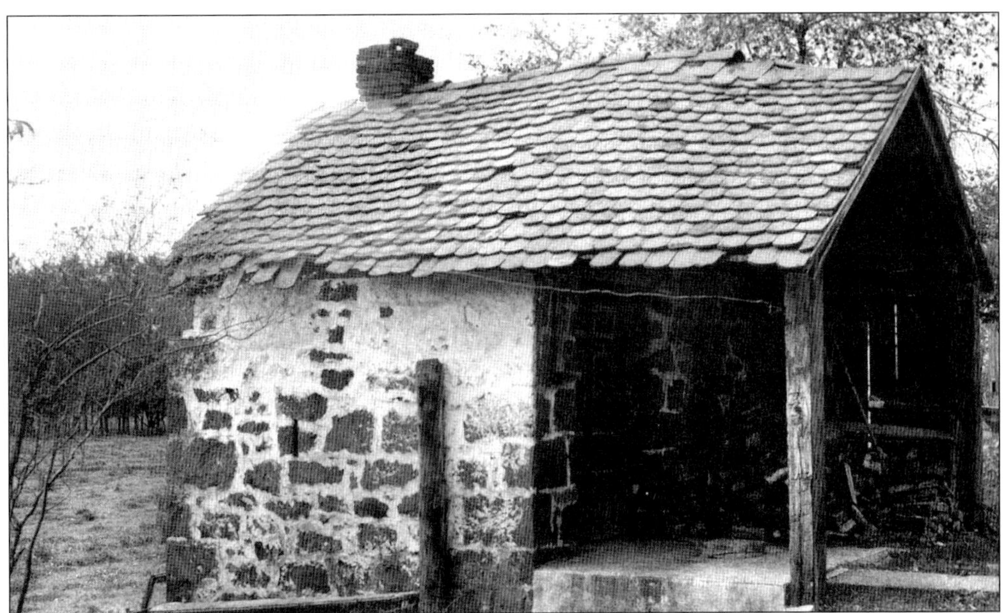

This 1956 photograph shows a bake oven on the Peter Bricker Farm. Clay tiles can be seen on top of the oven.

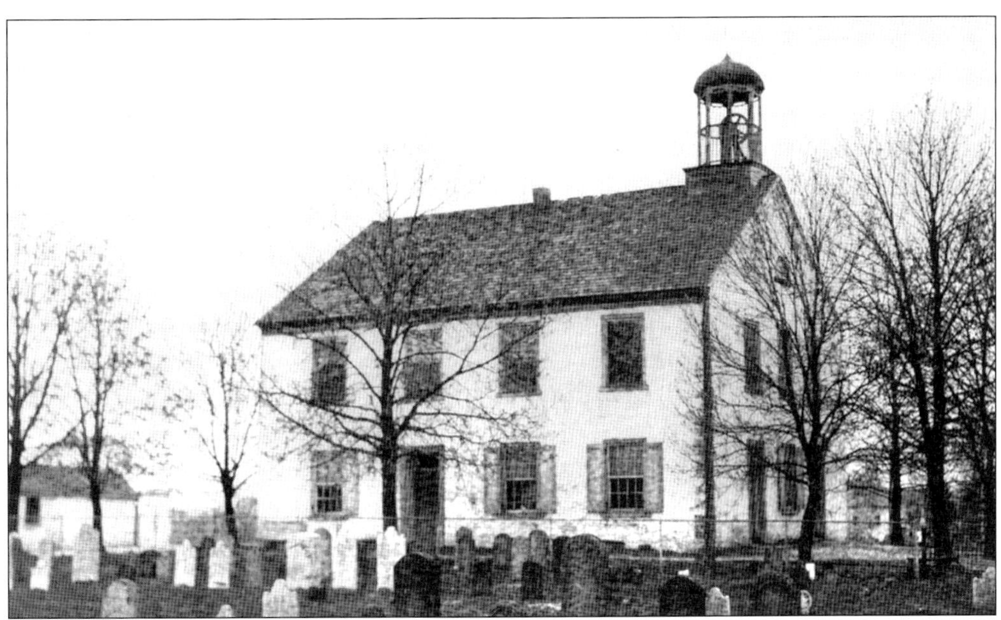

This church, now demolished, was located on Route 272. The church was originally built as a log house in 1732. A second church, built of stone in 1748, featured a hand-pumped pipe organ.

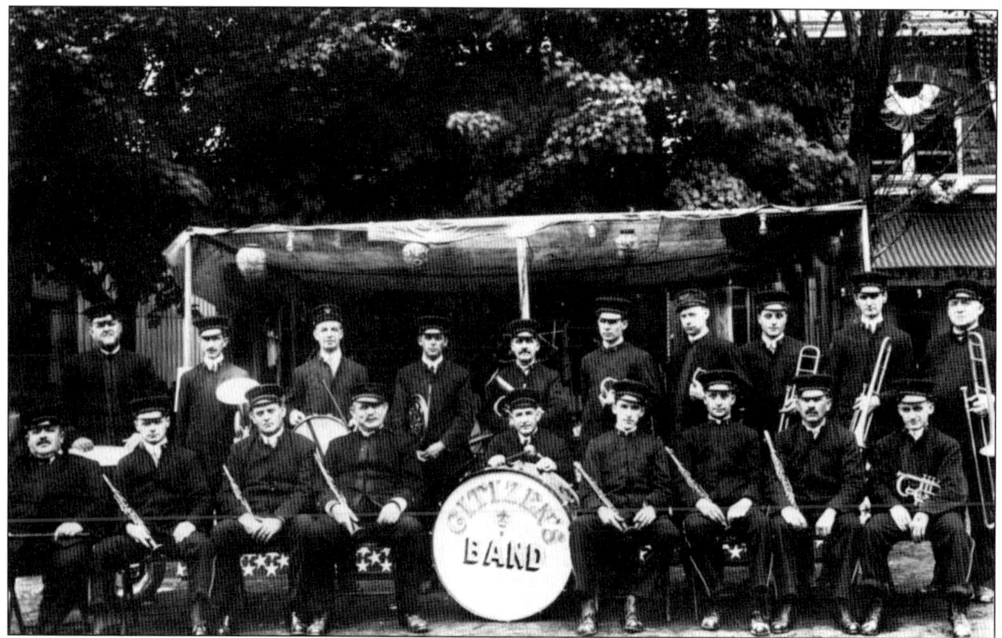

This unique photograph shows the Citizens Band Fourth of July celebration in 1910. Band members include Samuel Ulrich, Norman Hacker, Frank Eberly, Theodore Brady, Charles Beck, E. Romig, Dave Grant, Martin Ditzler, Gawd Showalter, Tom Miller, Elwood Barry, John Rathman, Streaker, Horace Mellinger, John Hacker, and Jacob Kilhefner.

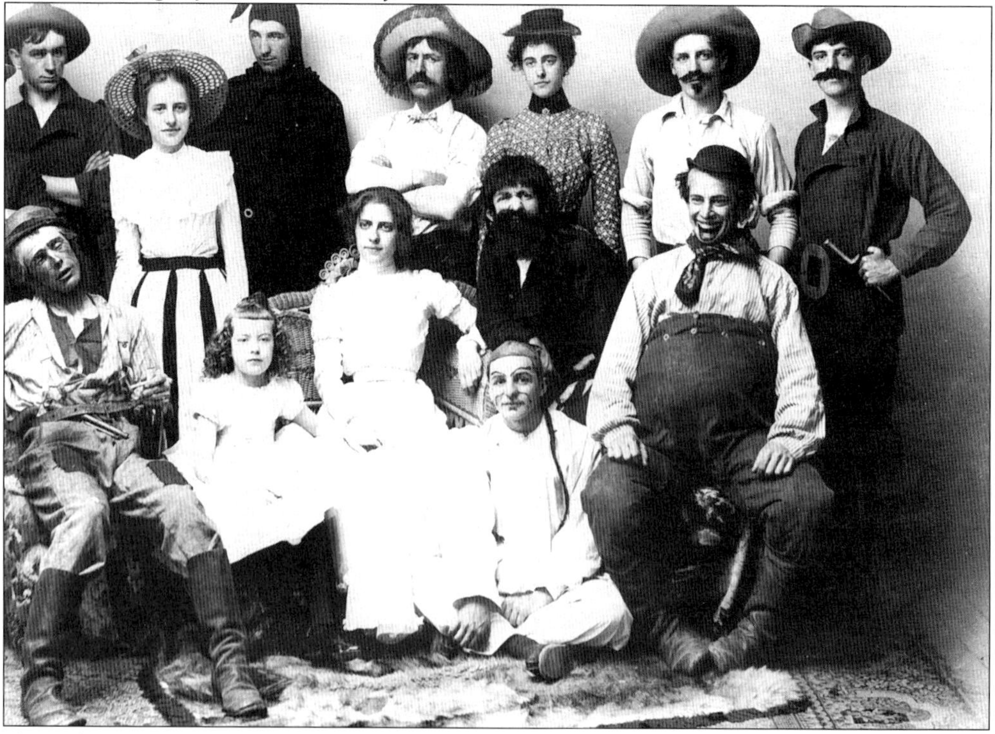

Shown here are members of the Mount Springs Rifles cast for a theatrical production in 1905. Notice that they have some very young members, who with a little makeup pass for much older.

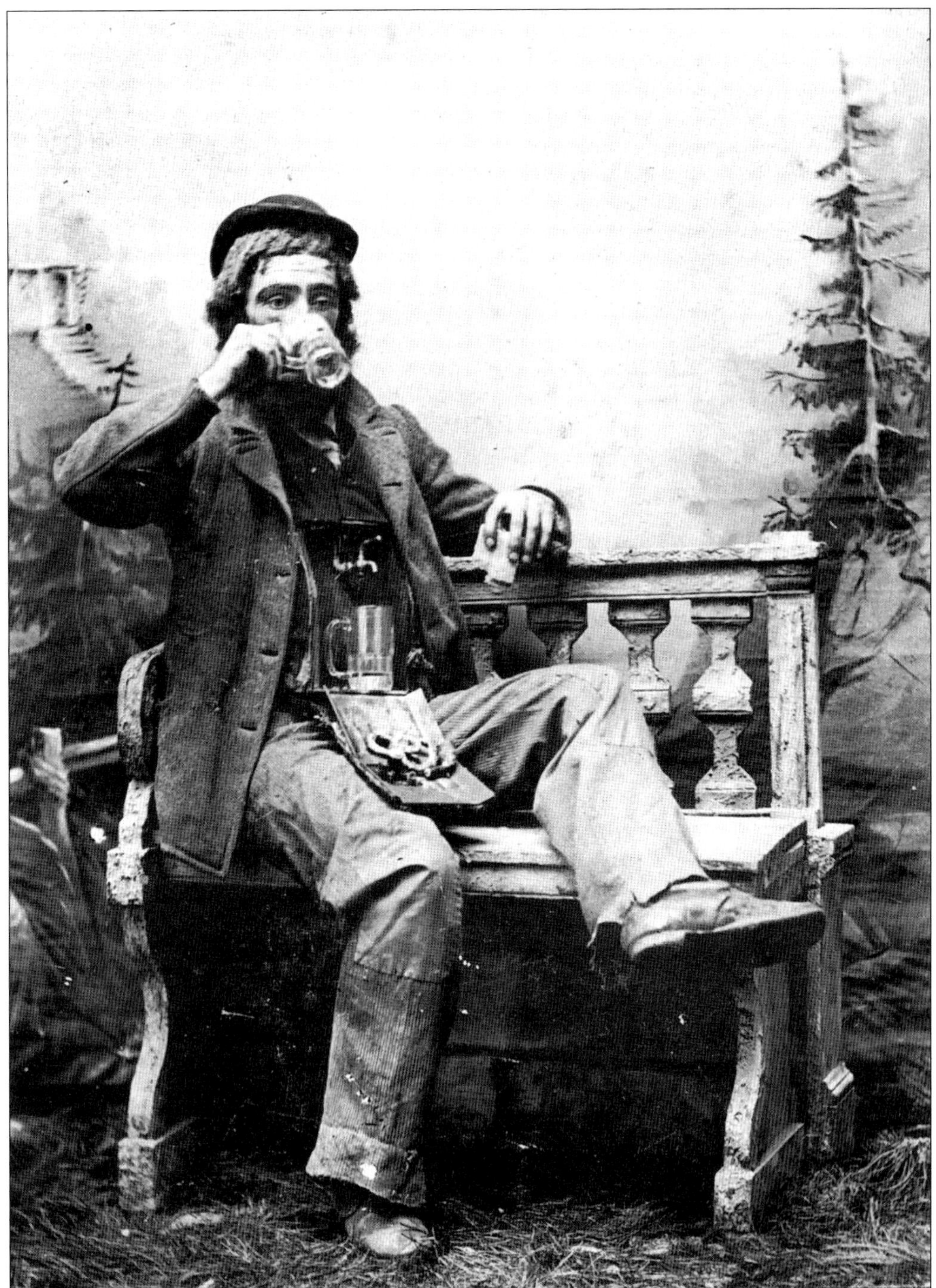

This most unusual photograph shows a member of the Mount Springs Rifles Theater in character. Notice that he has a full bar built into his vest as a part of his portrayal of the era's "wino." The word "wino" and portrayal of such was very common in this era, as alcohol was a big issue of the day, both ethically and politically.

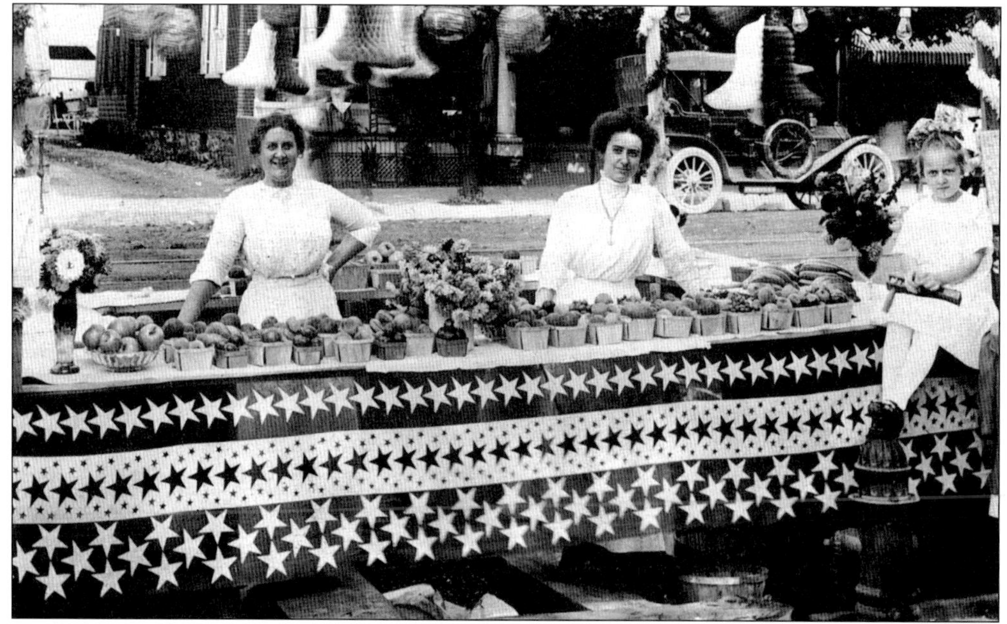

It was likely a very hot day with all of that clothing on at the 1909 celebration on the Fourth of July. Pictured here are, from left to right, Cora Keith Hilton, Mary Frankfort Garman, and Kathryn Myers, who is sitting on the stand, holding a noisemaker and not looking very festive.

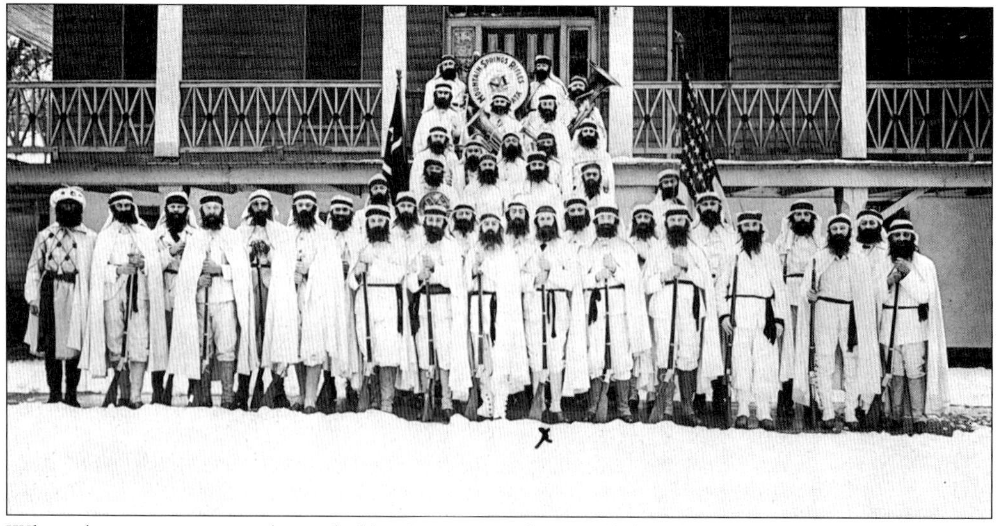

When the mummers parade was held in Lancaster, these Rifle band members rose to the occasion. This photograph of the band dressed in Arab garb was taken in 1910.

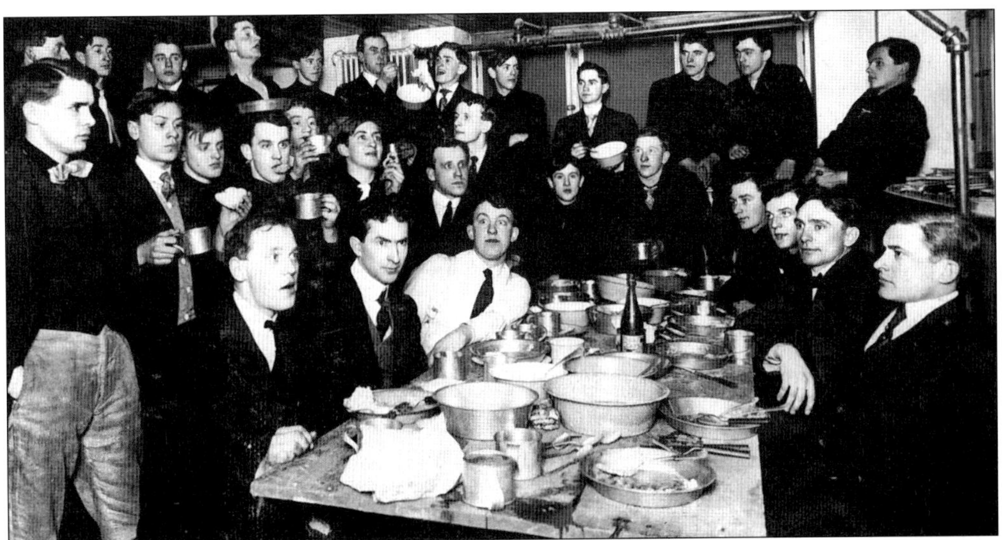

The Rifles band, seen here for once not in costume, are having fun over a sauerkraut-and-bean lunch on February 21, 1908.

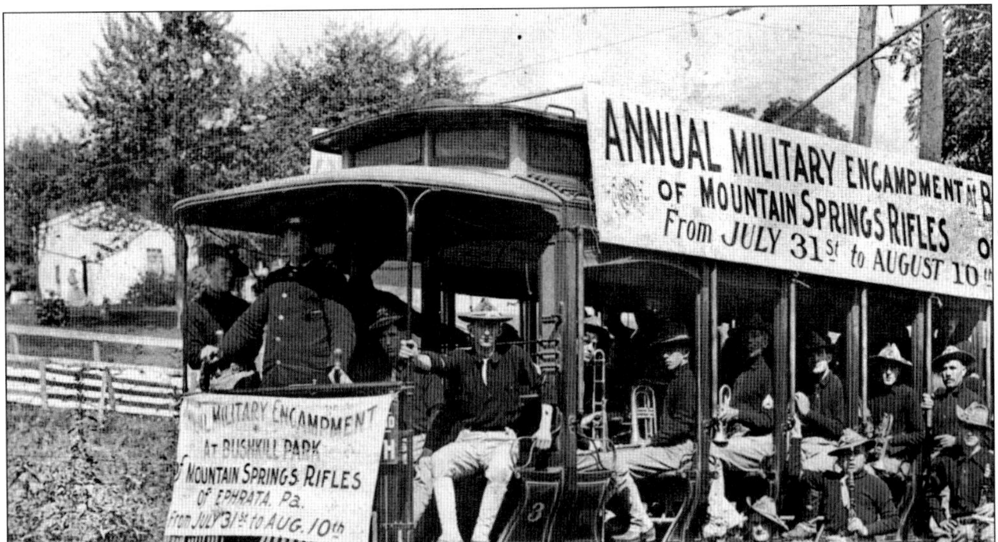

The proud members of the Rifles band pose for a photograph in the summer of 1907. The unidentified members were on their way to a military encampment.

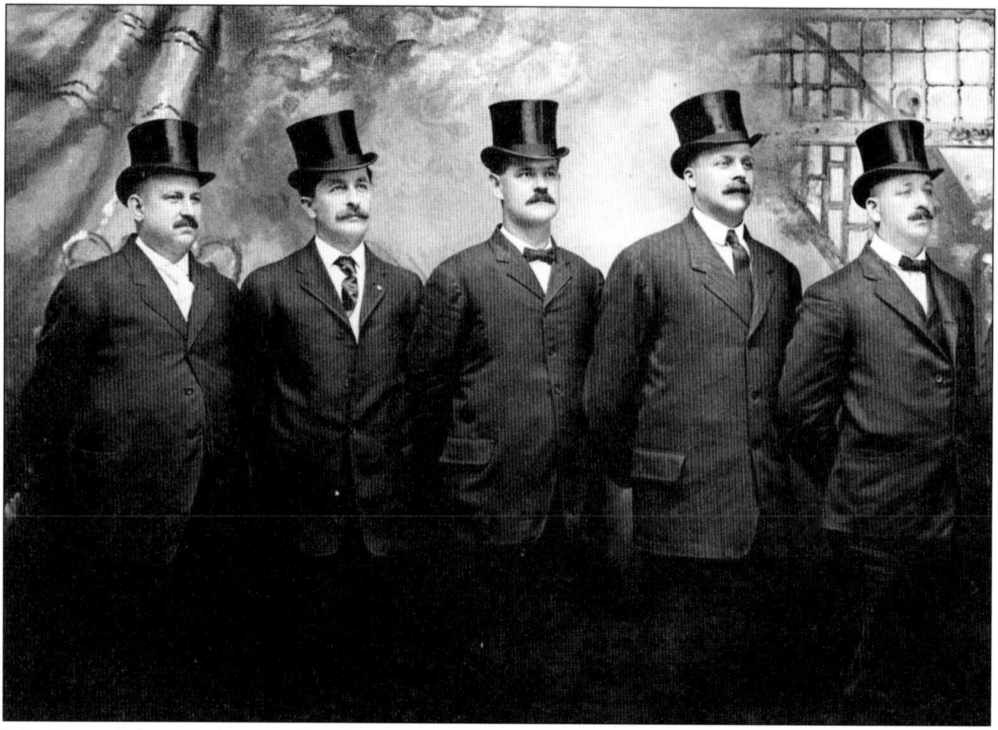

Members of the International Order of Odd Fellows are seen here. The organization is linked by ethical beliefs of love, friendship, and truth. From left to right are Adam Spangler, Robert Carter, William Strohl, Jacob Schlott, Francis Bolster, and an unidentified man.

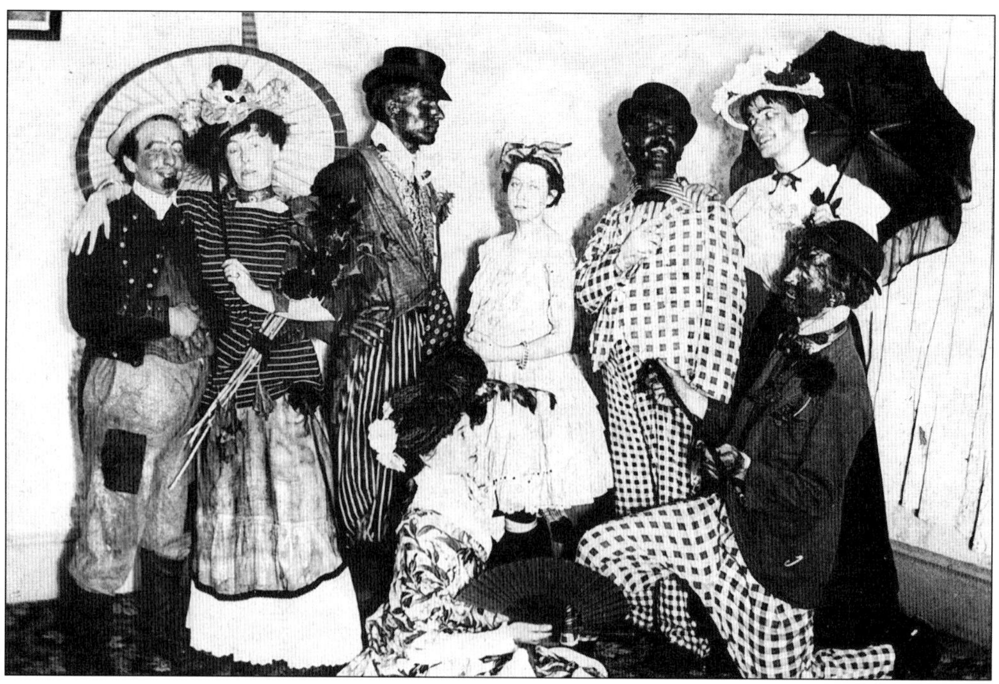

This amateur theater act, pictured in 1905, takes on a vaudeville look.

This undated photograph shows a peaceful lake in the area. The region is rich with many lakes and bodies of water, so narrowing the destination down proves to be almost impossible, given that the lake may not be in existence anymore, or it may be much more developed.

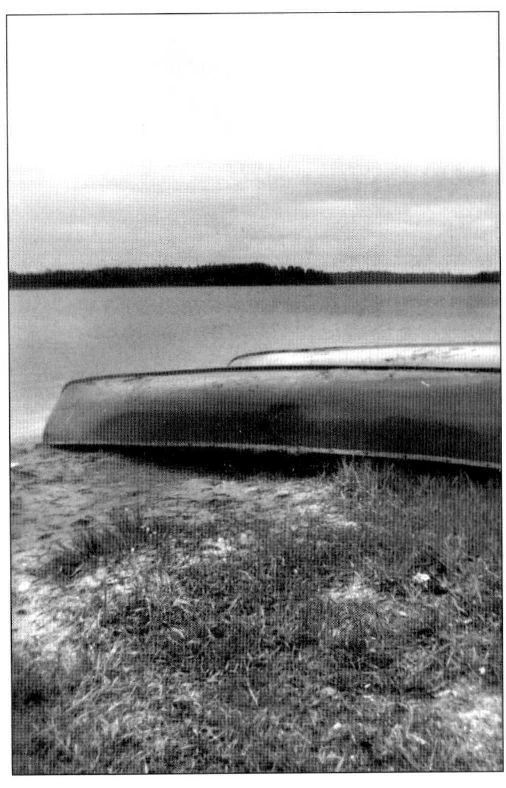

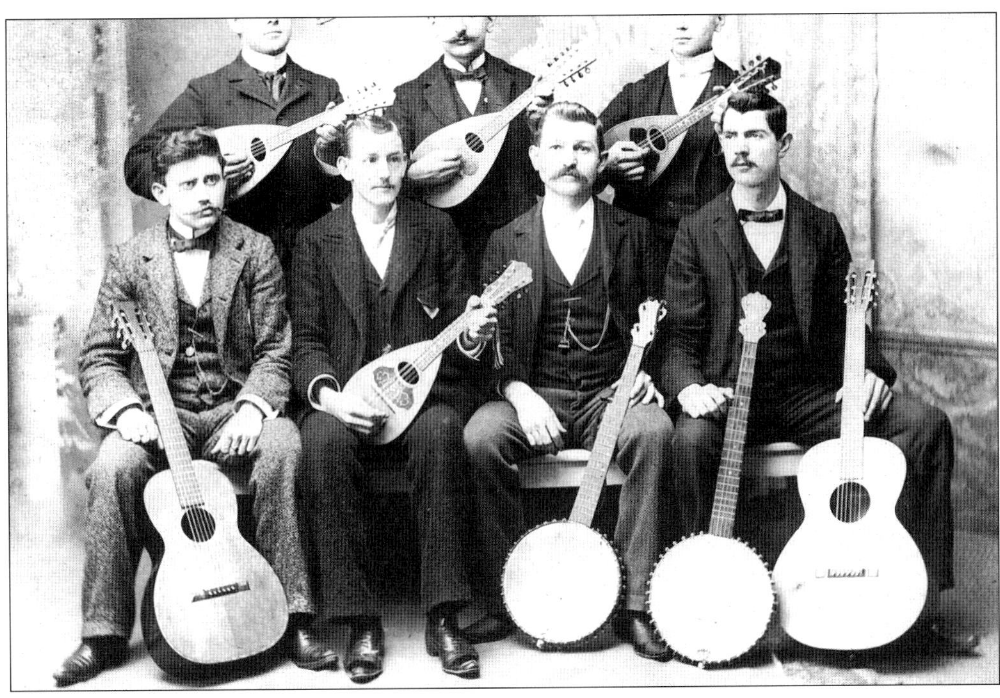

Members of an orchestra pose in 1900.

COMMISSIONERS' OFFICE, LANCASTER, PA.

$3 81/100

JOHN DENLINGER, Esq., Treasurer.

Pay Henry Musser Esq or order,

Three 81/100 dollars Clk fees in 2 Sessions at Apl Term 1863.

Allowed May 25th 1863.

Attest:

P G Eberman Cl'k Com'rs.

No. 305

John Doner
Wm Spencer
David Kemper

Commissioners of Lancaster County.

A unique element of history, this bail release from May 25, 1863, clearly outlines how people viewed murder in centuries past. No sooner did we look at the Odd Fellows on page 50 and learn of their strong ethics than we view this, a bail release of $3.81. The woman charged with the murder was found to be of unsound mind.

Lancaster County

To Henry Musser Clk Q.S.

To costs in case of Comth vs Mary Jane Sebastian ordered to Prison as of unsound mind on a charge of Murder, and released by the Court on report of Commissioner to inquire into the state of her mind

Filing papers in the case	.50
Motion for discharge	.25
Order for appointmt of Com.	.25
Commission to Dr [illegible] seal &c	.87
Copy of record & cert	.72
Recording return of com	.21
Stationery	.12½
Stamps U.S. Rev	.20
Taxing costs	.18¾
Certificate to Prison for disch	.50
	$3.81

Approved April 15th 1863 For Three Dollars & Eighty One Cents $3 81/100

[illegible]

Three

EDUCATION

Most students years ago attended class in one-room schoolhouses. The best-known schoolhouse in the area is the home of the Pequea Valley Public Library. This building should be on any tourist's must-visit list, as today these structures are a rarity.

Most schools operating in the one-room schoolhouses were coed, with boys and girls sitting on opposite sides of the room. Students of all ages were normally in the same room, but each had different assignments. Most mornings started with a biblical or spiritual teaching.

In years past, the central topics for education were reading, writing, and arithmetic. Students had to memorize much of what they learned, as there was not an abundance of paper and pens. Most students used chalk and slate, while some students did have the novelty of uses dipping pens with paper for special projects.

Students only attended school when the crop seasons were slow. During busy seasons, children of all ages were expected to help with crops, farming, canning, and other needed chores to help sustain community and family life.

Because of this, the students of the past had much more responsibility than children today, and they were expected to behave with more maturity. It was not uncommon for students to sit in a corner or be struck with an object if they were disobedient. Students were also expected to help the teacher with chores around the schoolhouse, such as bringing in wood for the fire, washing the boards, and assisting with the cleaning.

Teachers did not have it easy themselves. They were not only the teacher (usually the sole teacher in the schoolhouse) but also the janitor. They were responsible for getting water, keeping the school clean, keeping the school warm by making a fire (and often after walking in the snow to their job), as well as accepting a contract for low pay and sometimes stipulations that included a curfew for the teacher.

There were no buses for years, so if a family did not have a horse and carriage, which was rare, children had to walk to and from school. This was often a long trip, considering most families operated farms.

In later years, schools were constructed with more classrooms and more resources, but still to this day, some local cultures, such as the Amish, still operate one-room schoolhouses, and school is always closed during high crop time.

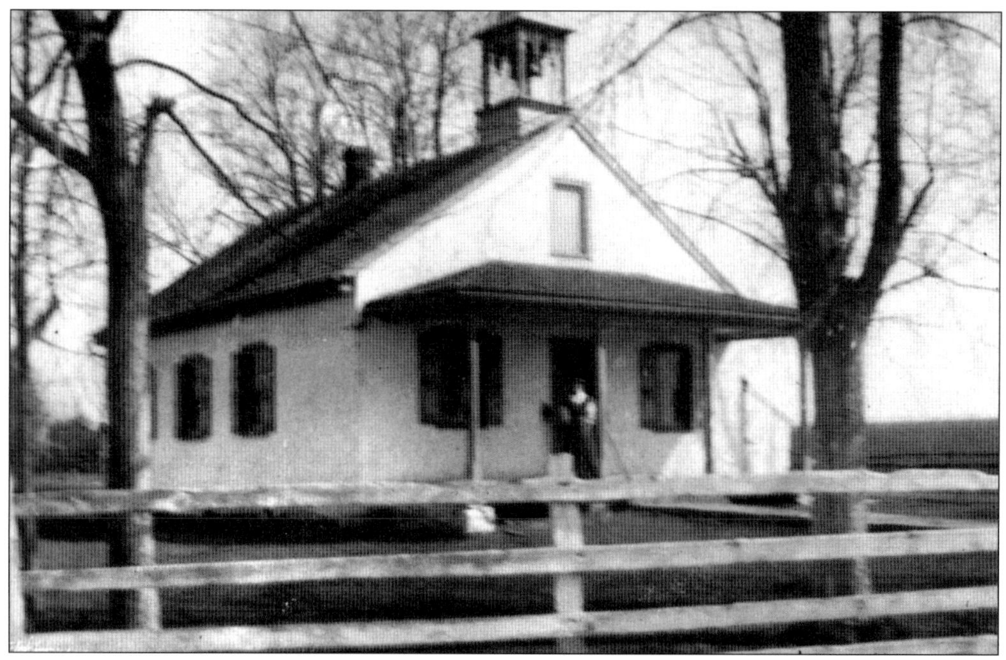

This is a fantastic glimpse of the time when the one-room schoolhouse was the foundation of education. This one-room schoolhouse was photographed in 1908. In the doorway, the outline of the school's teacher that year, Mary Reemsnyder, can be seen. Her salary that year was just $43, and she taught all ages and all subjects in addition to many other duties.

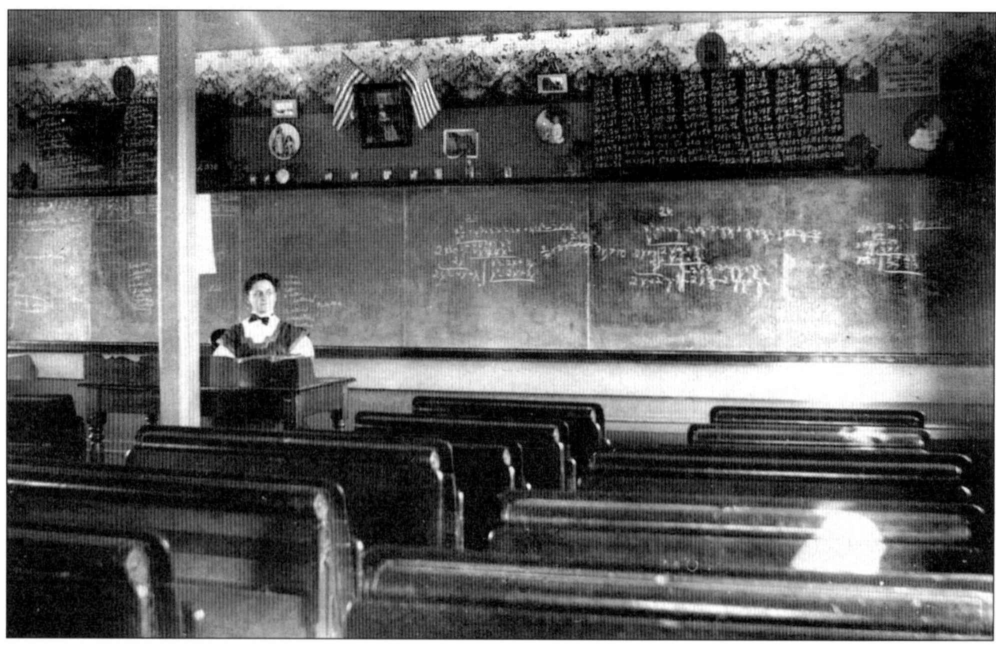

This photograph offers a rare glimpse into the interior of a one-room schoolhouse. The image also provides a closer look at Mary Reemsnyder, the teacher, sitting at her desk.

This well-kept program is from the graduation ceremonies for the Paradise Select School's class of 1888. The program is in excellent condition and seems to be made of true linen paper and bound very tightly.

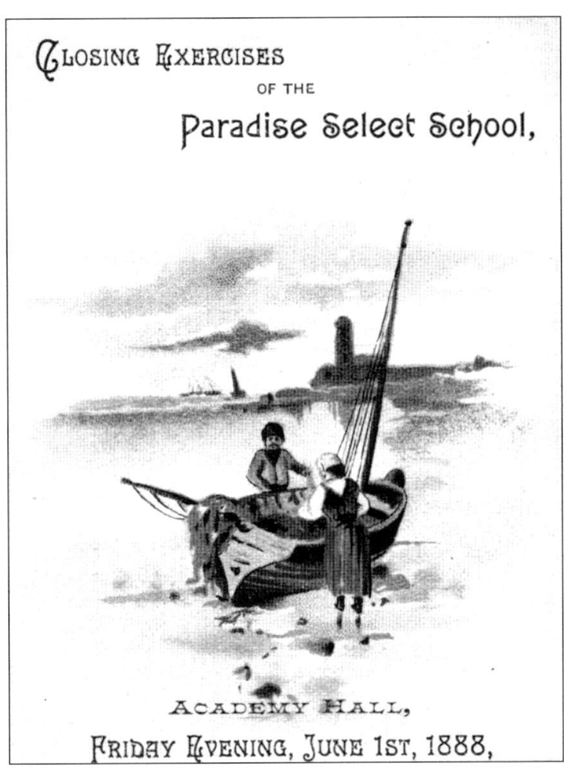
CLOSING EXERCISES
OF THE
Paradise Select School,

ACADEMY HALL,
FRIDAY EVENING, JUNE 1ST, 1888,

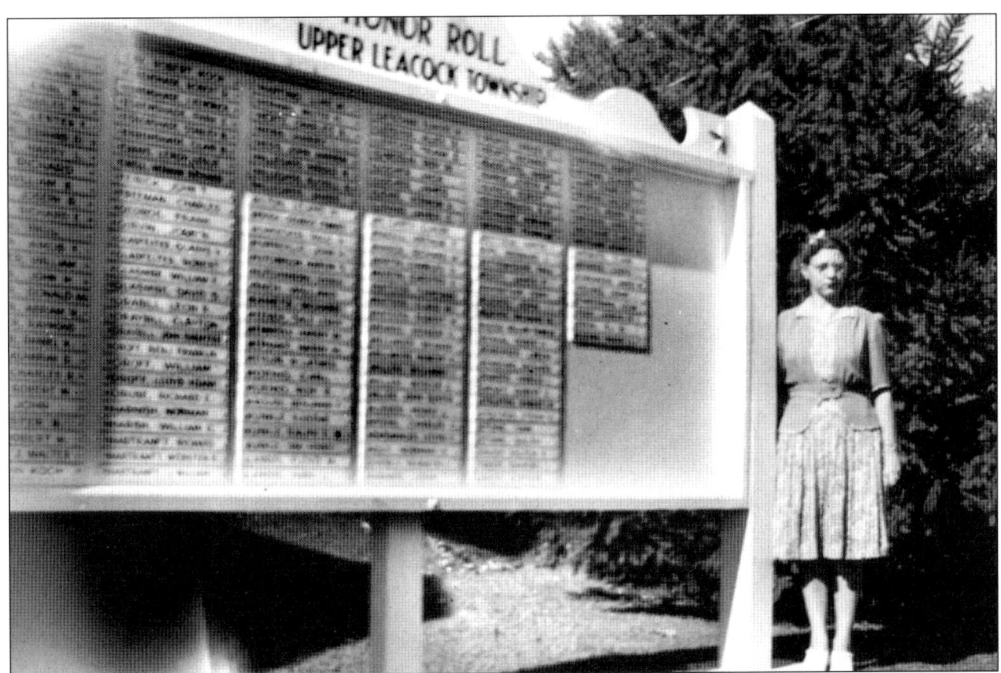

Captured here in the early 1950s, the Leacock honor roll sign looks quite urban. An unidentified young lady, apparently an honor roll student, stands next to the sign for her photograph.

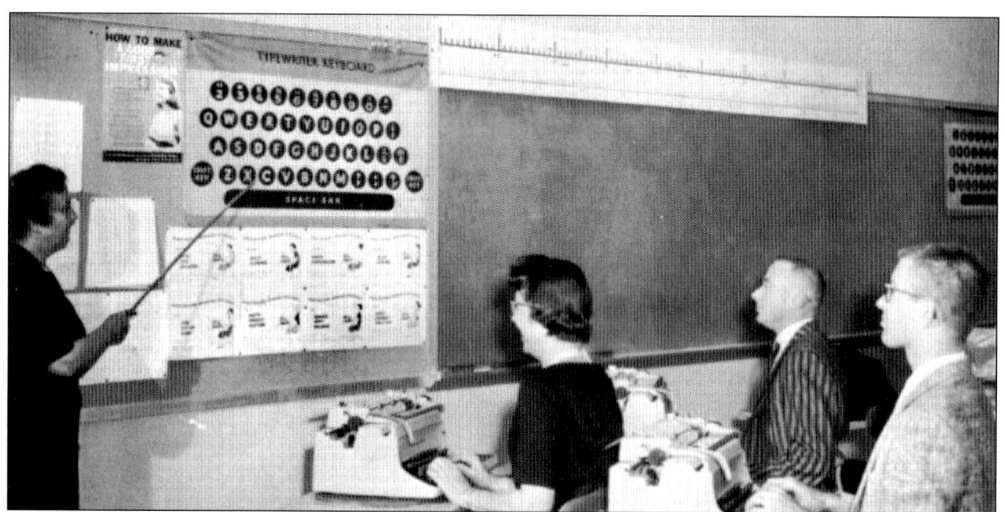

A typing class is shown in this 1950s photograph.

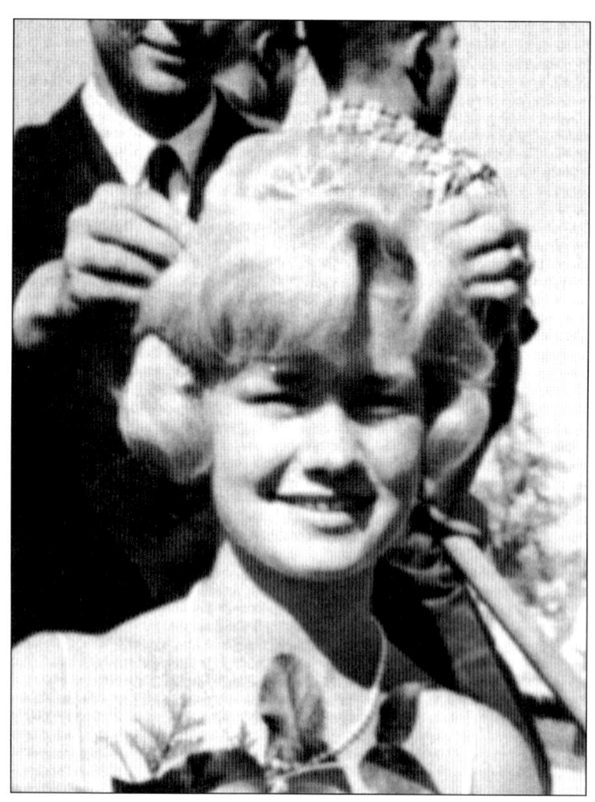

The homecoming queen for 1963, Jackie Royer, was crowned at the Conestoga Valley–Donegal game.

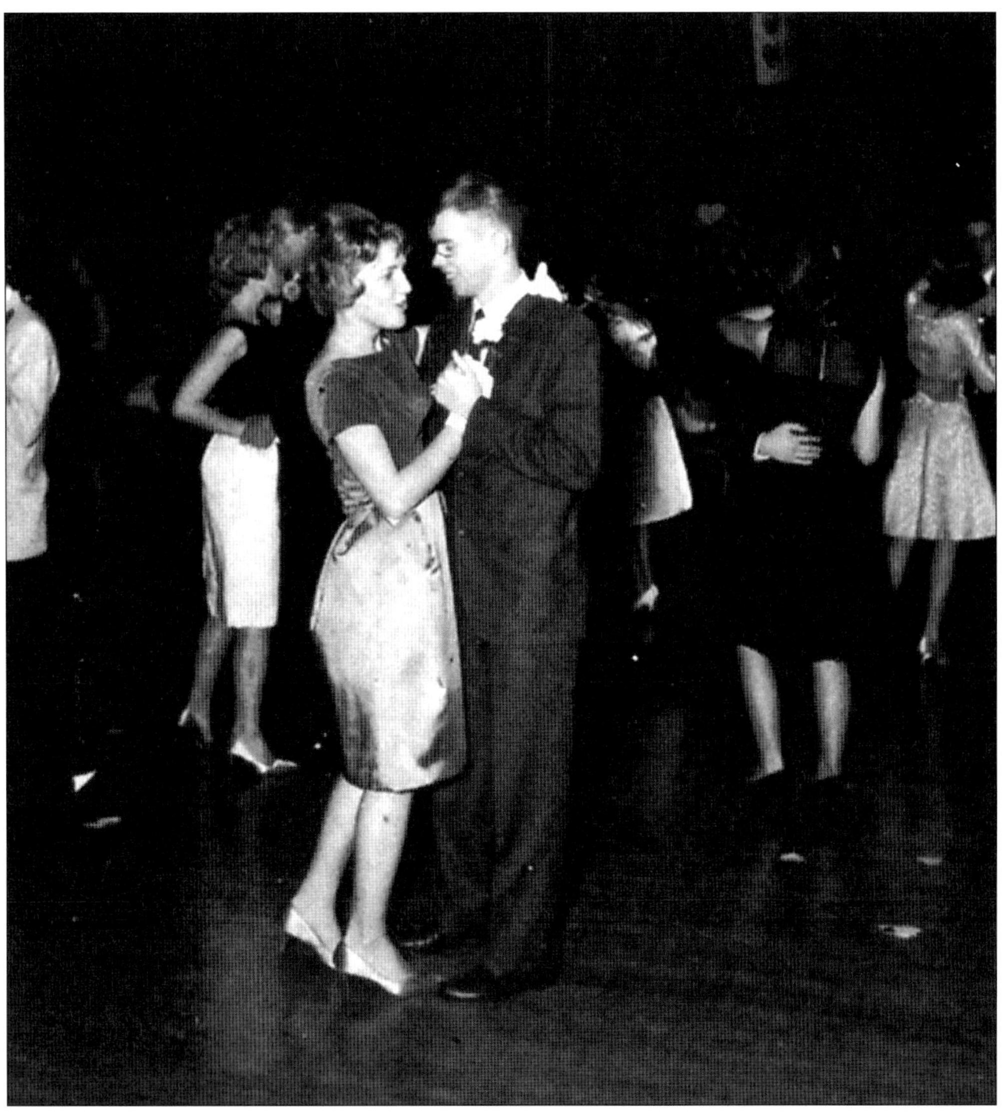

The old-fashioned school dances, where everyone dressed up, are a romantic and idyllic memory of the 1950s.

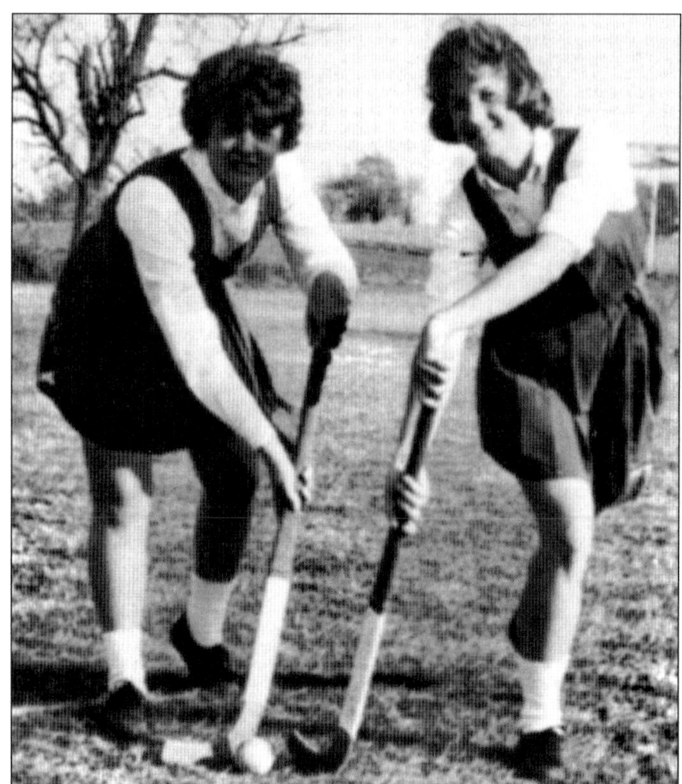

In the 1950s, females who played field hockey apparently needed no protective covering for their shins or knees.

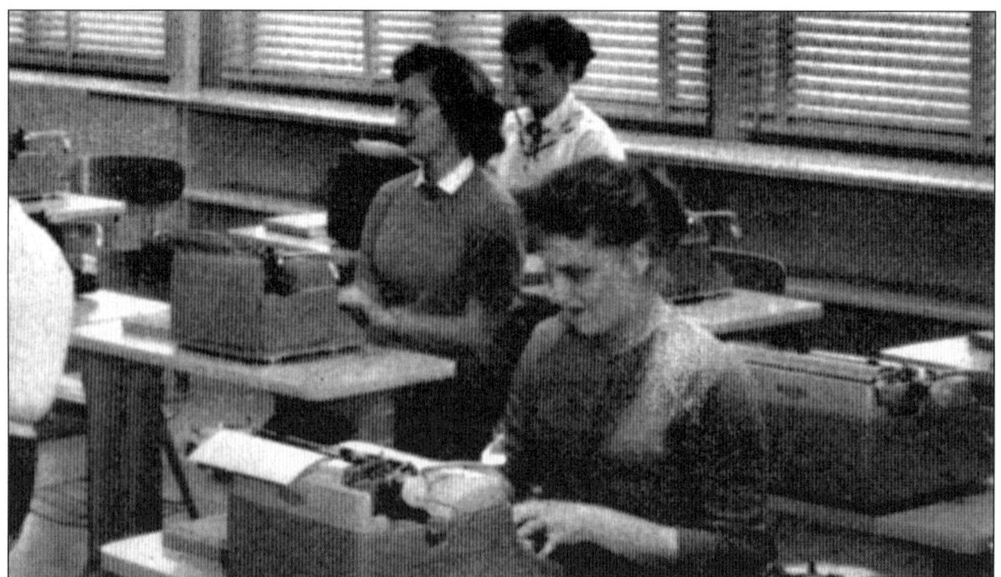

This photograph does not have a confirmed date, but it appears to be from the 1950s.

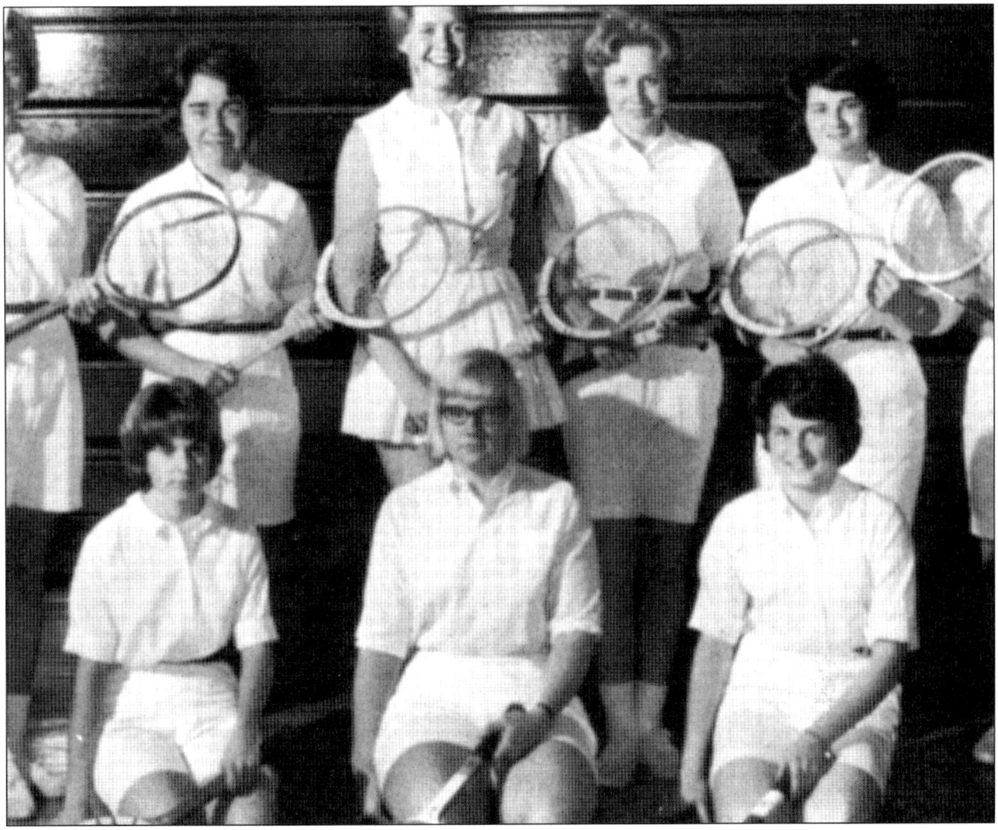

High school really was all about the cute outfits. Shown here is a tennis class in the 1950s with heavy wooden rackets, and unidentified players in great outfits.

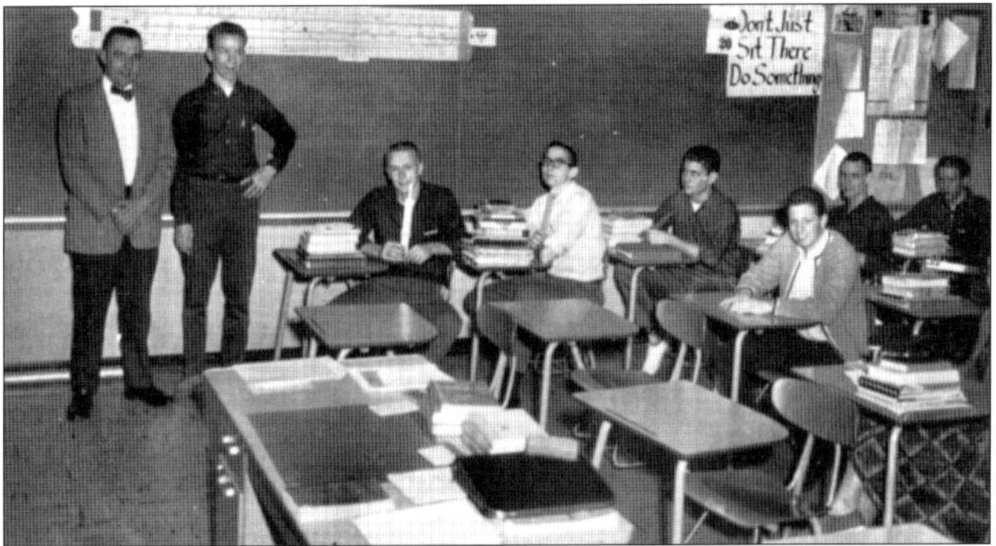

It is difficult to remember what class was like before calculators, but those who do remember this time should recognize the slide rule. In the 1950s, there was even a club designated to learn slide rule techniques.

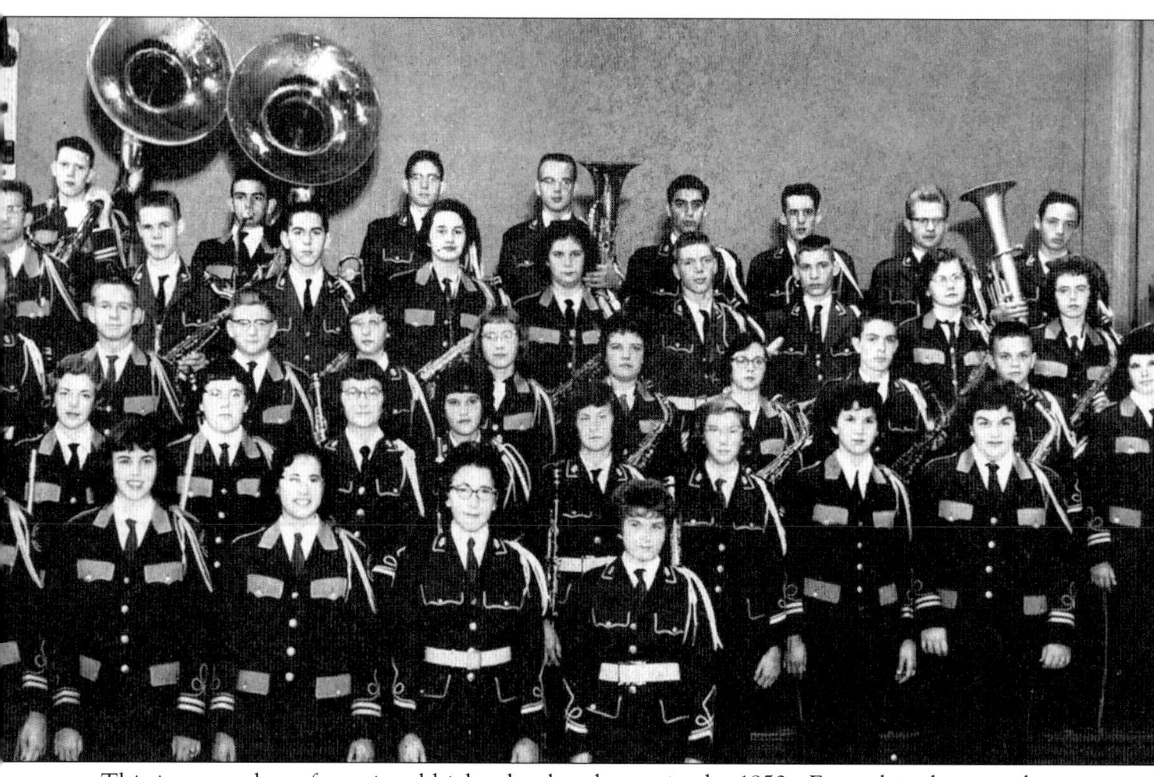

This is a snapshot of a regional high school orchestra in the 1950s. From this photograph, it is clear that not much has changed over the years in regard to orchestras—a reassuring fact, as playing music is a classic art form that should be carried on over time.

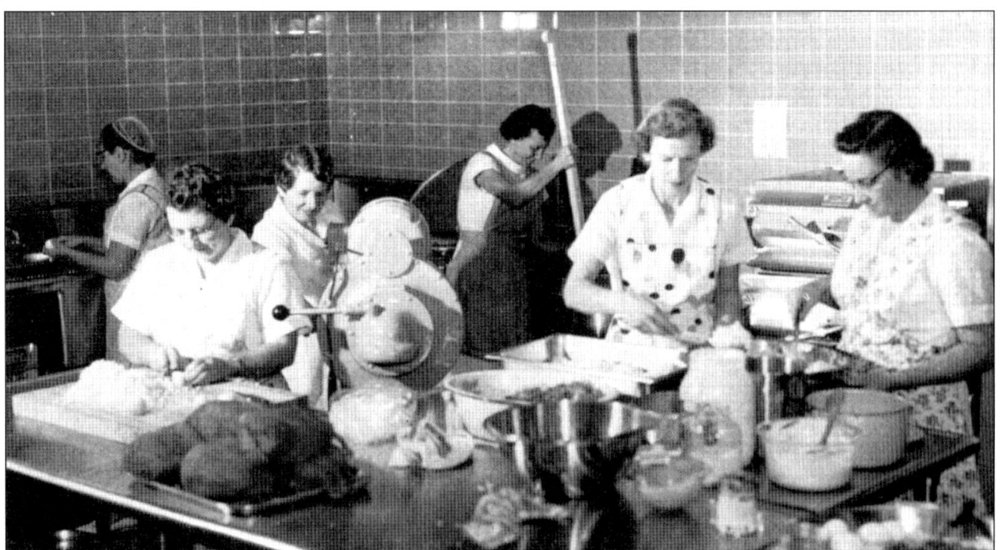

Taken in the early 1950s, this is a great action shot of the cafeteria staff. There are no hairnets and no gloves, and food is being freshly prepared. At least one of the workers is Mennonite, as can be deduced from her cap. From left to right are Irene Smoker, Grace Kane, Florence Andrew, Elizabeth Delinger, Ann Ackerman, and Lydia Kametz.

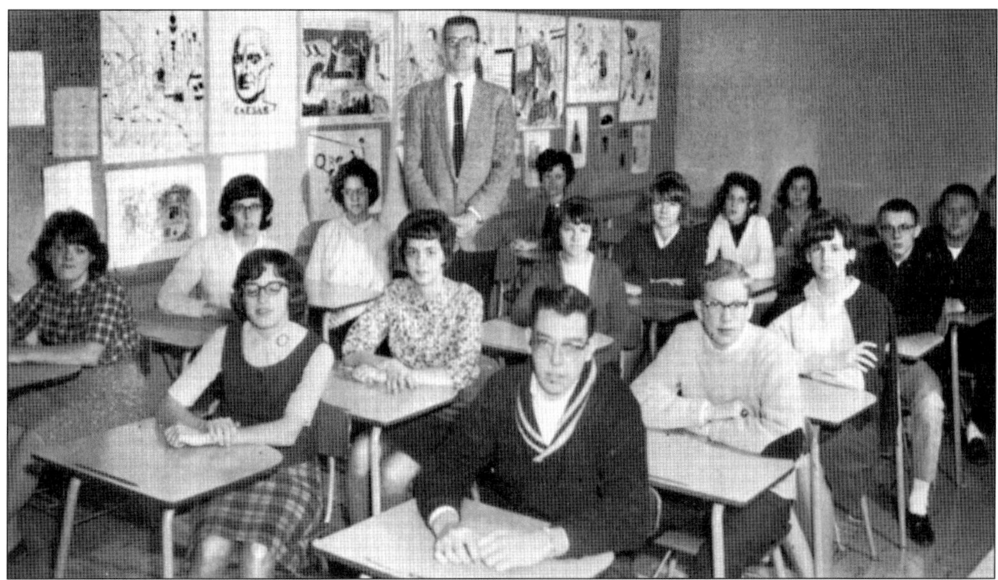

These studious youths are members of the business education club. They pose here with their teacher, Mr. Smith.

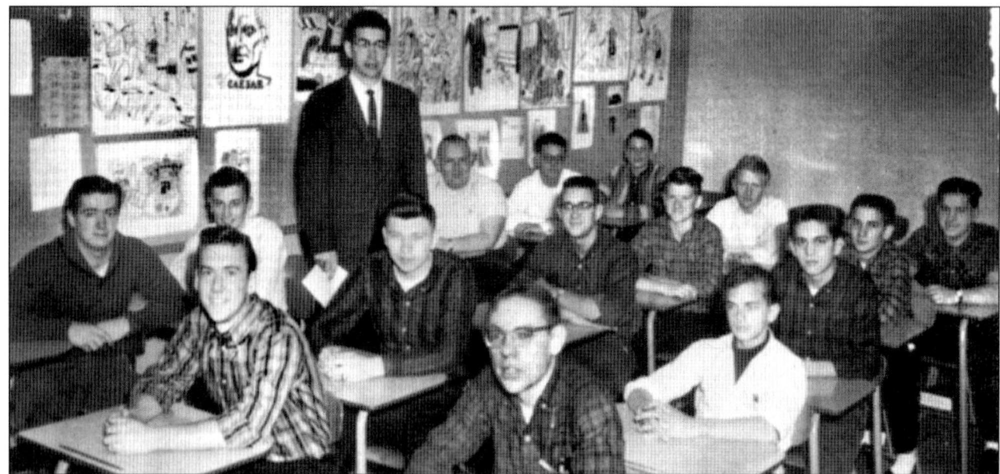

Mr. Brown leads this class of students in the projectionist club. The purpose of the club was to teach students how to operate projectors so that they could assist teachers who wished to show movies in their classes. In the early 1950s, this was considered high technology.

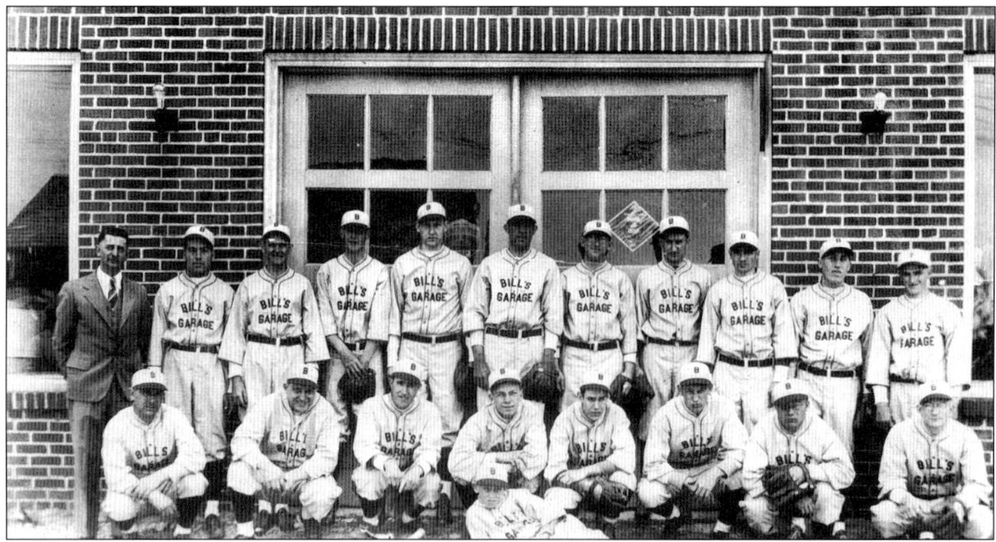

Bill's Garage sponsored this baseball team who posed in front of the garage in 1932 for this team photograph. Members are, from left to right, as follows: (first row) Mark Brubaker (mascot), Floyd Markel, Al Bensing, Luke Ochs, Earl Sweigart, Arthur Garner, Isaac Brubaker, Ralph Rutt, and Harry Bensing; (second row) William Schlappig (sponsor), Rudolph Claudy, Ralph Bechtel, Jerry Derr, Warren Kegerise, Earl Keiper, Ambrose Petery, Harold Burnner, Raymond Moyer, Horace Becher, and Harold Moyer.

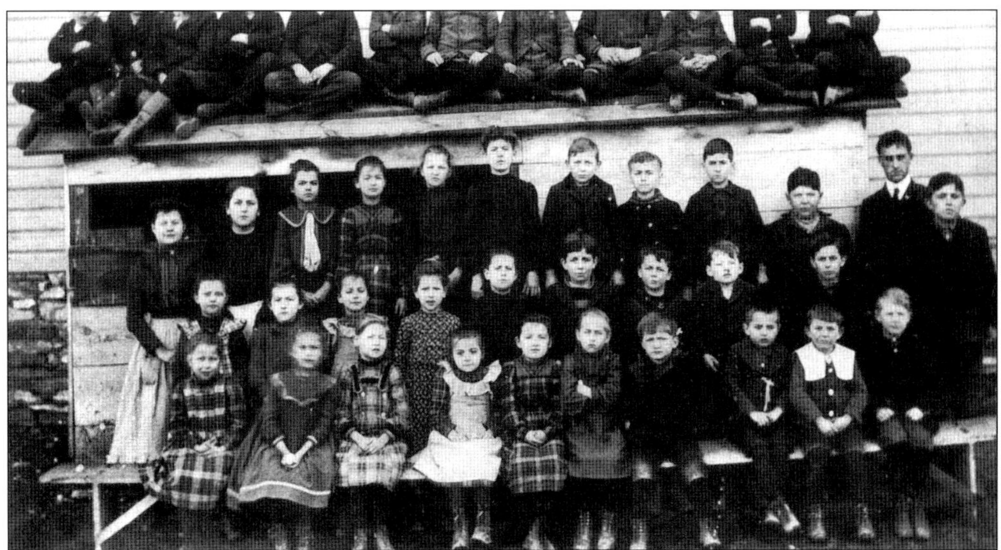

Seen here is the East Stevens School class of 1902. Notice that some of the children are sitting on the roof. From left to right are the following: (first row) Mame Horst, Daisy Wolf, Florence McQuate, Edna Weidman, Helen Stauffer, Katie Knoll, Wenger Hertzog, Harvey Noll, Andrew Wolfe, and Clayton Steely; (second row) Annie Ludwig, Alma Weidman, Carrie Weidman, Miriam Wealand, Maggie Bush, Sherman Hertzog, Emerson Miller, George Ludwig, Raymond Stick, and Lincoln Stauffer; (third row) Susie Ludwig, Amanda Pierce, Esther Miller, Minnie Stauffer, Emma Ludwig, Ella Buch, William Steif, William Weidman, Milton Buch, Clayton Buch, and Richard Dry (teacher).

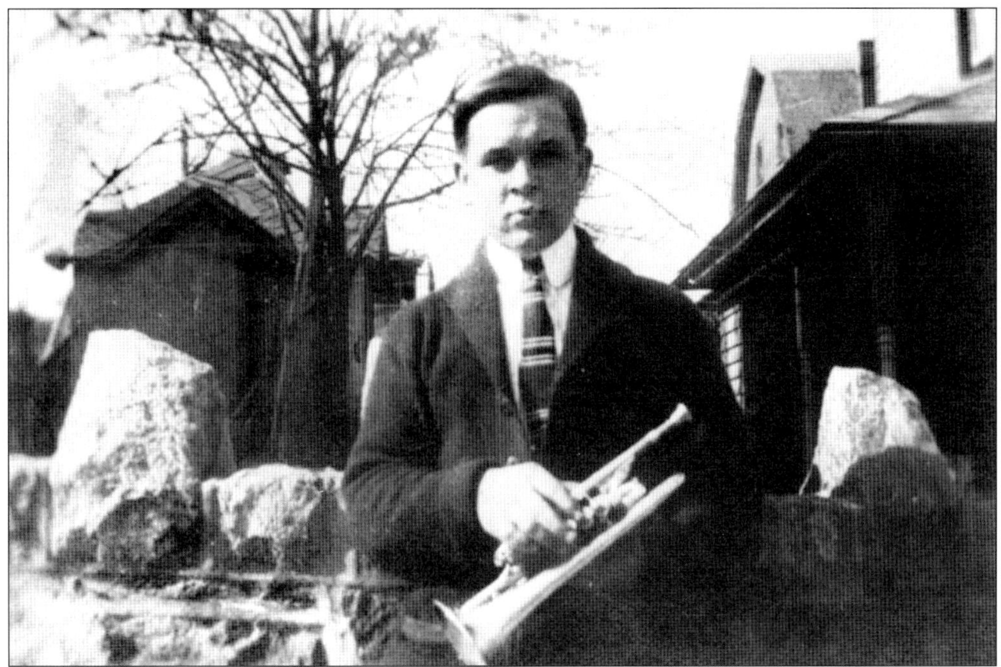

An unidentified young man poses with his trumpet. He may be on his way to a performance, given his more formal attire.

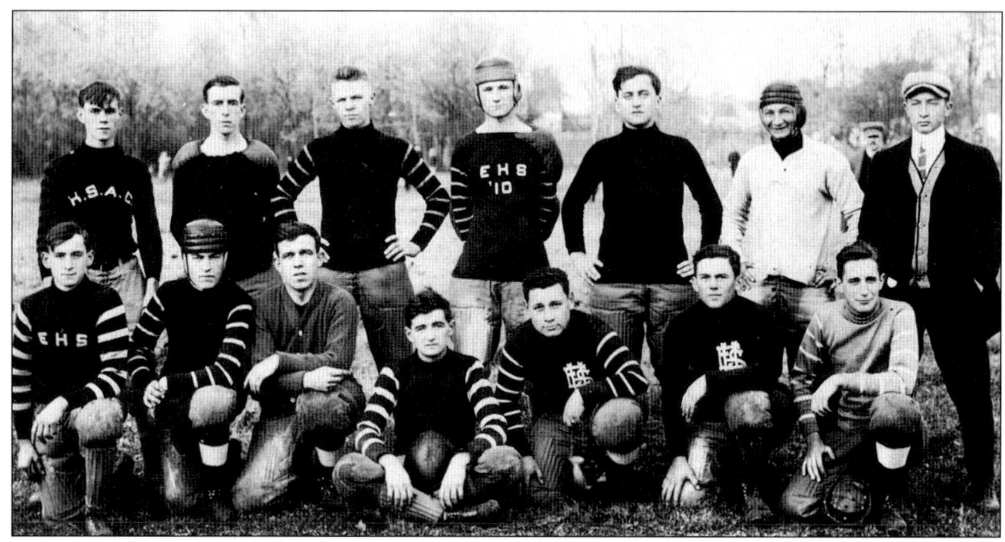

What a difference a decade can make. The top photograph is from 1910, and the bottom photograph was taken in 1920. Students above are, from left to right, as follows: (first row) unidentified, Lester McVey, Ira Usner, John Madlem, Deleth Mellinger, unidentified, and Baker Royer; (second row) unidentified, unidentified, unidentified, Clarence Glass, Martin Fry, William Krouse, and Ira Weise. The students in the bottom photograph are, from left to right, as follows: (first row) Jake Kilhefner, George Eichelberger, Roy Albright, and William Martin; (second row) Arthur Kilhefner, Walter Demmy, Charles Mull, John Rathman, Ivan Wolf, Howard Keeler, Marlin Good, and Harry Showalter.

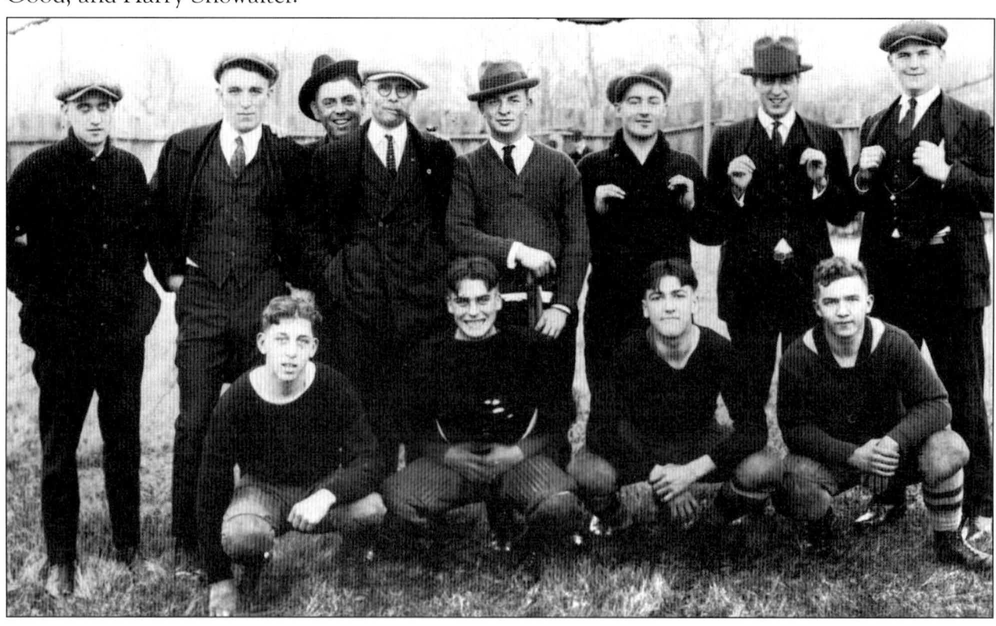

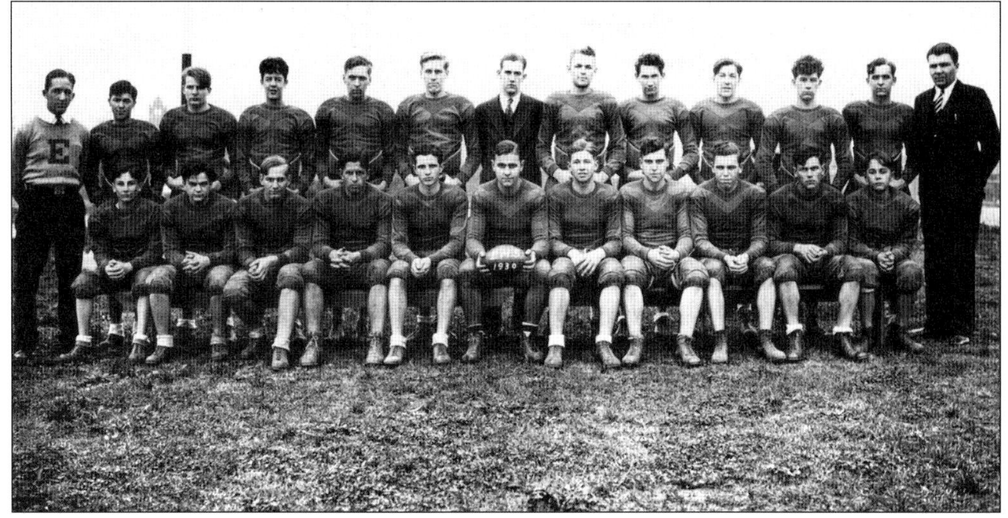

Another 10 years pass, and the difference is even more pronounced with these students. The date, 1930, is written on the football. From left to right are the following: (first row) Edgar Stober, John Longenecher, John Kiick, William Sprecher, Woodrow Ranck, Melvin Wenger, Robert Becker, Clarence Rettew, Abe Petticoffer, Christian Wenger, and Harold Hacker; (second row) Milton Fenninger (manager), Robert Wenger, Richard Sharp, Alfred Rettew, Ralph Fry, Robert Wissler, Harry Schwartz (manager), Edwin Gockley, Samuel Peiffer, Richard Fasnacht, Richard Russell, Earl Beck, and Henry Brubacker (coach).

Mass polio immunization of the oral Sabin variety will be administered at Pequea Valley High School gymnasium on Sunday, November 18, from 11:00 a.m. to 7:00 p.m. A voluntary contribution of twenty-five cents is being asked.

One of the interesting tidbits in the 1962 Pequea Valley High School newspaper, the *Pioneer,* was this polio vaccine announcement. Also of interest, but not pictured, is the announcement for yearbook orders for just $3 per book. The class officers were also announced. The senior officers were Bill Zimmerman (president), Paul Secunda (vice president), Joanne Kellenberger (secretary), and Chip Simpson (treasurer).

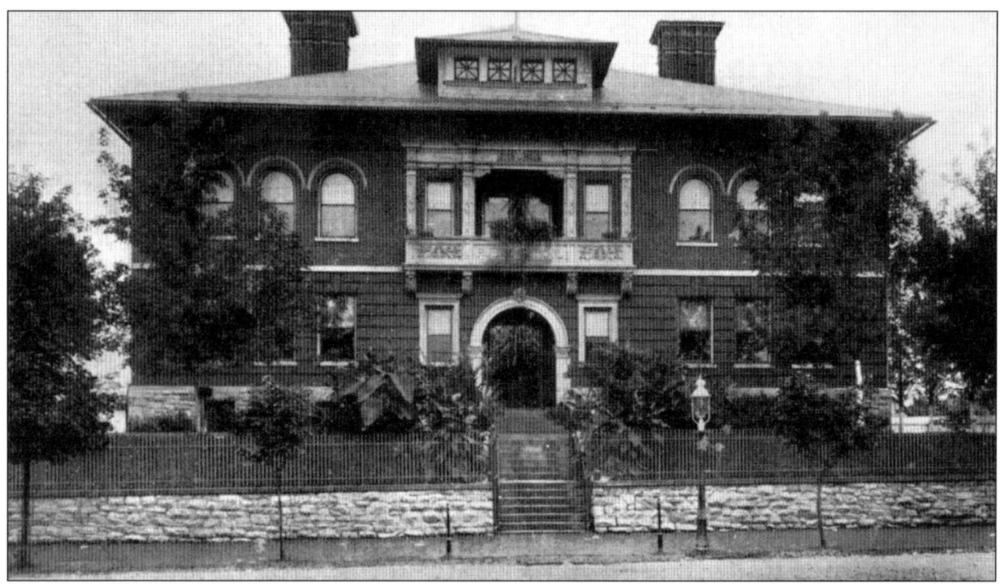

Pictured here is the Clay Street School in Lancaster. Many of the area youth traveled to Lancaster if they wished to further their education.

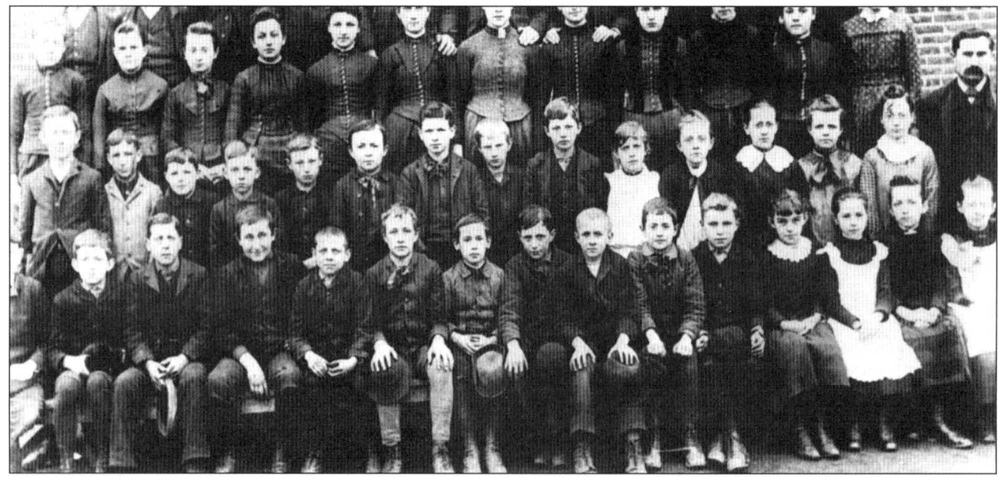

This photograph outlines a class *c.* 1888 at an area school. From left to right are the following: (first row) John Wise, William McCaa, J. Bitzer, Isaac Mentzer, John Leber, Elmer Binkley, James Lightner, Clem Bitzer, Harry Slick, Arthur Keller, Levi Cooper, Bare Bolster, Elmyra Allison, Fannie Barrington, and Naomi Seltzer; (second row) Daniel Breneiser, Elwood Garret, John Miller, H. Weaver, Pensrose Richwine, George Steinmetz, W. W. Halligan, George Sheasffer, Harvey Keller, Mame Weinhold, Mame Reddig, Lena Hertz, Minnie Leber, Bertha Richwine, and Levi Miller (teacher); (third row) Alice Fry, Sarah Landis, Von Nieda, Nora Connell, Emma Kramer, Maggie Eshleman Weaver, Ella Wise, Minnie Messner Hoover, Irene Royer Weidman, Mary Weaver, Allie Gemperling, Katie Strohl, and Minnie Gates.

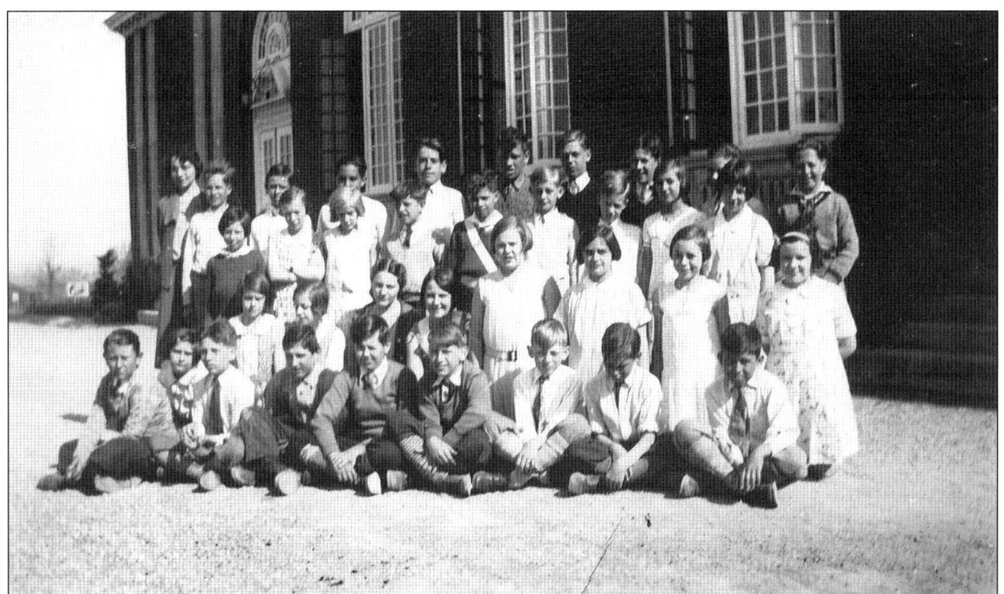

This is a unique glimpse of school students in a time gone by.

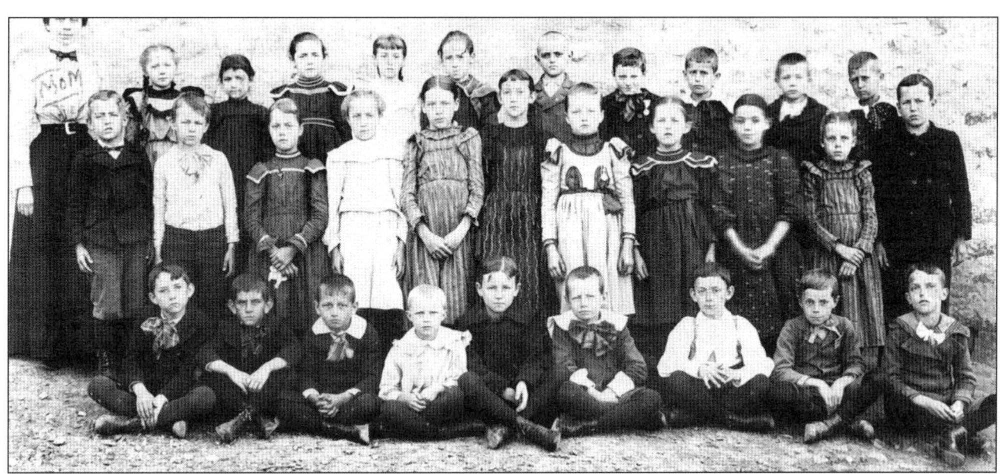

This is the class of 1897 from an area school. From left to right are the following: (first row) Colonel Regar, Robert Bare, Nelson Waltman, Robert Brugger, unidentified, unidentified, Elroy Lewis, unidentified, and unidentified; (second row) Ralph Schreck, Peter Doremus, unidentified, Cora Heinaman, Mohler, Seltzer, Hallie Hershberger, unidentified, unidentified, Mohler, and Clarence Roth; (third row), Emma N. Hassler (teacher), unidentified, Worley, unidentified, Pearl Shimp, Lillie Mohler, unidentified, unidentified, Milton Wise, unidentified, and Arthur Wise.

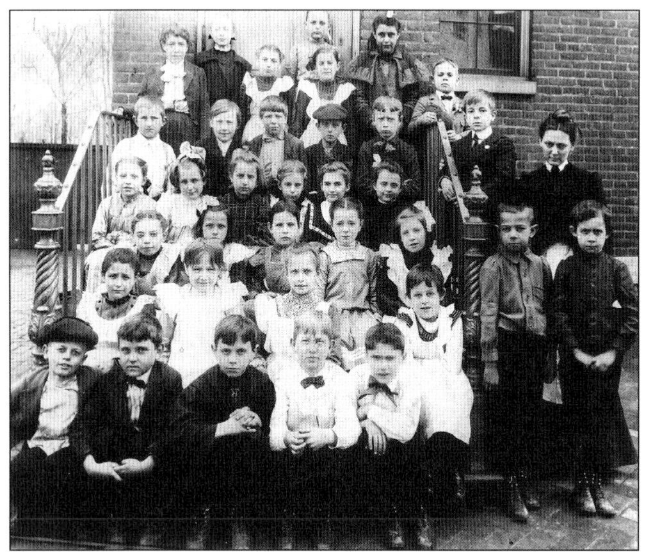

This is an unidentified photograph of a school class. Notice the teacher on the right and the very stern look she is giving to the camera. Perhaps she just had to settle some students who look a little guilty in the front row, or maybe she just disciplined the photographer.

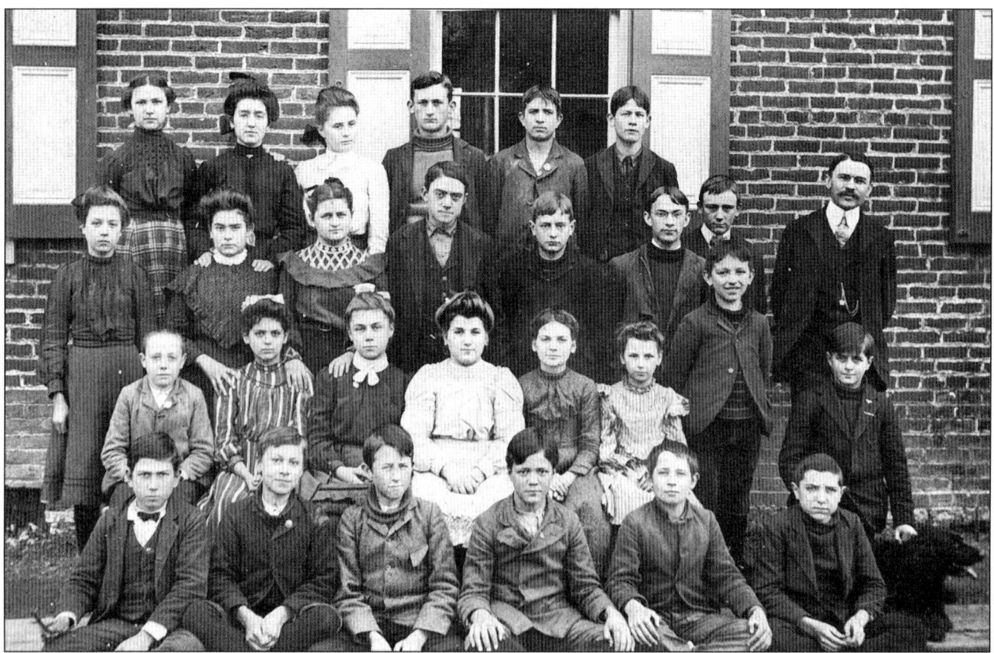

This photograph was taken in 1904, possibly at the Hinkletown School. From left to right are the following: (first row) Daniel Wanner, Samuel Hoeffer, Earl J. Snyder, John Frankfort, William McCarty, and Raymond Fassnacht; (second row) Nathaniel McCarty, Lydia Nixdorf Butzer, Alice Rhoads Dunn, Bessie Bard Bear, Sarah Weaver Stahl, Katie Good, Paul Glockly (standing), and Charles J. Reemsnyder (with dog); (third row) Fianna Brubaker, Edna Harting, Mary W. Reemsnyder, Harry Fox, David Burkholder, Cloyd Acher, Levi M. Bard, and Clayton Mussleman (teacher); (fourth row) Anna Brown, Mary Bard Myers, Lottie Sheaffer Treisch, Frank O. Butzer, Harry Garman, and Harrison Treisch.

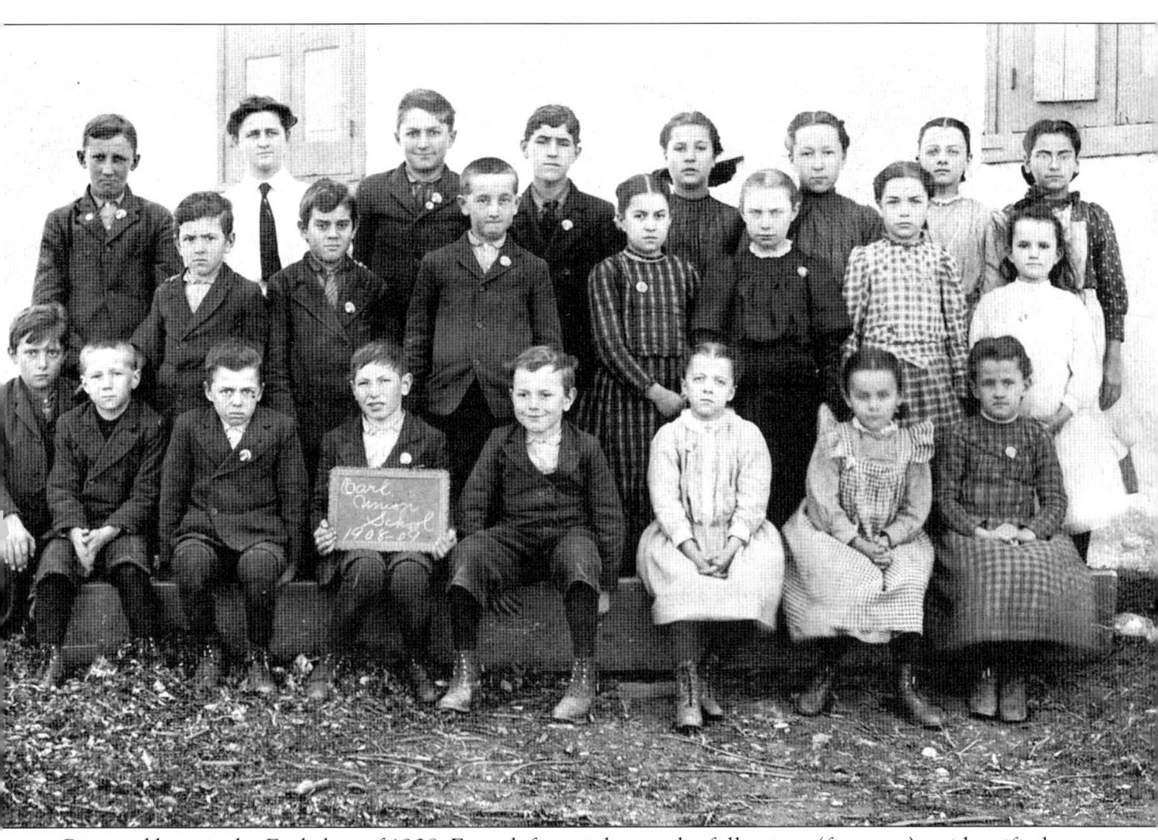

Pictured here is the Earl class of 1908. From left to right are the following: (first row) unidentified, Amos Newswanger, Ivan Senenig, William Kascaden, Jonas Martin, Anna Sensenig Horst, Alice Sensenig, and Ella Weaver; (second row) David Martin, Roscoe Burkhart, Peter Newswanger, Barton Sensenig, Lillian Rutter, Anna Newswanger, Mary Sensenig, and Anna Mary Nolt.

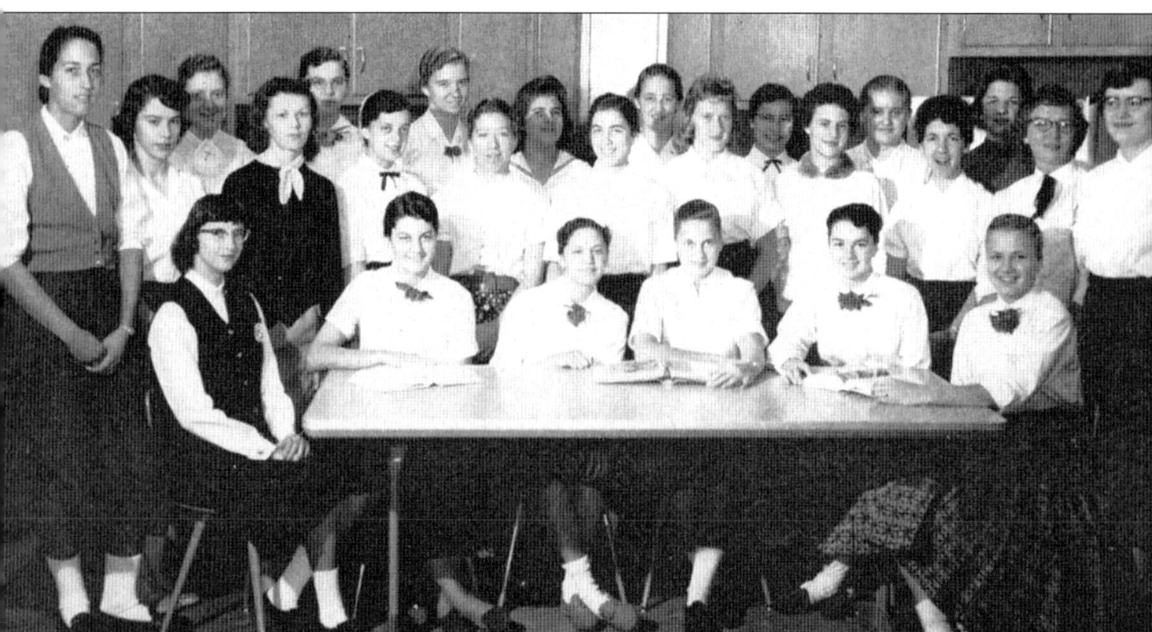

This is the epitome of an early-1950s club. This is the Future Homemakers of America club. The purpose of the club was to help girls become better homemakers. The girls learned how to sew, crochet, knit, and cook. From left to right are the following: (first row) Joan Szalak, Norma Leaman, Phoebe Dillman, Ruth Denlinger (president), Nancy Kreider, and Rhoda Denlinger; (second row) June Risser, Annette Hahn, Jeanette Myers, Mary Jane Stoltzfus, Lois Chubb, Ethel Hoover, Barbara Lohr, Brenda Weidman, Pat Kane, Joyce Denlinger, and Miss Latsha (teacher); (third row) Jeanette Hershey, Lois Boose, Barbara Martin, Nancy Longenecker, Joanne Mellinger, Verna Martin, Doris Groff, and Judy Thompson.

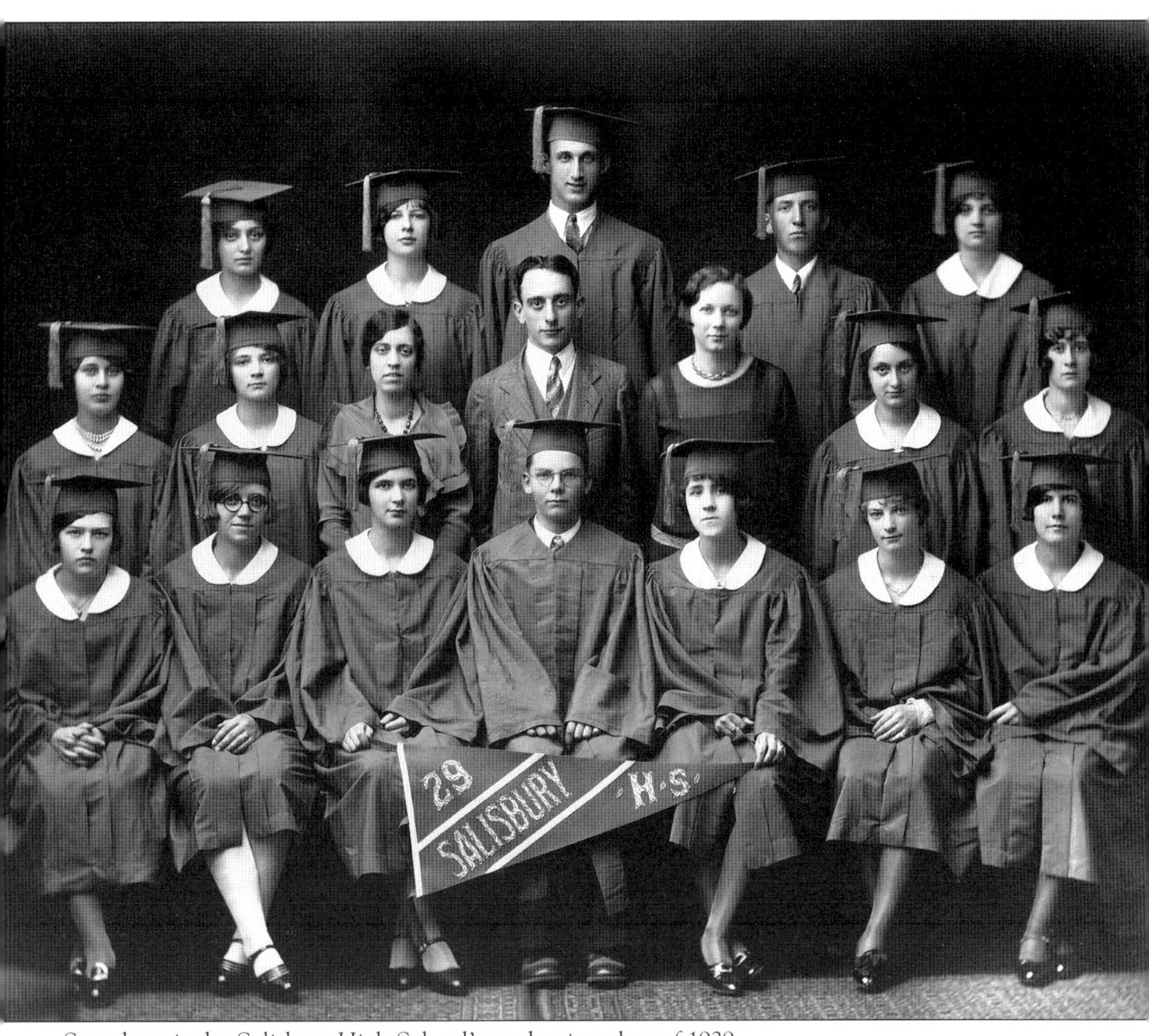

Seen here is the Salisbury High School's graduating class of 1929.

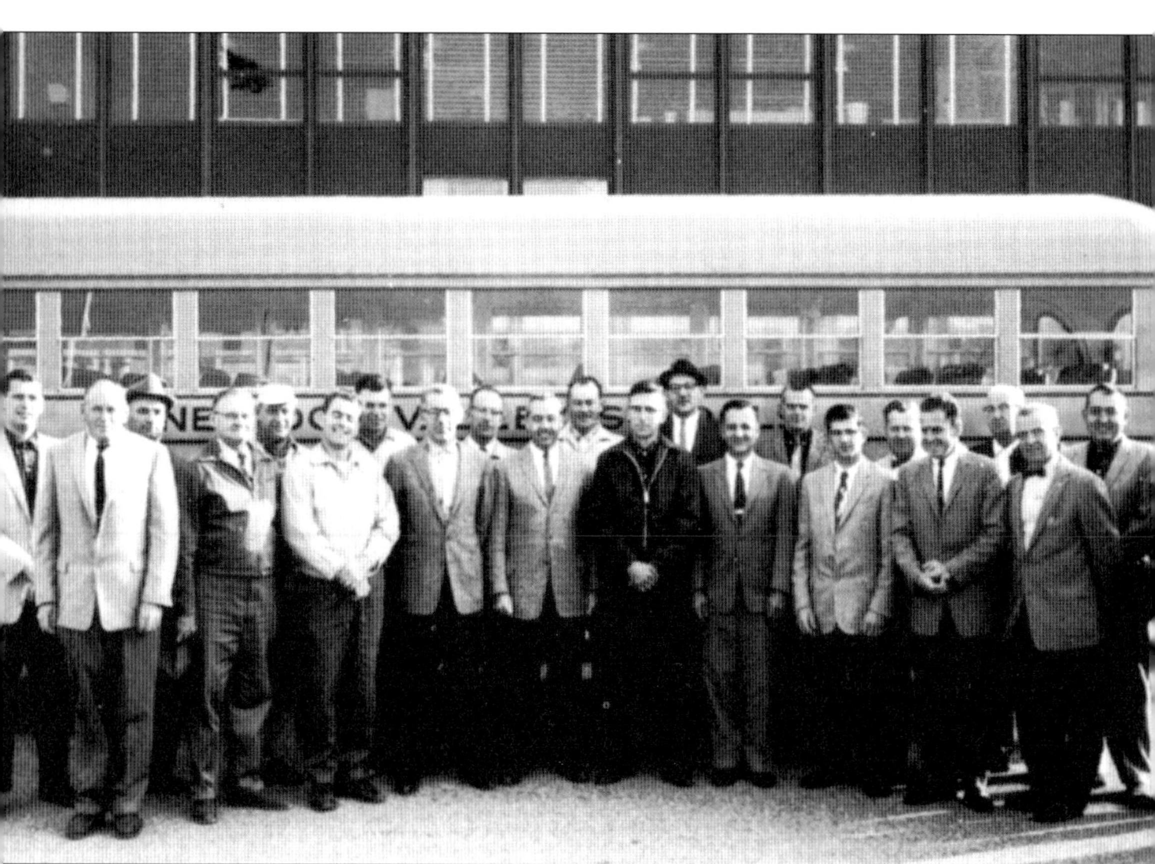

This photograph of school bus drivers is a great bridge between the education and transportation chapters. The bus, apparently manufactured in the early 1950s, probably did not have a stop arm or flashing lights, features that appeared on later buses. It is likely that the bus did have a ticking sound that alerted students and others that the bus was going to stop. Federal standards were not instituted for school buses until the late 1970s. From left to right are the following: (first row) P. Pickel, L. Zook, D. Myer, W. Wimer, D. Stoltzfus, L. Siegrist, E. Hollinger, R. Martin, L. Weaver, H. Brubaker, and F. Slabach; (second row) B. Steffy, H. High, H. Landis, C. Shennk, C. Boose. A. Esh, M. Bare, C. Rohrer, W. Buffenmyer, A. Shultz, and M. Sheaffer.

Four

Transportation

The people of the Pequea Valley often used the popular Conestoga wagon as a means for transportation. First developed in Lancaster County in the late 1700s, the vehicles were horse-drawn, four-wheeled wagons.

It is unclear as to why the name Conestoga was coined for the wagons. Some feel that the name stemmed from the name of local Native Americans, while others believe that the wagons were named after a river or valley.

More often than not, locals viewed wagon trains, which were really nothing more than a multitude of wagons, going from Philadelphia to Lancaster and beyond. Usually, there was a wagon master to aid with the long journey.

It is documented that the first need for wagons was to transport goods for trade, and it is noted that William Penn was one of the first to ride from Philadelphia to the Lancaster area, passing through the town of Intercourse.

The wagons were first made of a variety of woods, some of which were better than others for various parts of the wagon. The harder, more cured wood was best for the wheels.

A typical outing to or from Philadelphia to Intercourse and surrounding areas could take a few days at minimum, more if the haul was larger. Modernized wagons, streetcars, soon dotted the embryonic dirt roads, carrying not only goods but also passengers to and fro.

In the early 1900s, many roads were developed by the state, and motor vehicles were able to utilize these roads to visit various communities throughout Pennsylvania. More often than not, the top speed limit was 25 miles per hour, which may seem slow in terms of today's roadways, but it was not that far-fetched for drivers during this time, as that was the fastest most were able to travel anyway.

Although Route 340 is still in existence, it was not adequate for the amount of travel that was required in later times, and thus the turnpike in Pennsylvania was born. Additionally, the Route 30 bypass was built, and it continues to be upgraded.

Today, in Intercourse and surrounding areas, the Amish and some Mennonites still use horse-drawn buggies as their means of transportation.

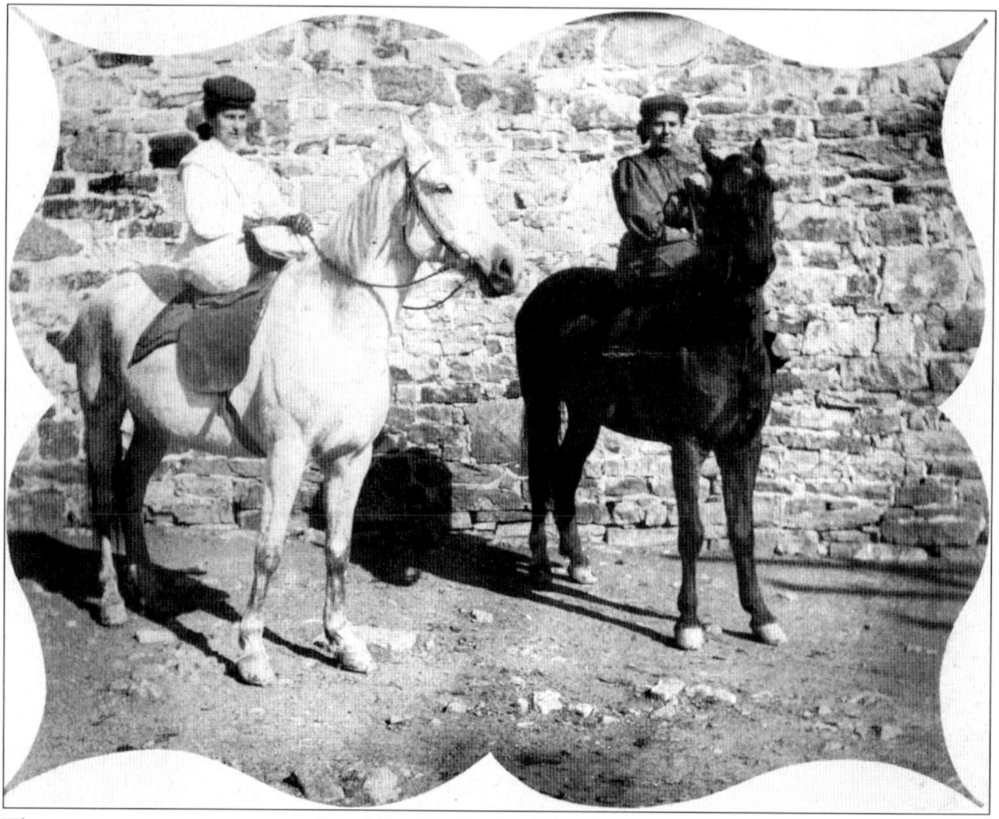

These two women are sitting sidesaddle. The back of the photograph reads, "Mary's horse, Caolie (White one)."

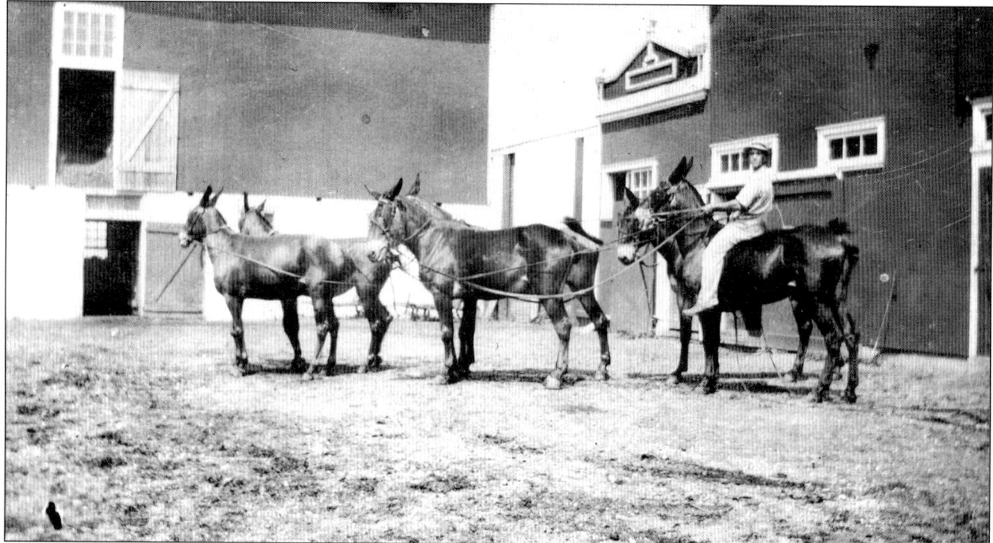

The back of the photograph reads, "Charles 40," which may be the age of the man in the image. Perhaps the horses were a birthday present.

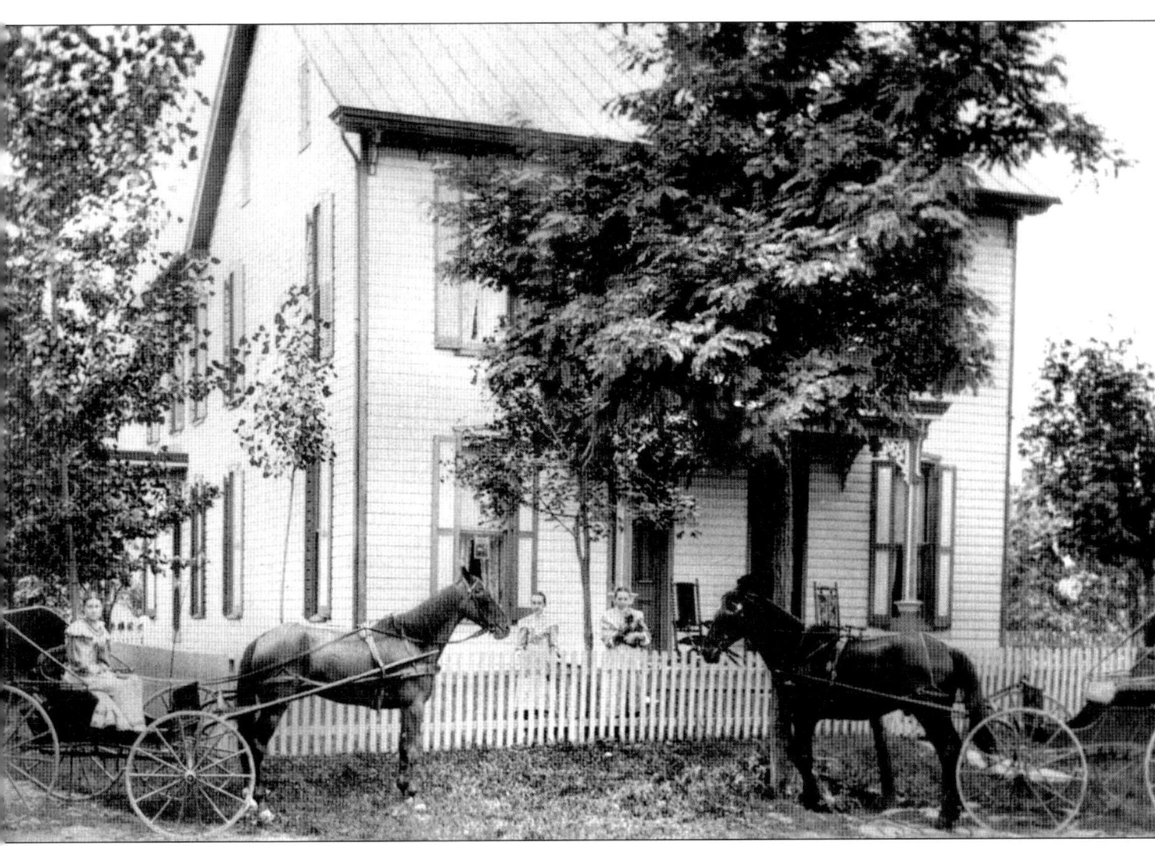

The home, carriages, attire, and pets in this photograph all lead one to believe that Israel Widder, powwow doctor, was well-to-do. A powwow doctor was originally a Native American term for a healer. When European immigrants arrived, if they were a proclaimed doctor or healer, they were called powwows.

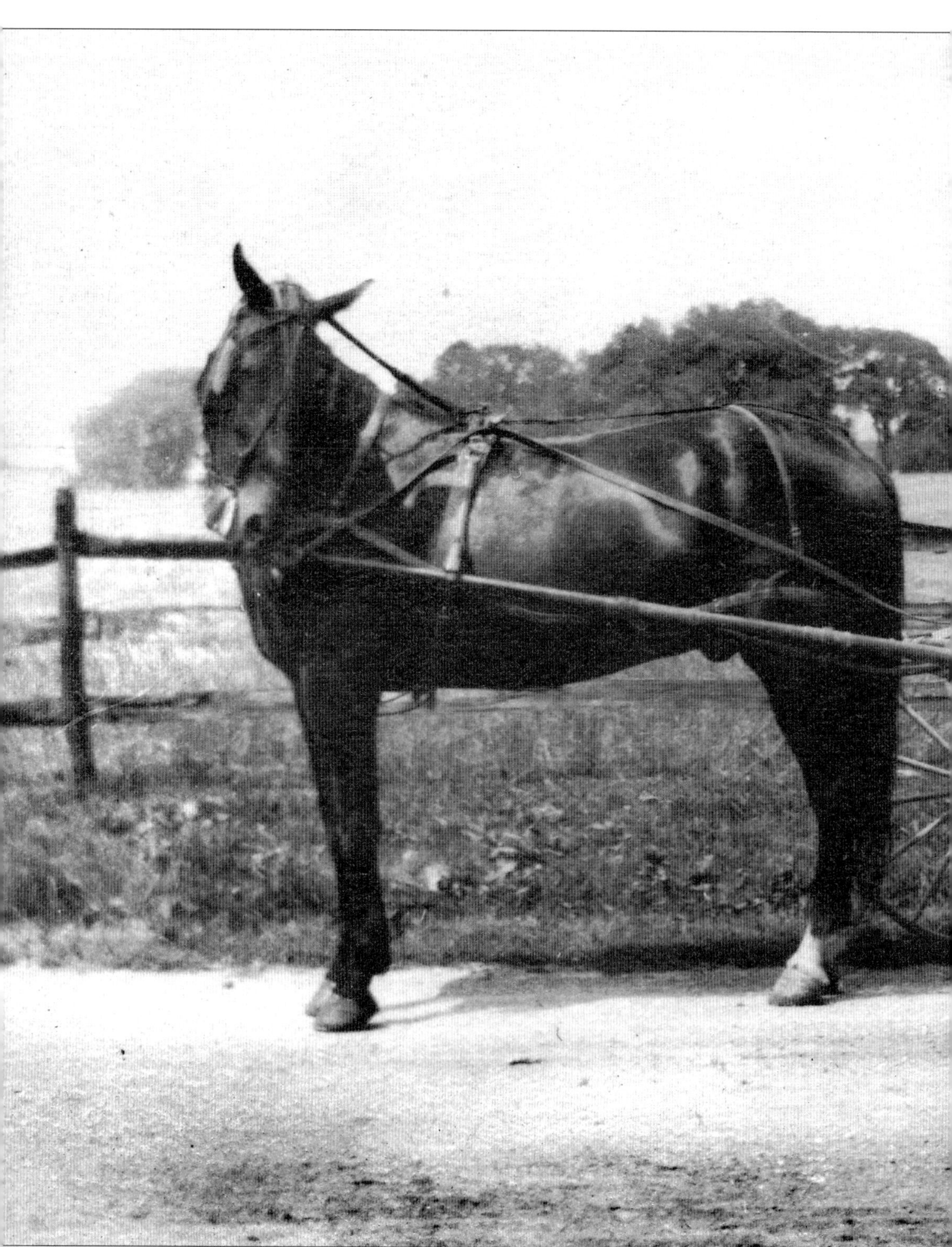

This unique photograph from the mid-1800s outlines the country roads, the country-style fence that is still seen often in the region, as well as the mid-level carriage. The girl's expression is priceless,

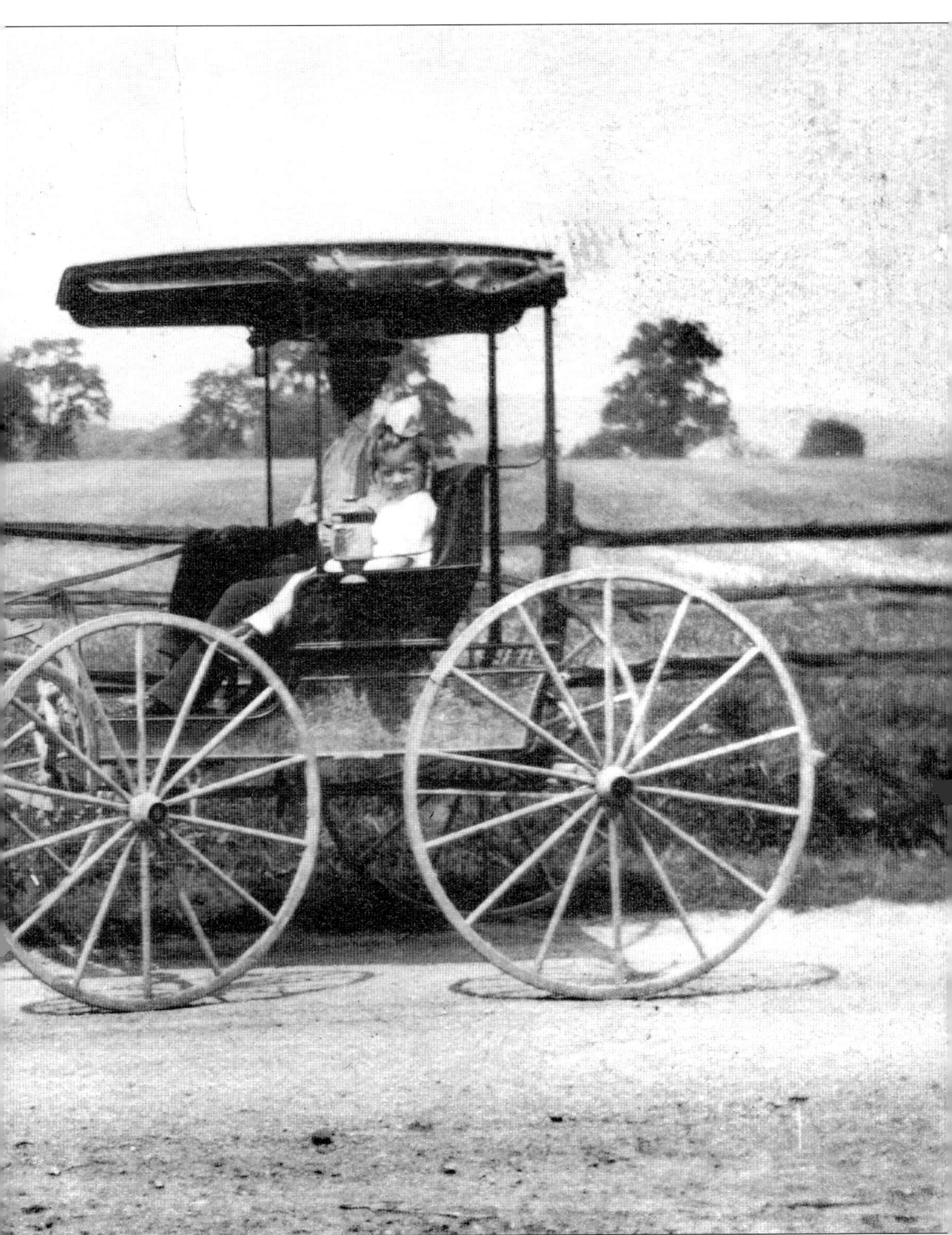

and it appears that the gentleman is taking her to a party or outing, based upon her attire.

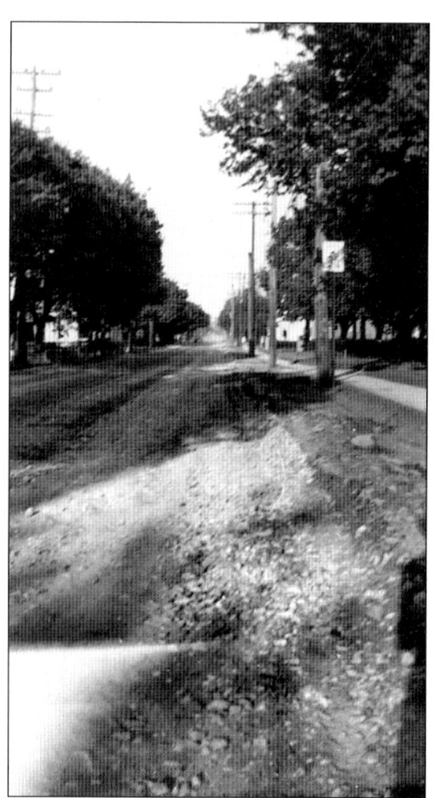

This is a typical view of a road in the region before the roads were blacktopped. You can see that there were already telephone poles and sidewalks in the area. This photograph could have been taken as early as the 1920s. To the lower right is the shadow of someone who was standing near the photographer when the picture was taken.

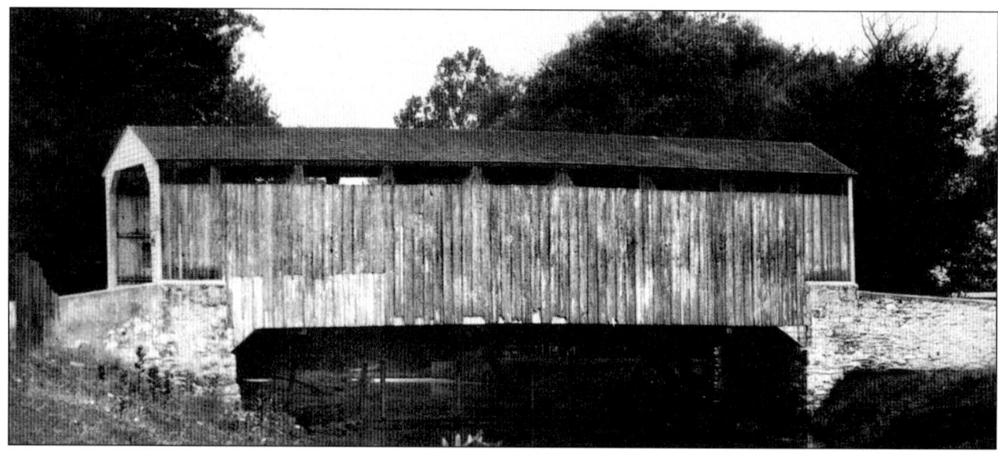

One of the last bridges in the Pequea Valley and surrounding regions, this bridge was built in 1891. The bridge is formally called the Kellers Mill Bridge, but it is informally referred to as the Guy Bard Bridge, as a prominent judge by the name of Guy Bard once lived in the area. The bridge is wooden, as all bridges were in that era.

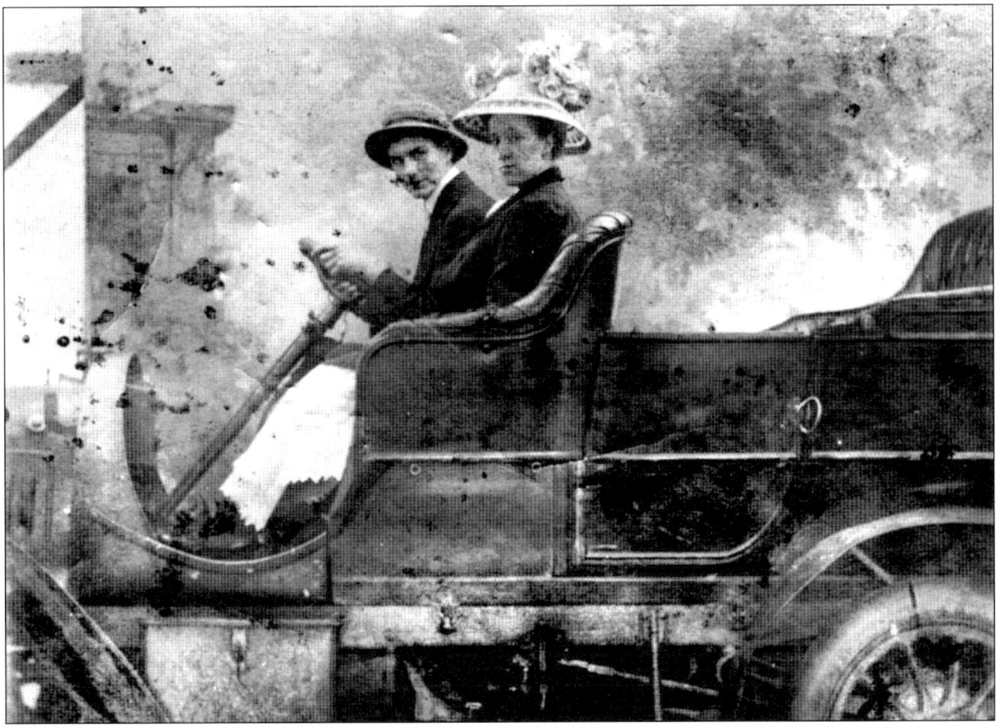

This photograph of a couple in a car was taken in September 1911. The back of the photograph reads, "Not yet married as pictured." The couple is identified as Charles Christman Sr. and his wife. The people below are all unidentified except for Israel Widder, who is seated in the front, wearing the lighter coat.

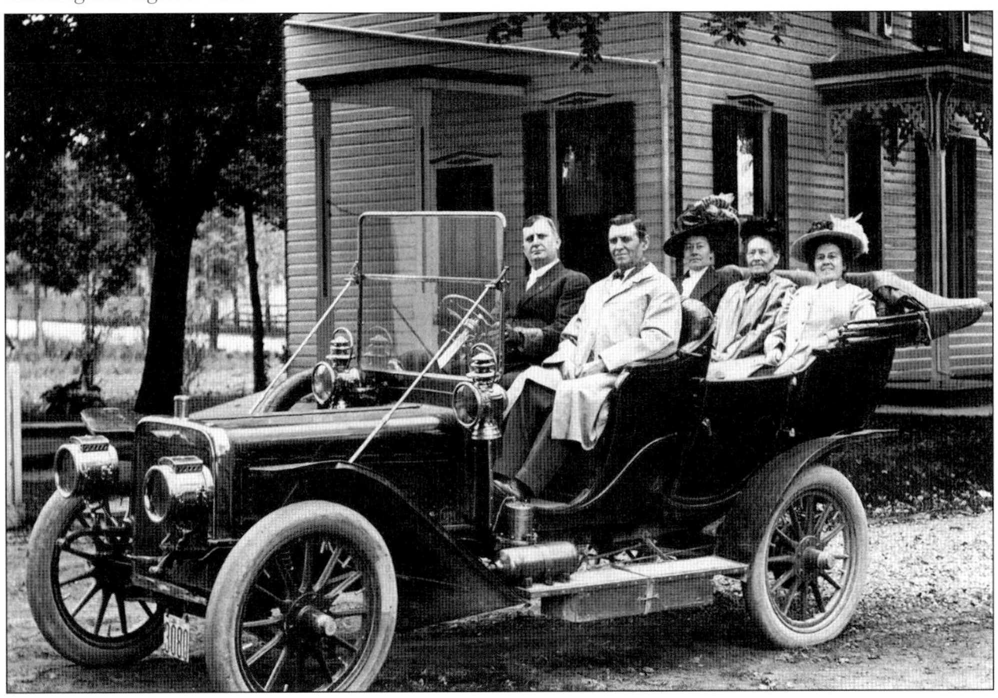

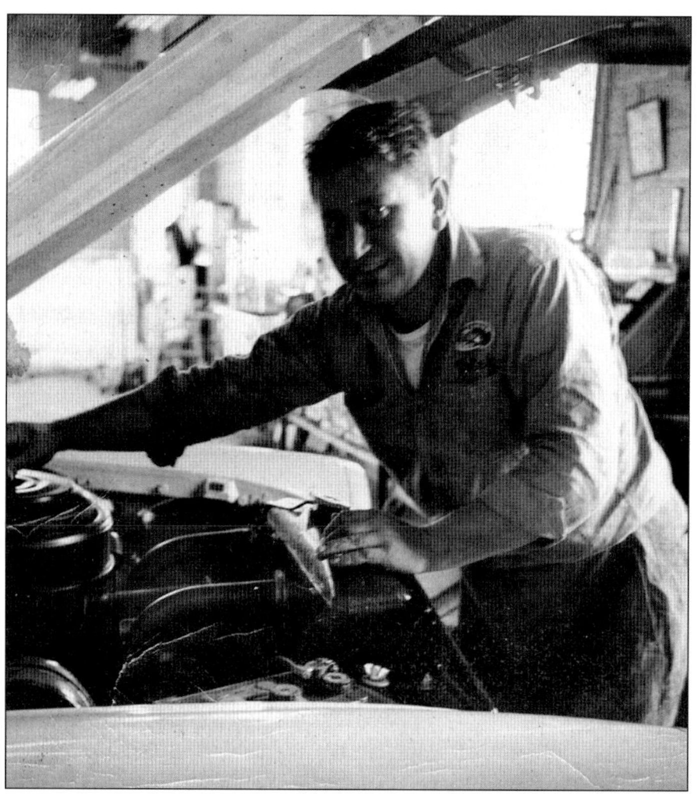

With the influx of manufactured vehicles came an increase of jobs. This *c.* 1950s image shows an unidentified man working on a car.

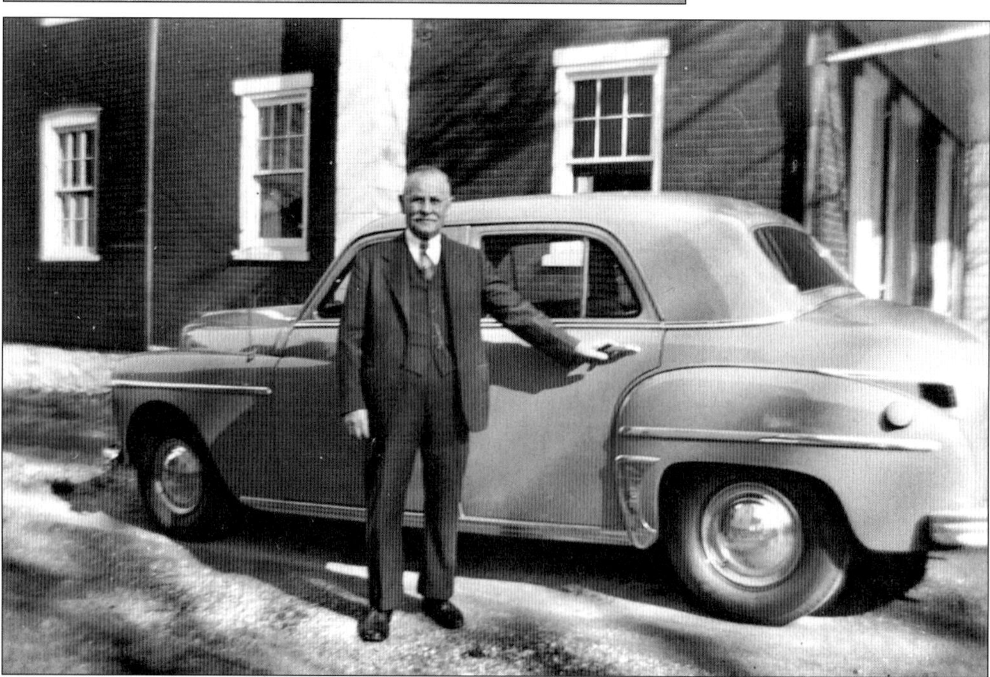

One thing that never seems to go out of style (in the early 1940s and in the present) is people posing with their cars. This proud man is posing with what appears to be a brand-new car, given the glossy exterior, which was actually fairly rare in that era.

Cars play a large role in many lifestyles. Here we see a woman loading or unloading something into the trunk of her car. We also see, in the other photograph, two unidentified men, one of whom is probably the proud owner of the car. The front of the photograph reads, "My New Car." In both images, you can see the spare tires; note the considerable difference in just a few years of the tire width and design.

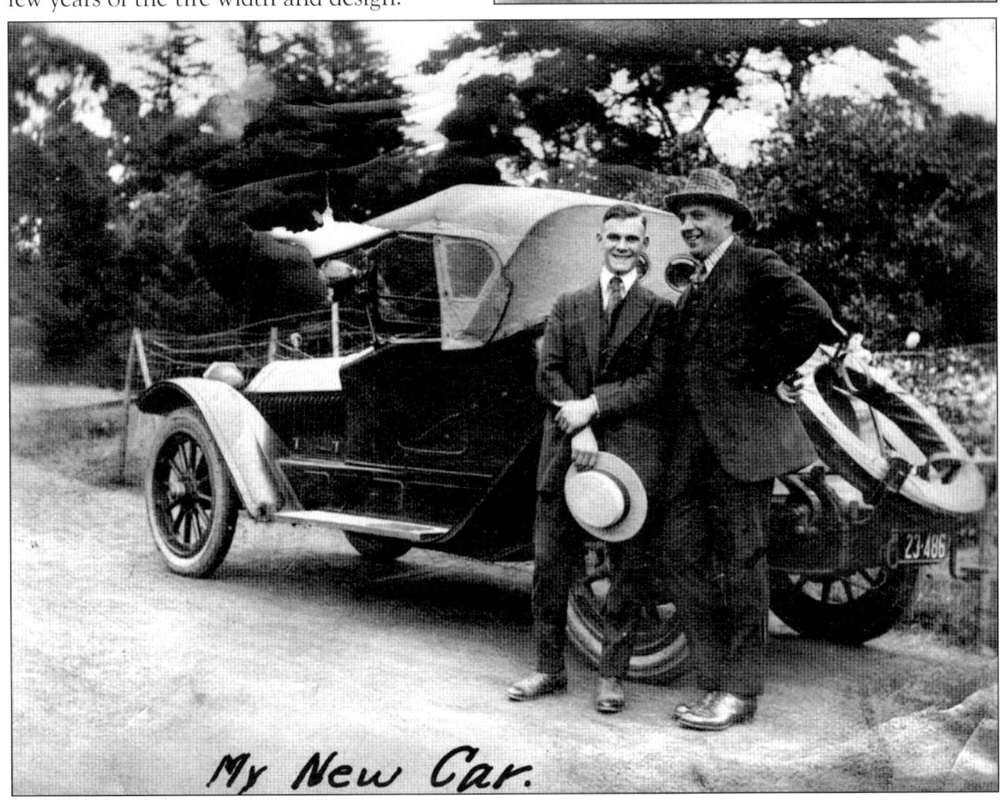

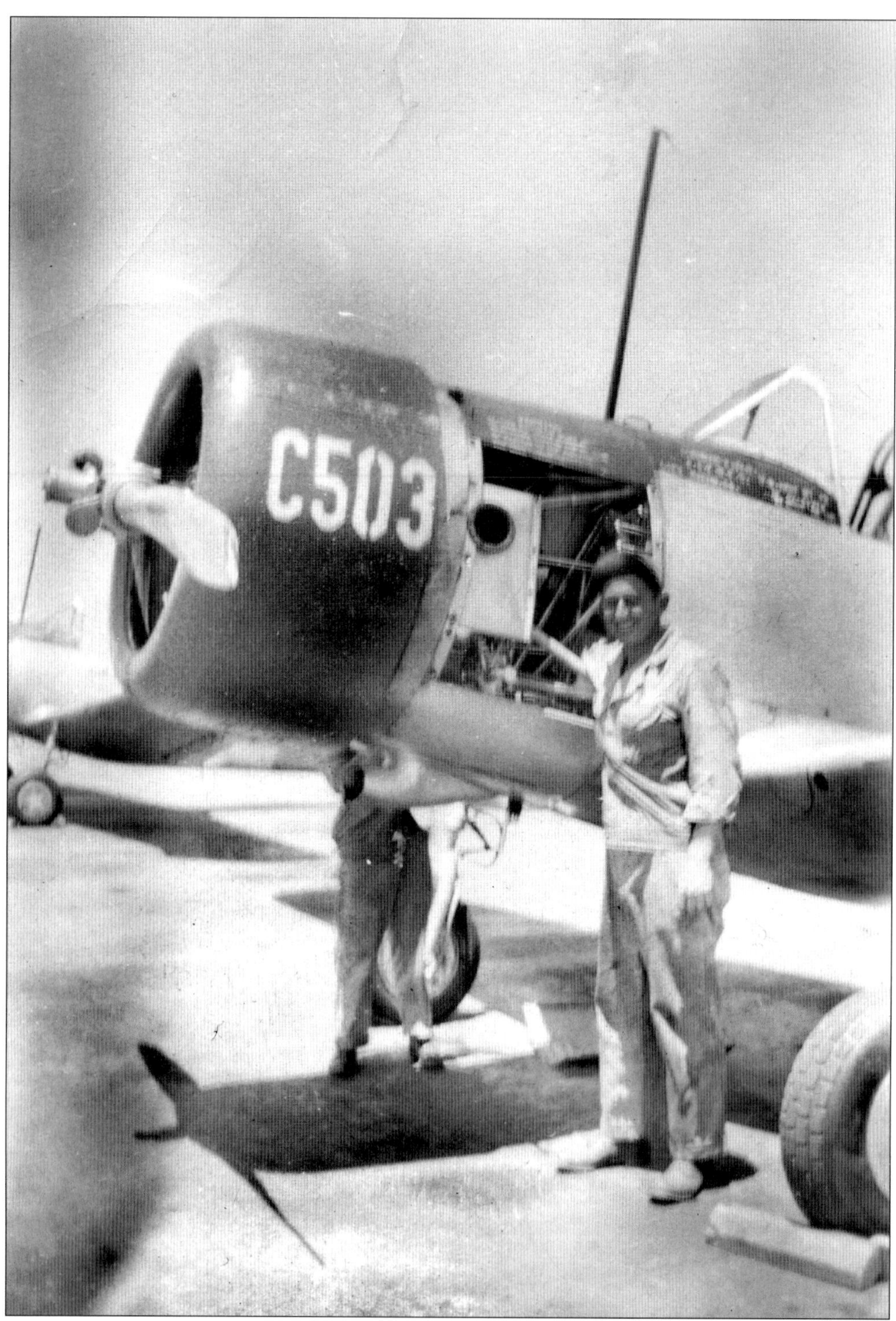

It is believed that this photograph was not actually taken locally but that the pilot or mechanic, who is unidentified, was a local resident. Note the man who appears to be hiding on the other side of the photograph. It looks like the plane has legs.

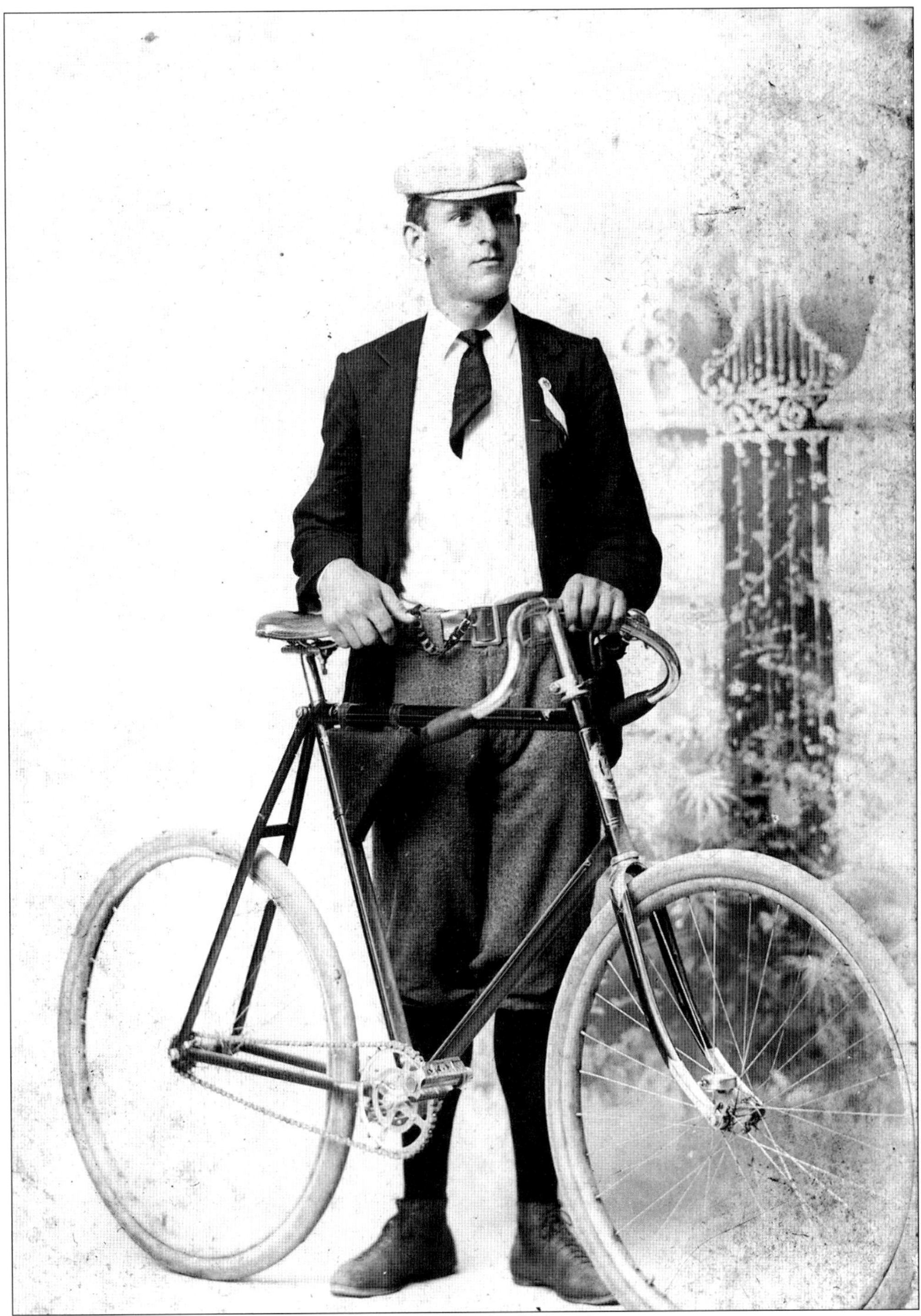

This bicycle looks to be brand new, and the young man who owns it looks quite proud, dressed in his best. The bike could be a Crawford or a Cresant style from the 1890s, but judging from his attire, it appears the photograph was taken in the 1920s. In the early days, bicycles were often called bone shakers or ordinaries.

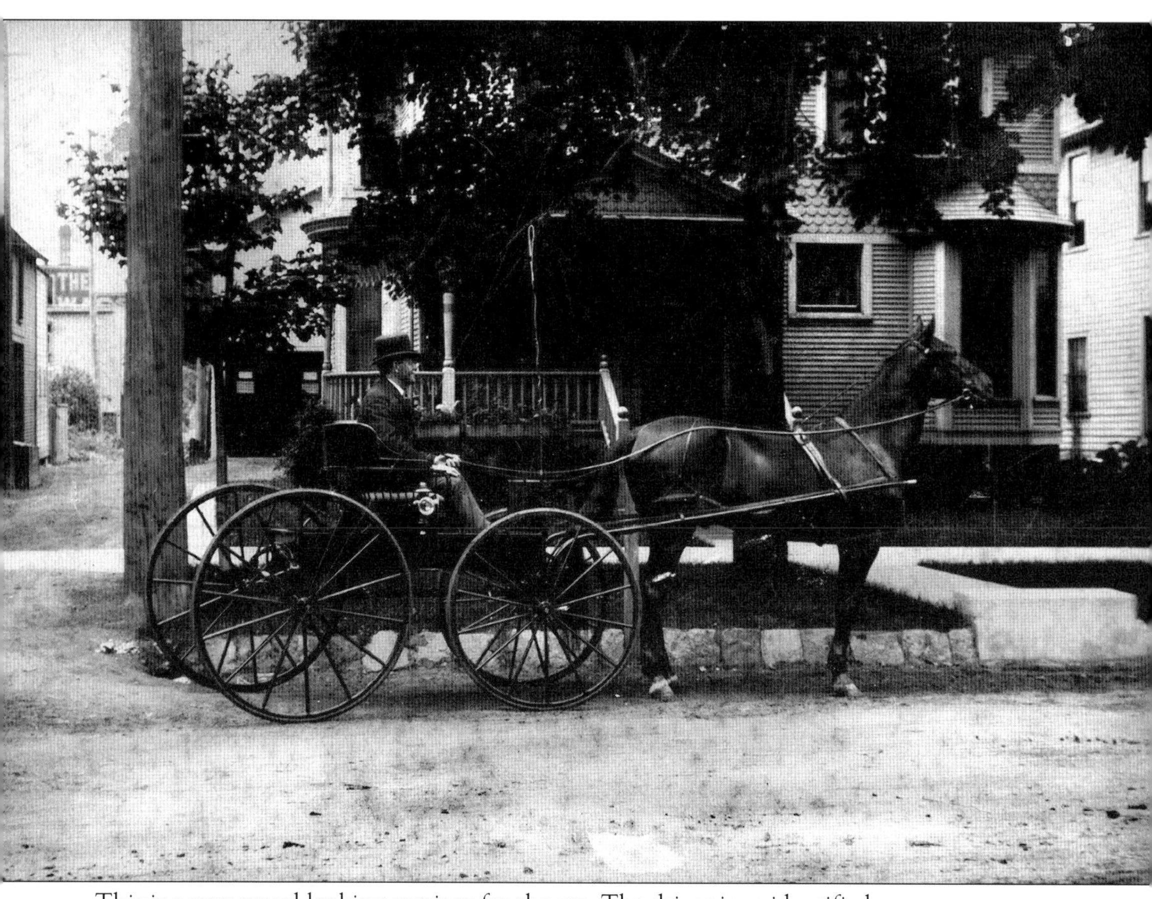

This is a very grand-looking carriage for the era. The driver is unidentified.

Five

Transportation at Work

Horses and wagons were the primary means of aiding workers in their occupations and trades during the early years in the region. However, in the early 1900s, the tractor was born.

Although you can still see many landowners utilizing horses, wagons, and combinations of farm equipment that are horse drawn, there is still a movement to use new and improved farm equipment—mainly, the tractor.

The purpose of the tractor was to boost manpower and decrease manual labor for farm workers. Another goal was to provide additional power and strength that the horse or bare hand could not supply. While the tractor was not cheap, it was realistic to own for the farmer who saved. It was an affordable, attainable extension of farming, and it was high tech in that era. Oddly, the very first tractors were not called tractors at all, but rather automobile plows. Many of the local tractors were built by the Ford Company and were called Fordson tractors.

In the early 1900s, the United States manufactured more tobacco than any other country, and much of that was produced on the East Coast. This region was a hub for tobacco farming, and it was often a family business. Although some crops of the United States were originally imported, tobacco is native to the area. Although rare, photographs of early tobacco farmers can sometimes be found, and within this chapter, images document what was considered a family business with very young children helping to harvest tobacco.

With the end of the Civil War came a doubling of tobacco demands, and business boomed. It was not until the Depression era that politics stepped into the picture and regulated the tobacco industry.

Beyond the field, as time marched on, many other business owners saw the need for work cars, work trucks, and different styled tractors. From apples to yarn, trucks were used to sell, transport, and advertise goods and services.

Some common local industries that utilized transportation as a part of their business include flour mills, dairy farms, ice-cream sales, meat sales, fruit and vegetable sales, fertilizer, poultry, eggs, breads, and of course, tobacco products.

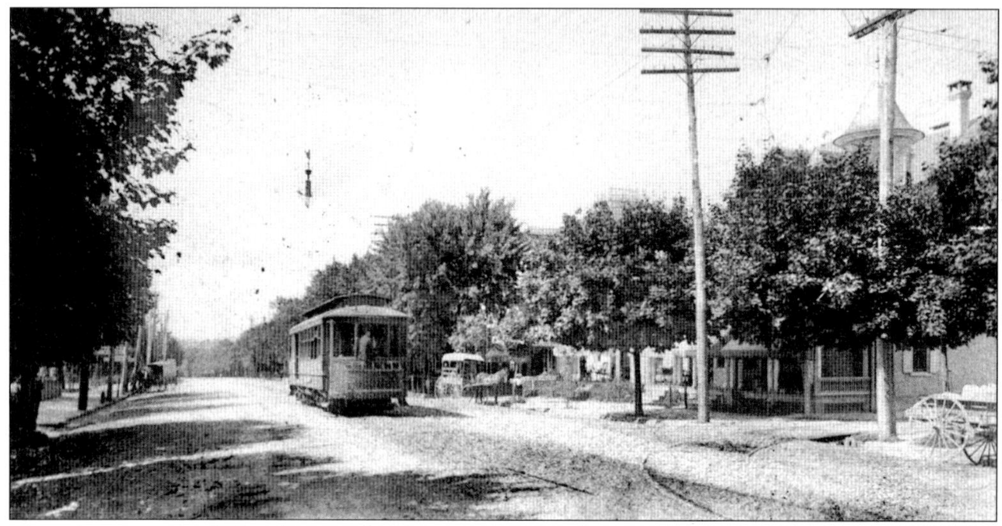

This photo postcard, dated 1906, depicts a portion of the town of Ephrata. It is hard to believe that at one time the main roads were home to trolleys. Notice on the far right that there is also a wagon, and in the distance, down the road on the left, there is a horse and buggy tied to the side of the road.

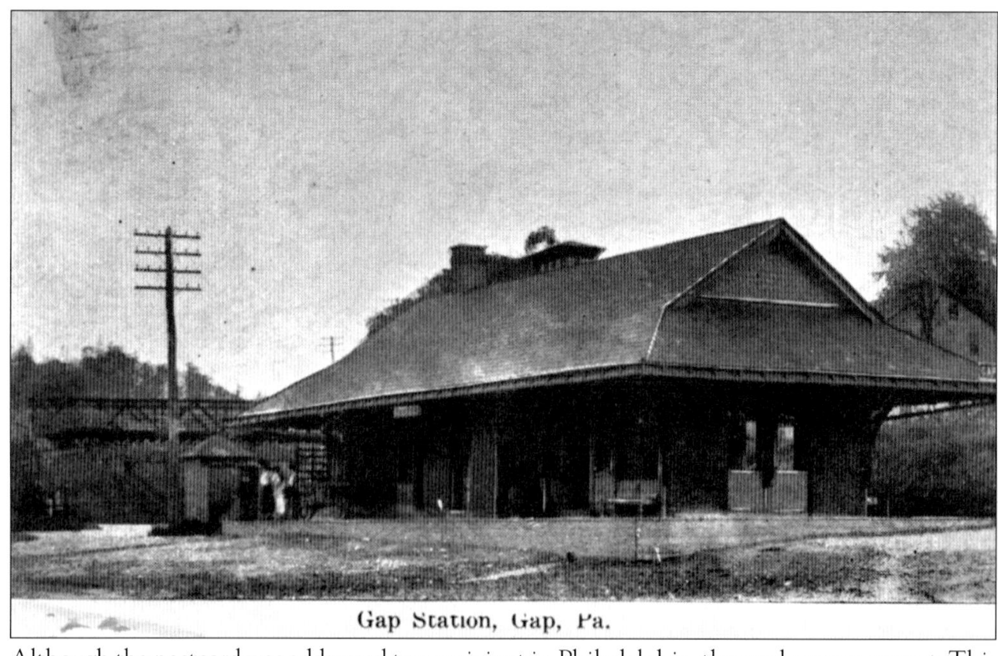

Although the postcard was addressed to a recipient in Philadelphia, the card was never sent. This photographic postcard depicts the Gap station, in the nearby town of Gap.

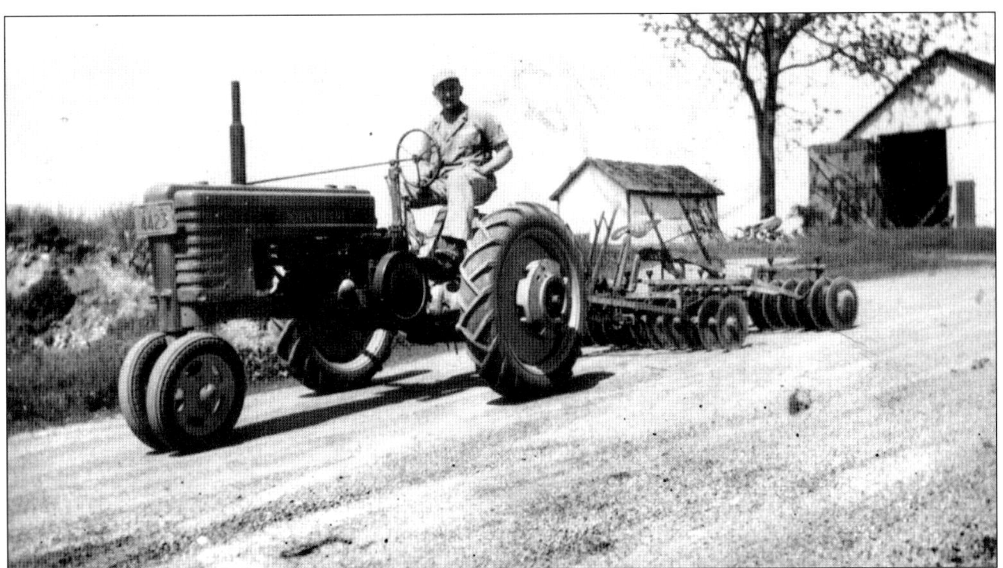

An unidentified tobacco farmer poses with his tractor and machinery. Notice the large barn in the background with a smaller structure next to it. His driveway is a dirt drive.

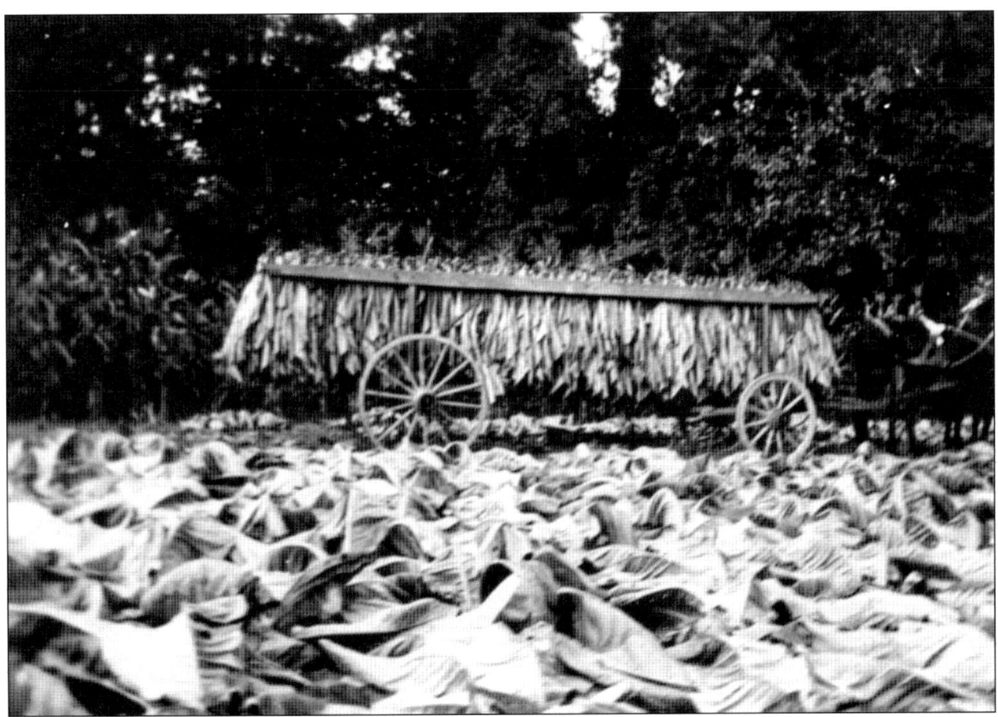

Some machinery was high tech in the early industry of the area, and some of the farm aid was more primitive. Here is a wagon on which the tobacco is strewn and hung. Barely visible is the horse that leads the wagon. Notice how large the tobacco leaves are.

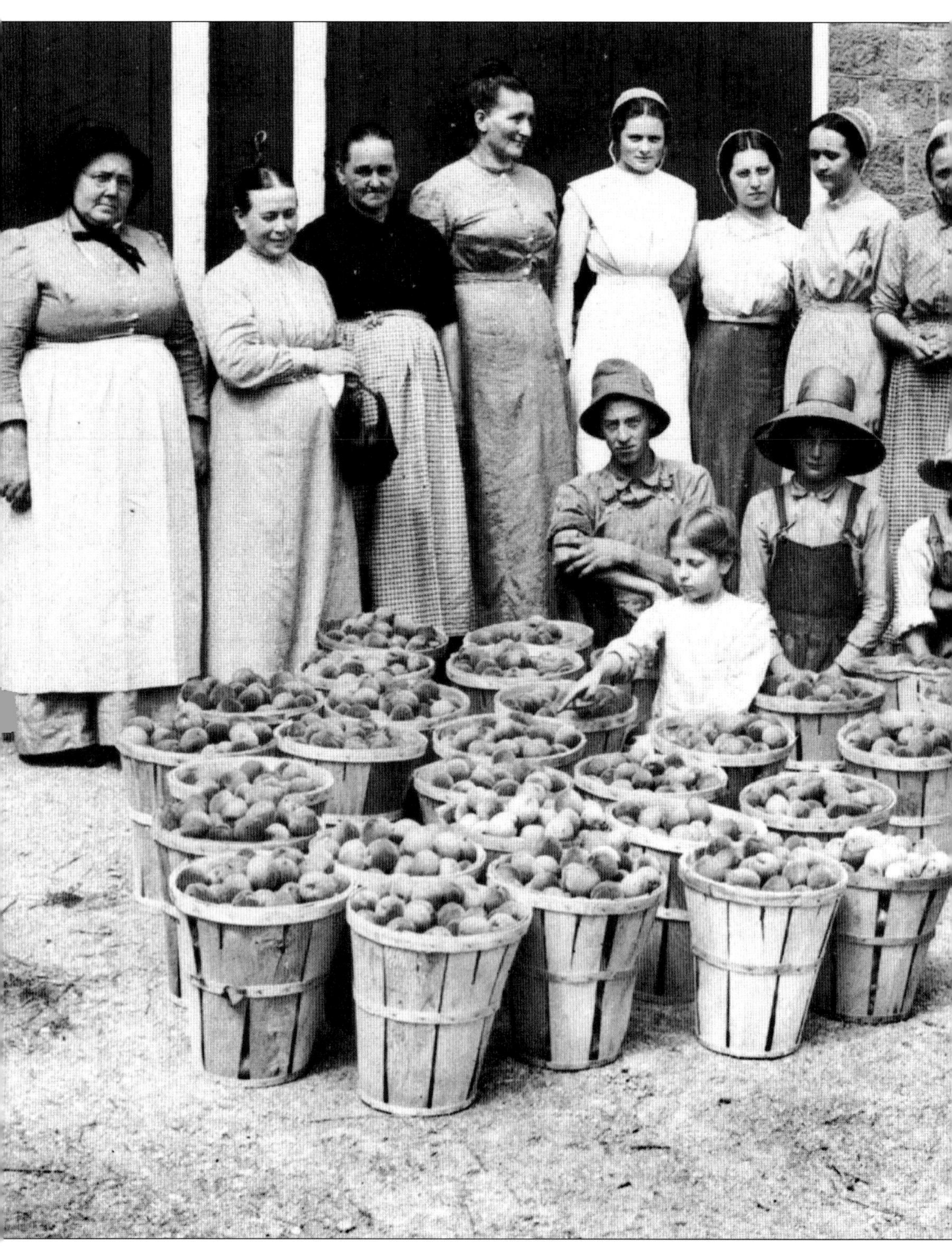

This peach wagon, with a combination of Amish and Mennonite farmers, was photographed on September 1, 1914. Peaches cost about 50¢ a bushel at that time. The farm is that of

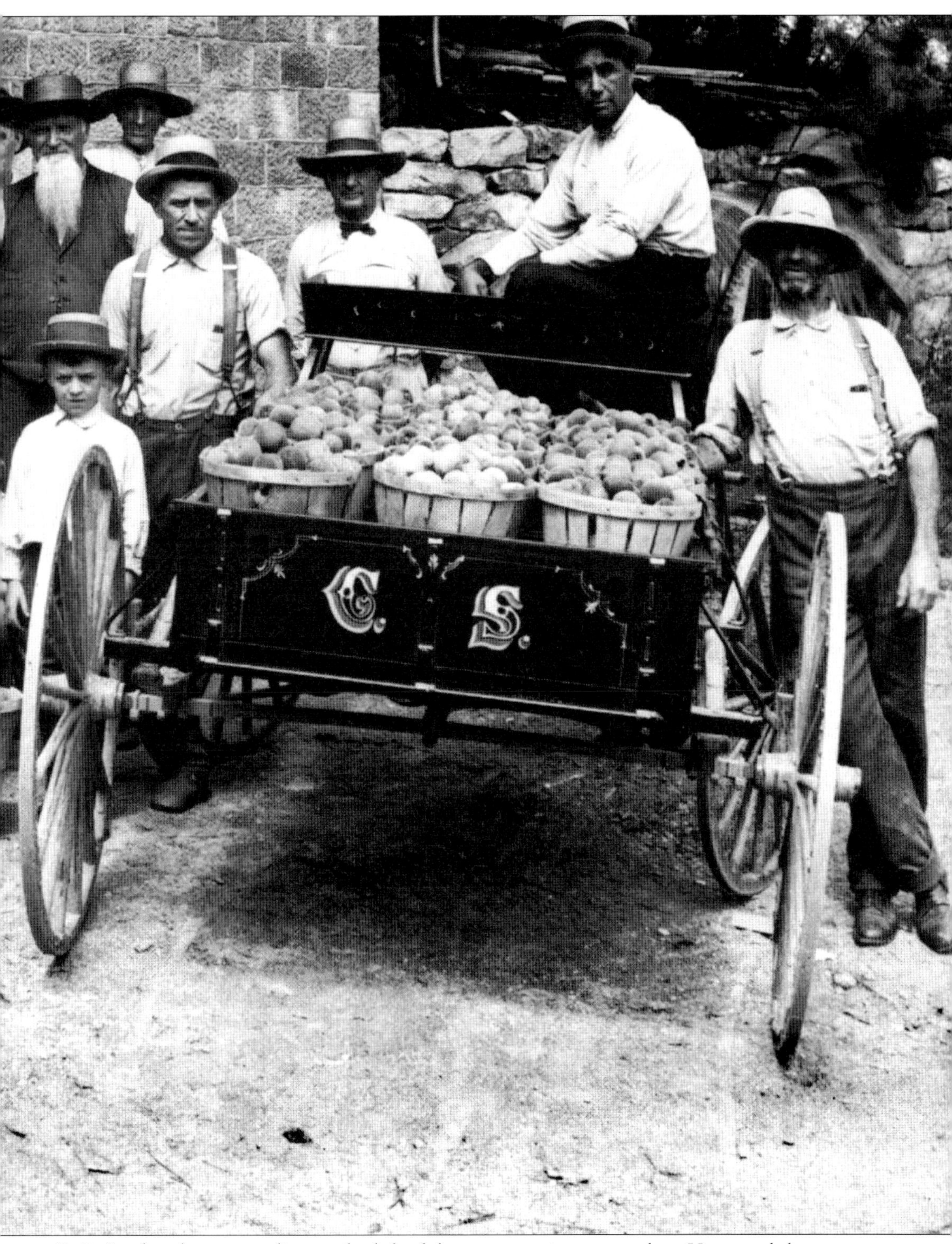

C. B. Snyder, shown standing to the left of the cart, wearing suspenders. He owned the wagon and business.

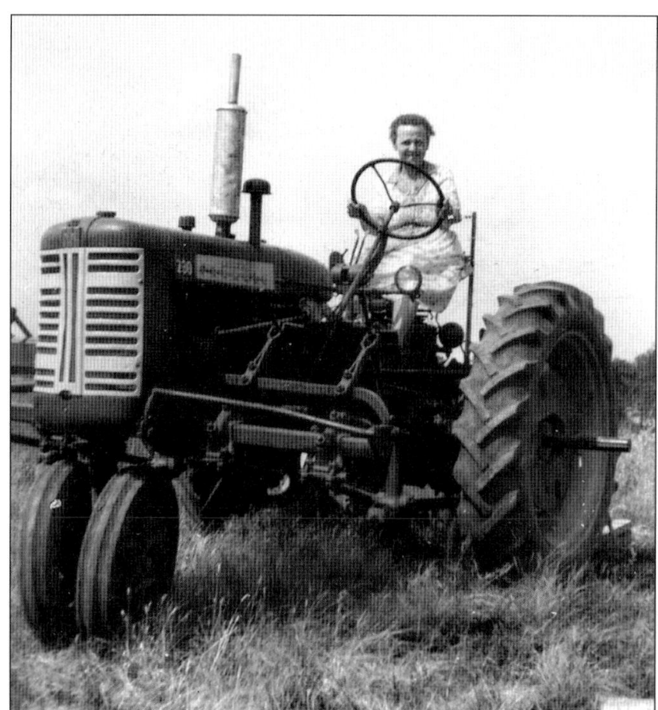

This unidentified woman is seen riding a tractor c. the late 1950s, proving that women working on farms wore many hats.

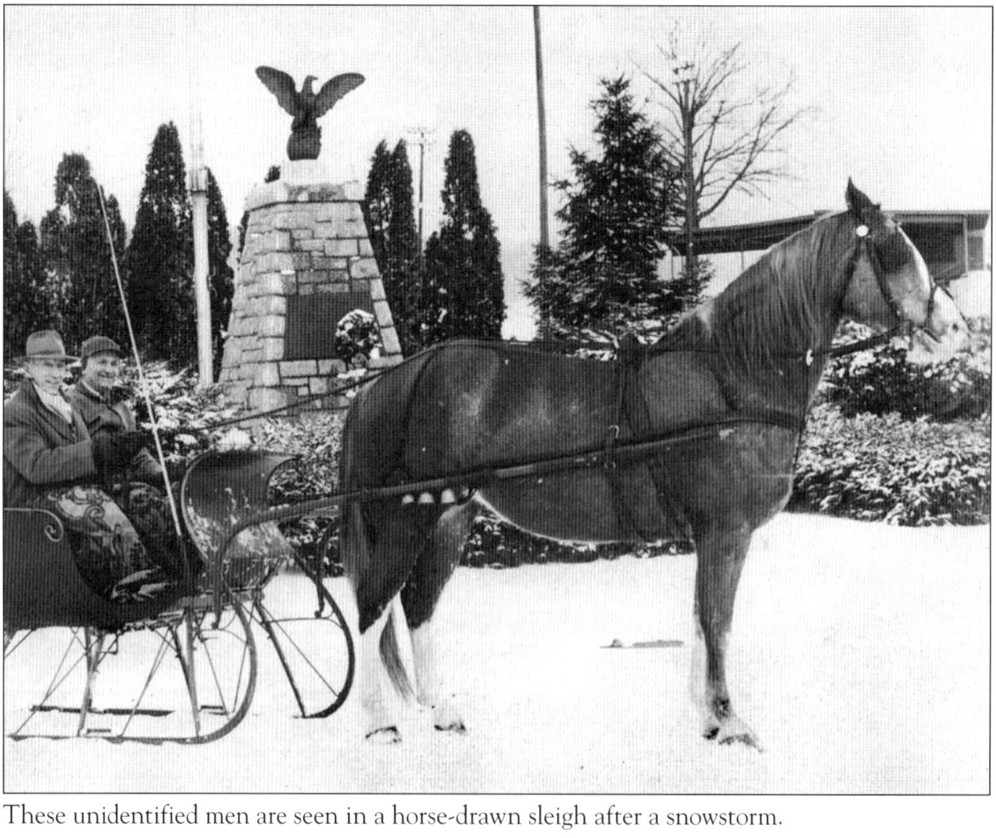

These unidentified men are seen in a horse-drawn sleigh after a snowstorm.

The 1952 presidential campaign passed through the region on the way to Lancaster via the railway.

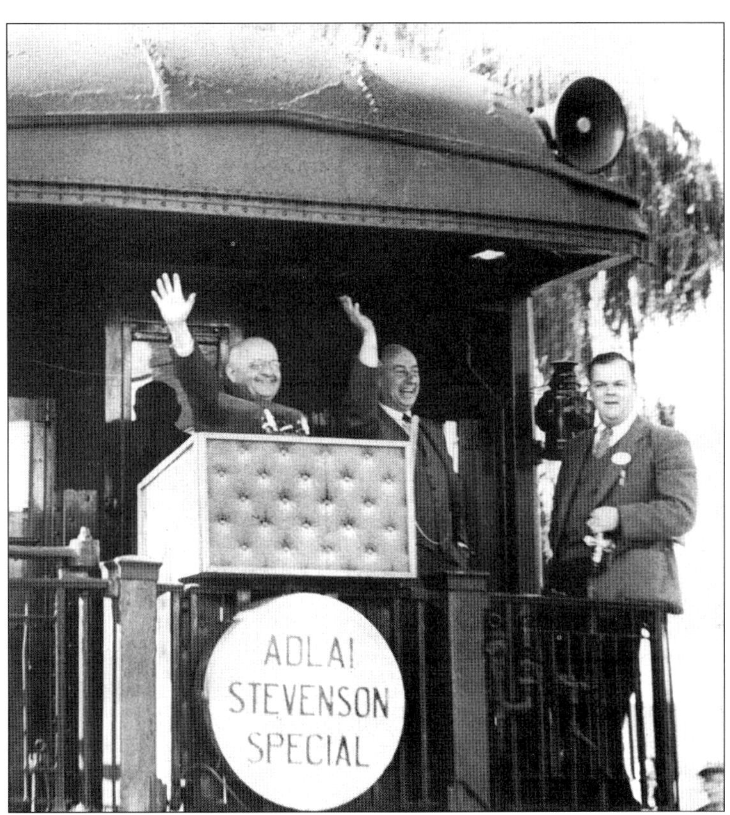

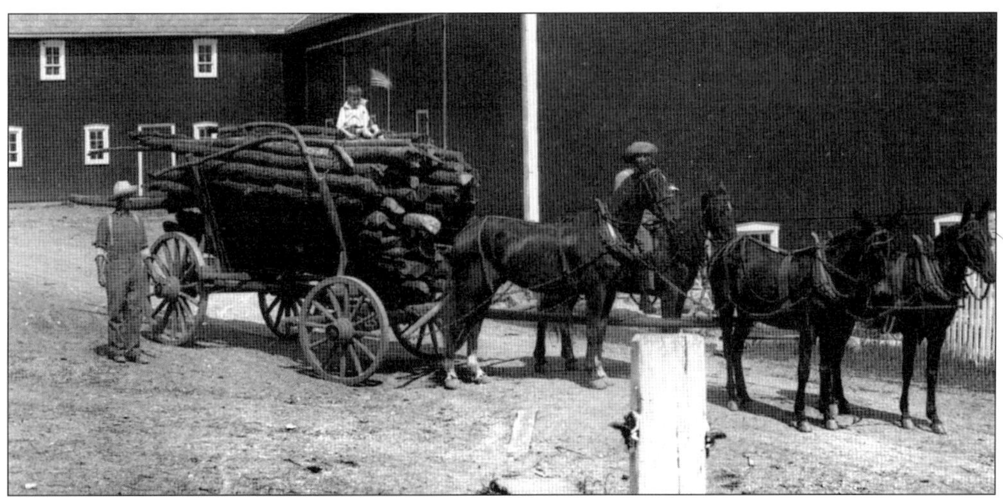

This photograph is dated June 2, 1914, and the child on the rails is Simon Snyder. The other individuals pictured are unidentified.

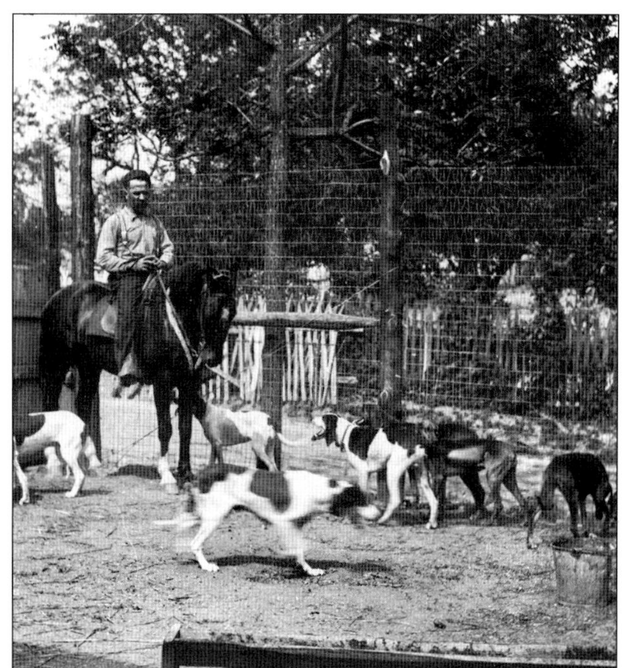

The photograph to the left, dated 1911, shows a Mr. Nessinger with his hunting dogs. Notice the picket fence and how differently these fences were constructed in this era compared to today. Horses were not just for personal wagons and hunting. Below we see horses pulling a country produce wagon *c.* 1912.

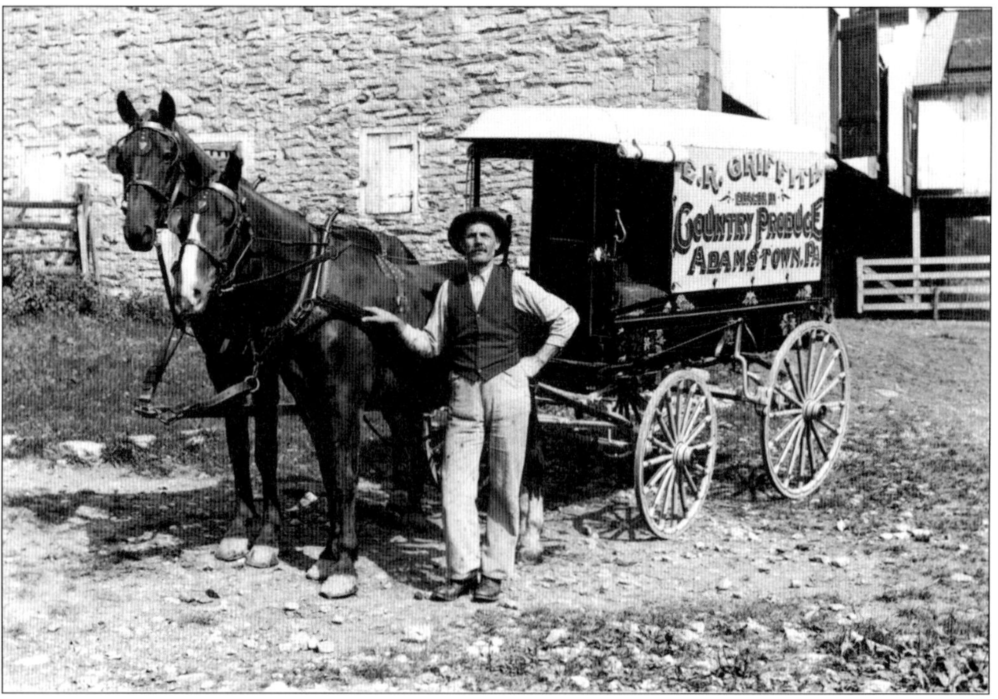

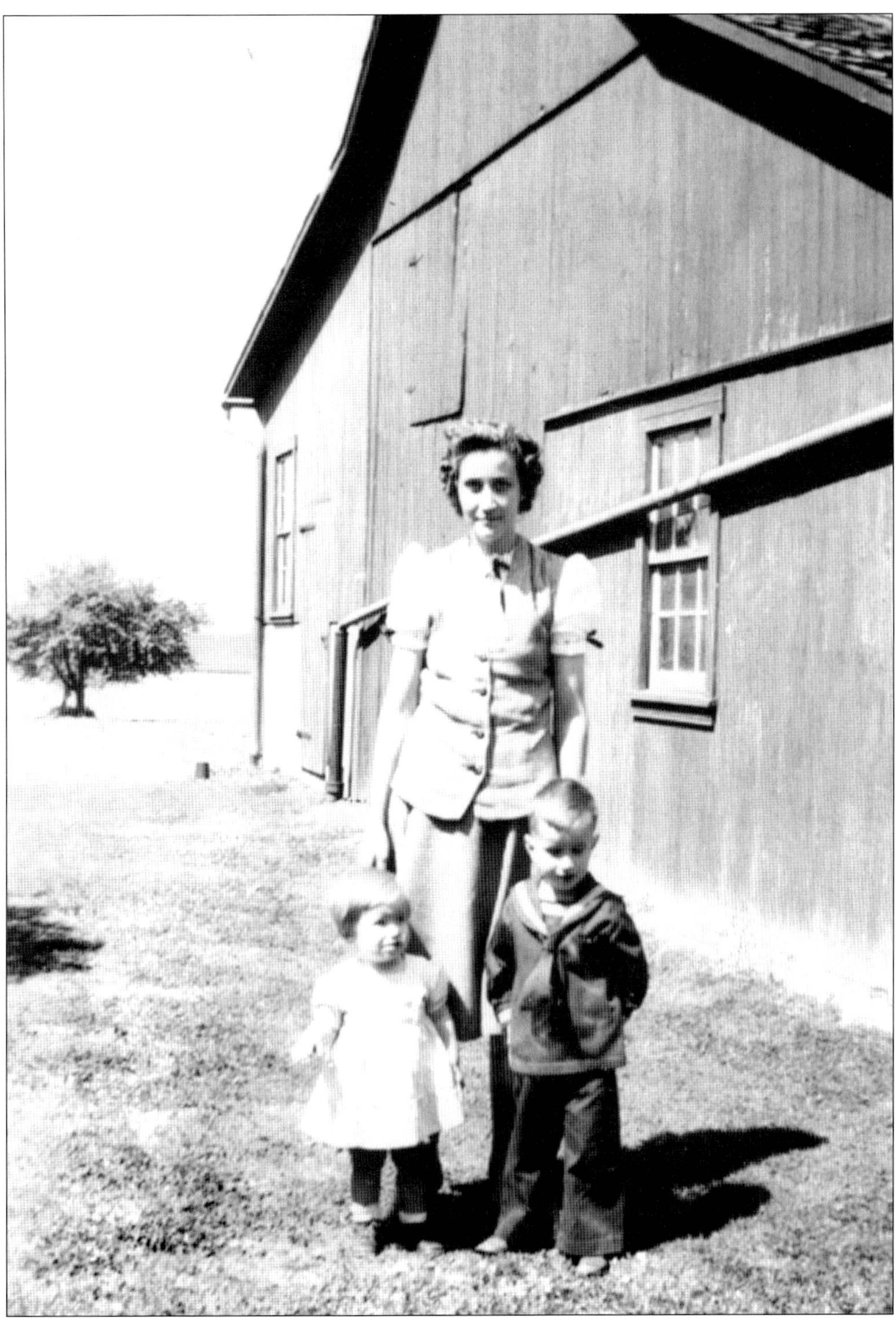

Pictured here is a farming family. The barn in the background was designed to hold tractors and other farm equipment. Toward the top of the barn is the door that was used to throw hay and straw down to be transported.

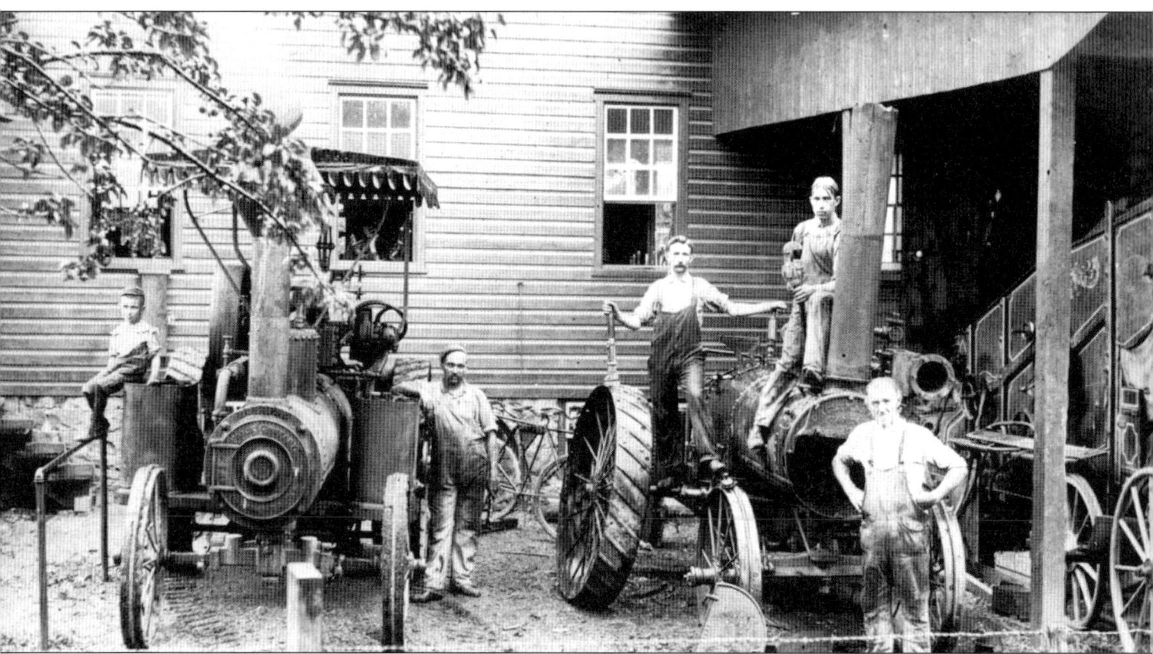

The machines seen here are very primitive. The photograph was taken in 1910, and the machinery is very much used and worn. Take notice of the boy sitting on the far left on top of the tractor. In this day and age, that would be considered a very dangerous maneuver for a child. In that era, the boy was probably already working. Workers are, from left to right, Samuel Erb, unidentified, unidentified, Edwin Erb, and John Erb (owner of the Erb Farm).

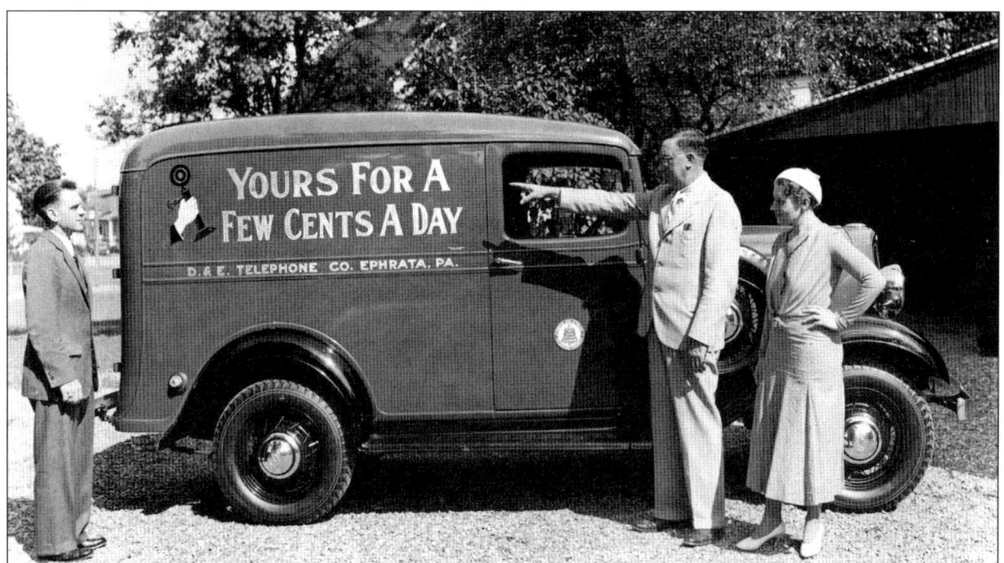

Still in existence, the Denver and Ephrata Telephone Company is seen at work *c.* 1932. Old advertisements for telephone companies were very common in print, often advertising that "you could pick up the receiver and talk to anyone, instantly, even a mile away." From left to right are Wayne Fair, Christian Eaby, and Bertha Brossman.

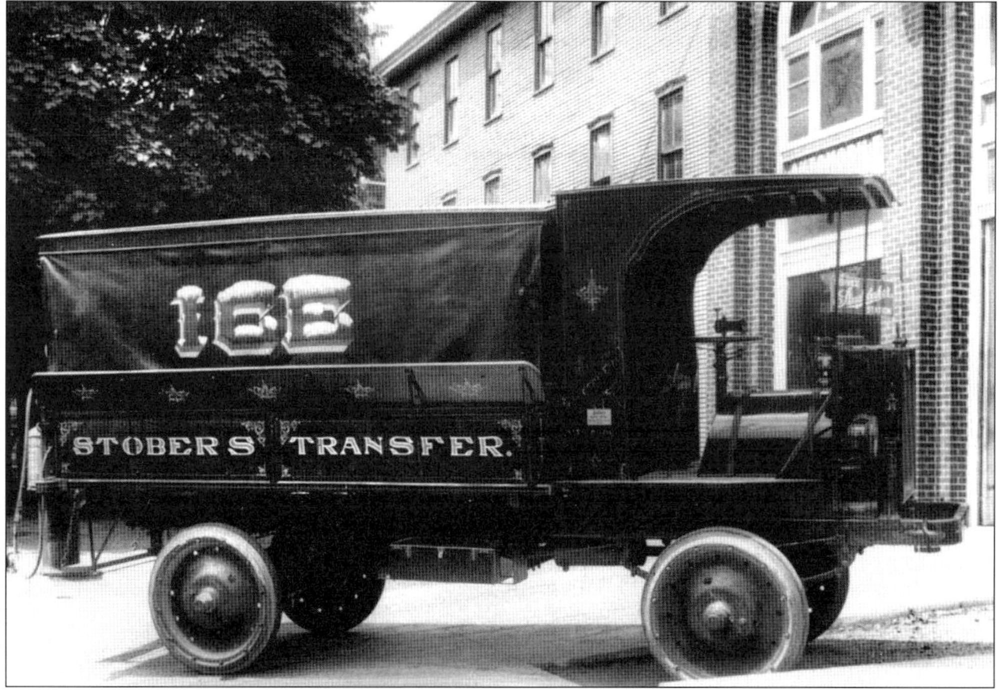

A Stober's ice-delivery truck is seen here in the 1930s. At that time, most people had iceboxes to keep their perishables, and ice trucks delivered ice to the families and businesses that depended upon them. In the background to the far right, a sign advertising Studebakers is visible.

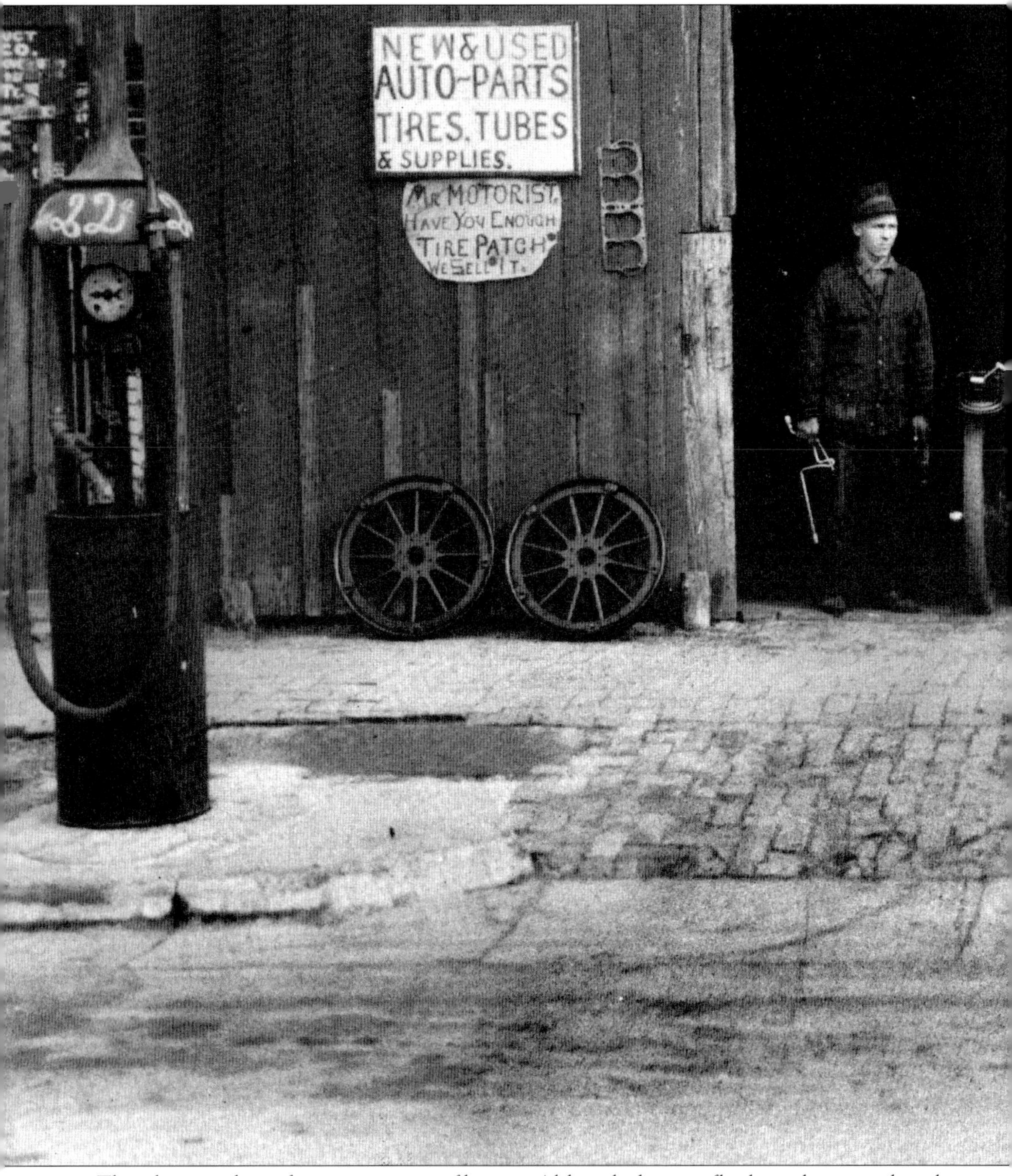

This photograph is a fantastic capture of history. Although the men flanking the car within the garage are unidentified, they are likely mechanics. The man to the far right is likely a customer

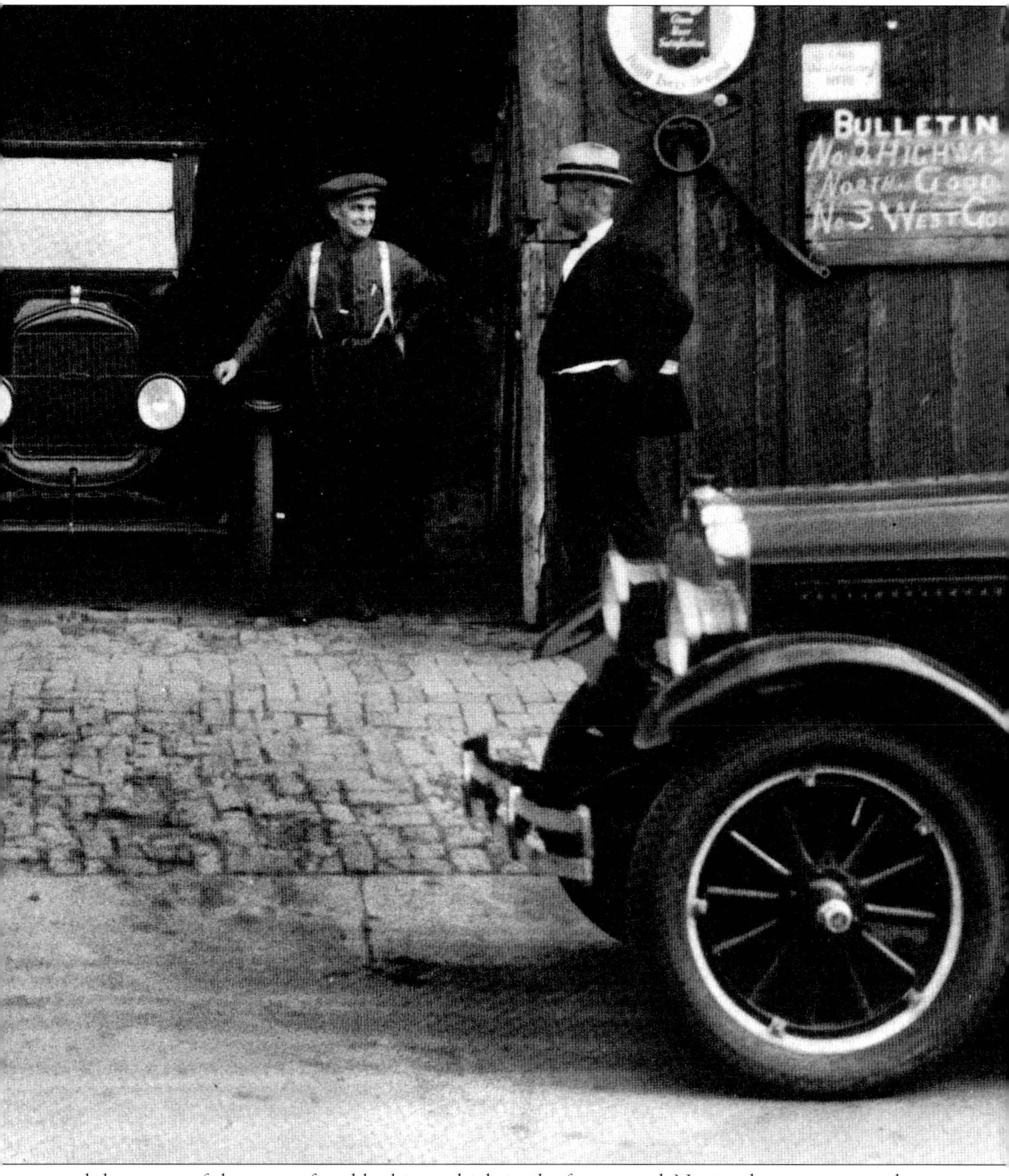

and the owner of the very refined-looking vehicle in the foreground. Notice the gas pump to the far left, with the gauges. Gas at this time cost a whopping 22¢ a gallon.

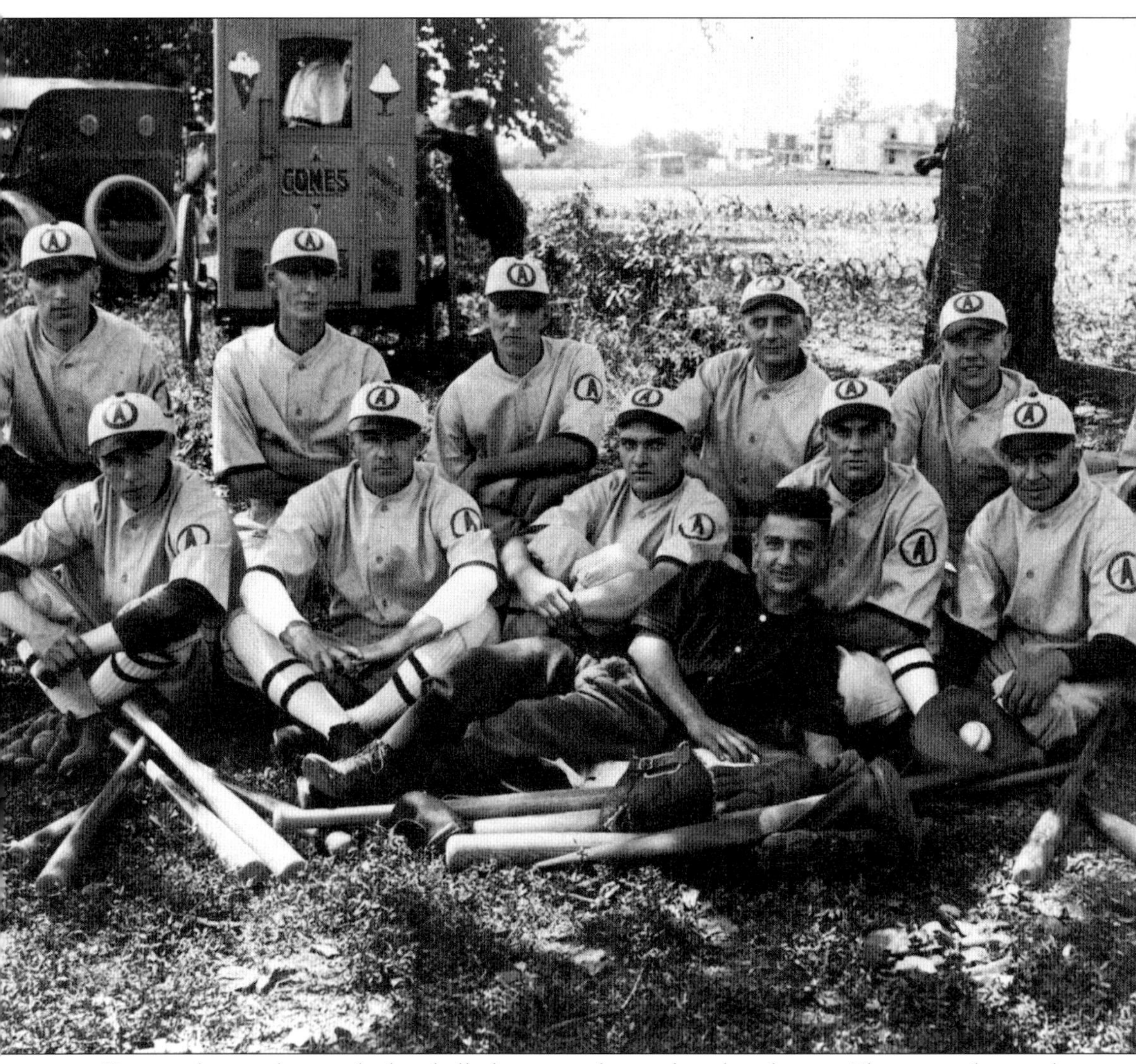

You may be wondering why baseball players are featured in this chapter. The reason lies in the ice-cream truck behind the team in this *c.* 1918 photograph. The birth of the ice-cream cone was in 1904 at the St. Louis World's Fair, and it became very popular across the nation. Just a decade later, ice-cream trucks were touting cones to ice-cream lovers around the nation. The unidentified players are a part of the Akron baseball team.

Six

BUSINESS AND INDUSTRY

The first inhabitants of the area, the needs of those people, and the resources available were all variables that were reflected in the business and industry that cropped up over the region.

The tobacco industry was a fairly early and prosperous endeavor of the early settlers. As opposed to the tobacco grown in some parts of the United States, this area has boasted some of the finest cigar tobacco available within the nation.

For the most part, the immigrants were the first farmers of all crops. But now when you sightsee among the region's many acres, you will notice that it is more the Amish or Mennonite way of life to farm the large crops.

Still, supportive residents will often purchase vegetables and tobacco from the area farmers. There has been a market for locally grown products that stretches to New York and Boston, especially for the tobacco crops.

General stores were also very popular in the past. General stores were the first true retail store, and they offered a small yet varied selection of many items serving the needs of the local residents and occasional traveler. The first general stores often carried everything from medicine and cooking supplies such as flour and sugar, to hardware and mechanical supplies.

Dotted along Old Philadelphia Pike were many inns for weary travelers, as the towns themselves were born of a need of growth stemming from the Philadelphia area. For locals, the inns served as fine meeting places to sit talking with neighbors after a hard day of work and unwind with a drink of ale.

Also dispersed within and around the region were various mills, blacksmithing shops, and wagon shops.

With the popularity of mills and flour in abundance came the natural progression of bakeries. The diverse cultures of the area immigrants offered a variety of baked goods and breads that were not only treats but mainstays at many meals for area families.

The wagon and carriage industry was born in this area, and to this day, the Conestoga wagon has a significant place in the history of the Pequea Valley, the nation, and even the world. Not only did the wagon boom help travelers, locals, and farmers live and work with more ease and convenience, but it is said to have helped the economy of the area as well. Employees were needed to build the wagons, and there was enough work not only to hire local residents but also to import fellows from Philadelphia as well. Also within the region was a myriad of new business, from jewelry, clothing, and music to sewing machine stores. There was a young community being built economically that continued to grow and prosper for years to come.

READ what these Studebaker truck owners say about performance and economy

WISCONSIN

My former trucks could not begin to approach the low operating cost of my Studebaker. You are building a fine truck and I am proud to be the owner of a second one.

TEXAS

This unit has cost less to operate than any vehicle ever owned by our firm, so far as major overhauls and minor repairs are concerned. Our gasoline mileage averages more miles per gallon better than any other unit we have operated.

NORTH CAROLINA

The last three trucks I have owned have been Studebaker half-ton pickups. I drove the first . . . for 49,000 trouble-free miles. My second . . . was driven 50,000 miles . . . my third Studebaker was driven 78,000 miles and gave me dependable, low-cost operation so necessary to my work.

NEBRASKA

. . . about one year and a half ago we purchased our first Studebaker . . . Since that time, we have purchased five more of your Studebakers and, in plain vernacular, "are tickled pink." They have been most serviceable and have operated with most economical efficiency.

ILLINOIS

Our Studebaker trucks have so far outperformed any trucks we have ever used that we herewith place an order for a 100% Studebaker fleet.

NEW YORK

Being contractors, we had to have a sturdy model, one in which we could be confident of safe duty; yet we also wanted something with style. Your Studebaker rings the bell; smooth performance, style and efficiency, all in one package.

LOUISIANA

It is easy to handle under all conditions. We could not ask for a better vehicle.

CALIFORNIA

The performance and adaptability of this equipment in my construction business is more than satisfactory, and having driven other types, you can rest assured I am entirely sold on Studebaker equipment.

IOWA

I am especially proud of its power and performance which seem endless. Using a truck for wrecker service, we are called upon to use every bit of power it has. It has yet to stall the motor for lack of power in this truck.

MINNESOTA

I am hauling 2000 gallons of fuel oil, making commercial and domestic deliveries. My Studebaker hauls this load without any strain. In fifteen thousand miles, I have had no repair bills and maintenance costs have been lower than on any truck I ever owned.

WASHINGTON

As our field of operation includes out of state as well as local hauls, we feel that Studebaker's ability to give top quality performance combined with low operating cost has more than adequately supplied our requirements.

KANSAS

With over a quarter million miles of service our records prove our upkeep costs are much lower than any trucks we have ever used.

Have you seen the NEW 1954 Studebaker trucks?

Thousands upon thousands of users everywhere have acclaimed Studebaker trucks for long-lasting, low-cost performance. Now, in '54, this operating economy plus rugged new truck styling, new cab features, new chassis features, new engine developments, and new low prices give you the best truck buy in Studebaker history. See us, see the NEW 1954 Studebaker trucks today!

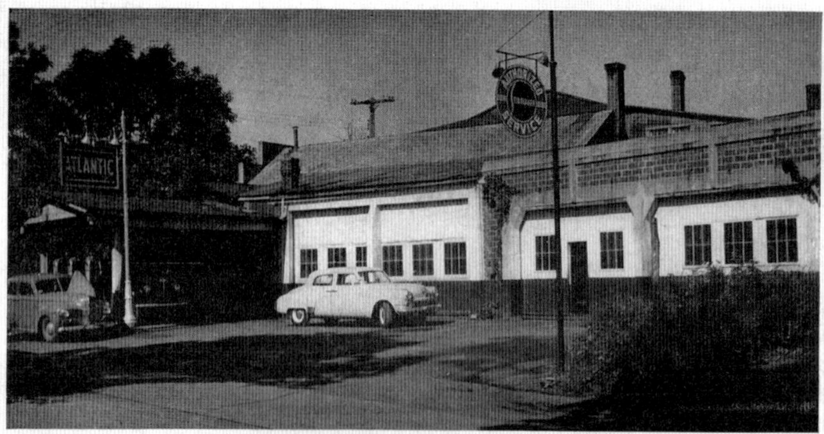

WEST SALISBURY GARAGE

Main and Railroad St., W. Salisbury, Pa., Tel. Salisbury 2426

This is a classified ad for the West Salisbury Garage and Studebaker trucks from 1954. Although the trucks were designed in the late 1930s, the model was not put into production until November 1940. The Studebaker company was already looking to wartime production as a priority, so although the design and production were successful, not many were produced before World War II. This advertisement boasts new features and developments, focusing on power, sturdiness, and performance.

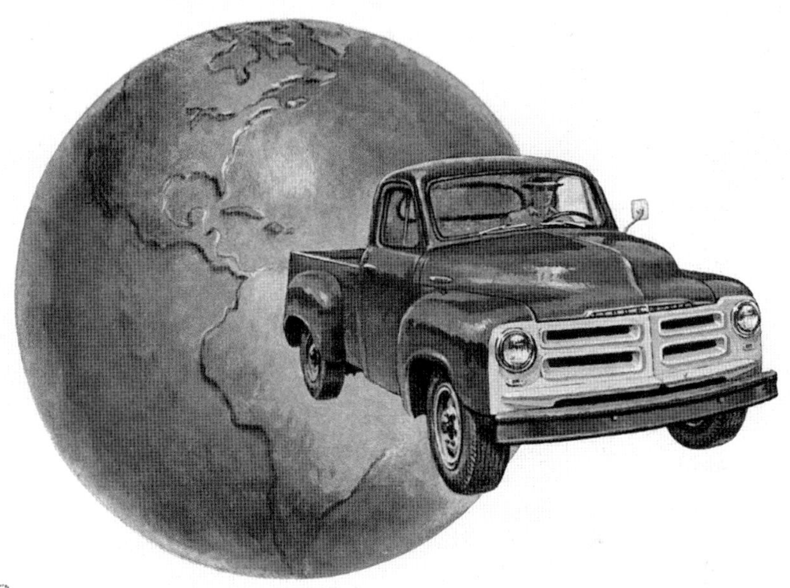

This advertisement reflects strong competition with its slant of group cohesiveness in owning the vehicle. With the war over, there was a strong competition for car and truck sales. Prewar, it was enough to just own a car for social status; however, after the war, it became the norm for each family to aspire to own a car, so the competition for buyers was much more influential. Manufacturers had to start targeting buyers in creative ways. Some manufacturers looked at the family person, while others like Studebaker focused on performance and dependability and a tougher owner.

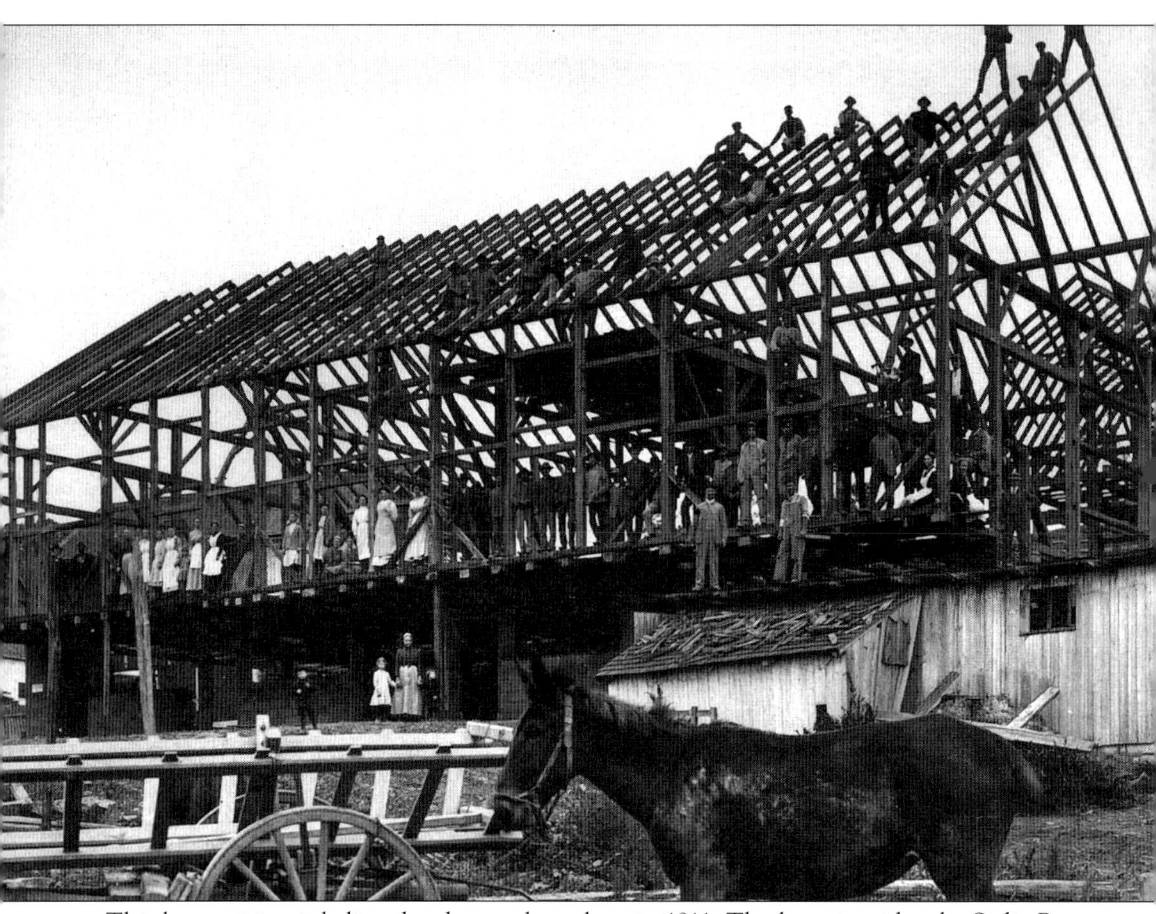

This barn raising is believed to have taken place in 1911. The barn is said to be Sadie Rupp Snyder's farm. As you can see, men and women took part in the barn raising, though most of the construction was actually completed by the men. Many people took part in the project. At the far right are two daredevil young men showing off their bravery, balance, and love of heights. No machines are present, as all of the work was done with bare hands and human strength.

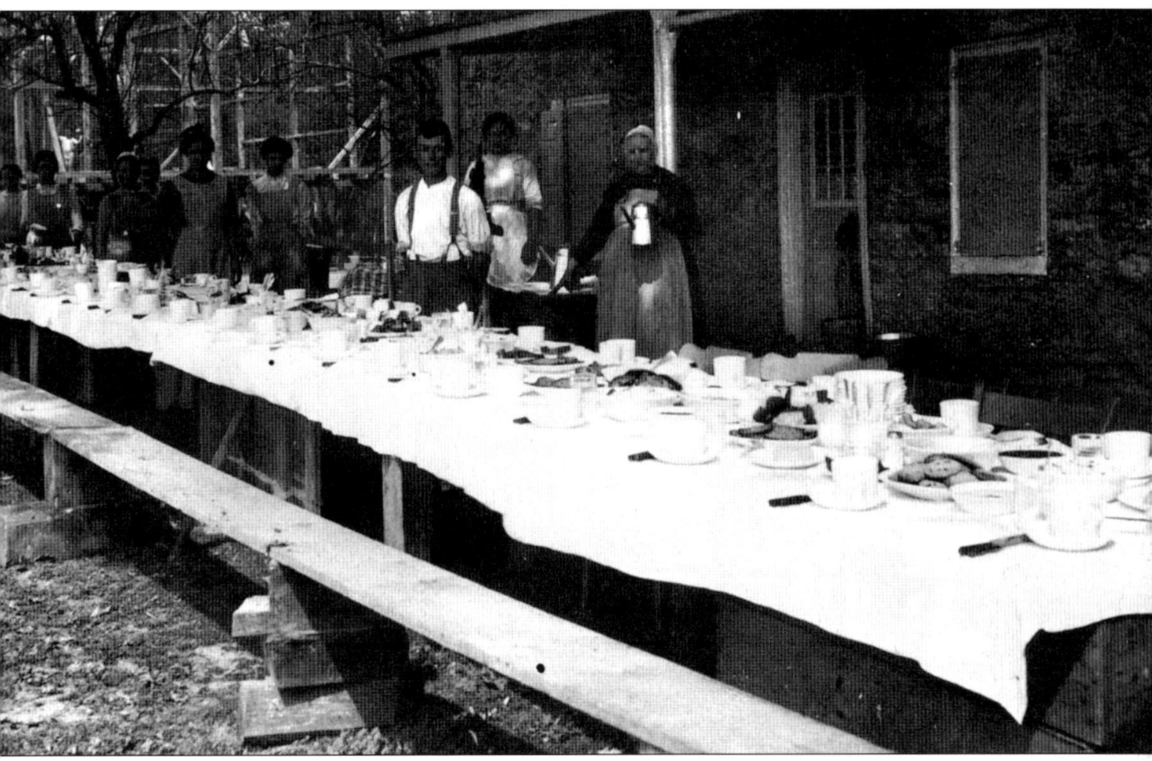

This photograph was taken on the same day as the Snyder Farm barn raising. While the men of the community worked, the women of the community prepared meals. Notice that there is a hot beverage table. Notice the fine table settings. You can almost reach out and grab a cookie that appears on the far right of the table. Also notice this is not your typical lawn furniture. The seats are timbers to be used for the barn, and they are held up with blocks of wood, as is the table.

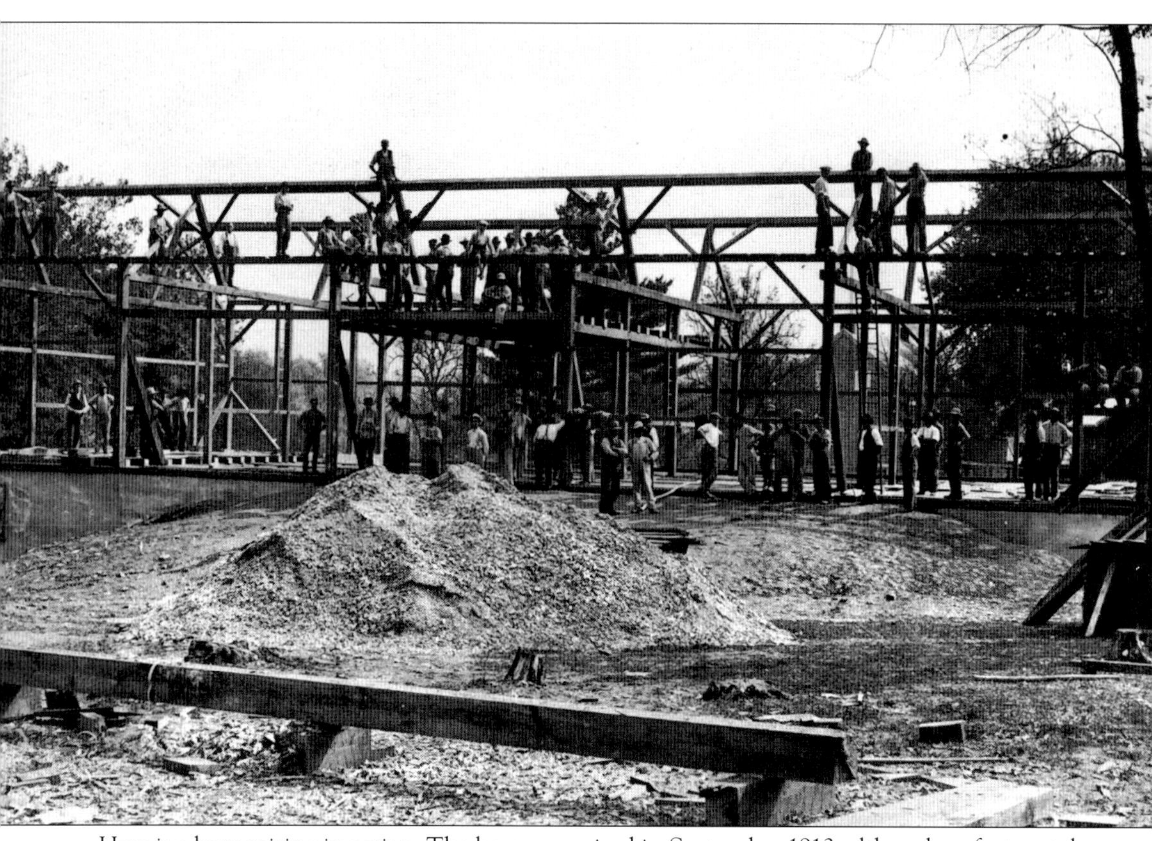

Here is a barn raising in action. The barn was raised in September 1913, although unfortunately it was destroyed a few months later in the summer of 1913. The barn was located near what is now known as Route 322, and the farm was owned by the Widder family.

Not at a barn raising or of Amish culture, these roofers work on a hotel in May 1902. The man photographed in full is Harry Givler.

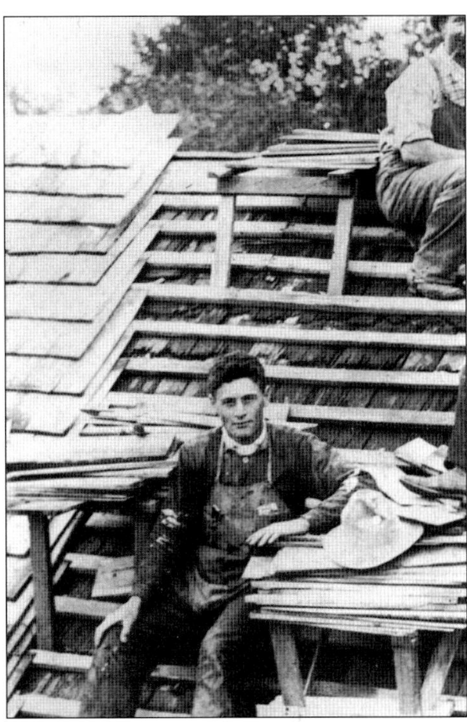

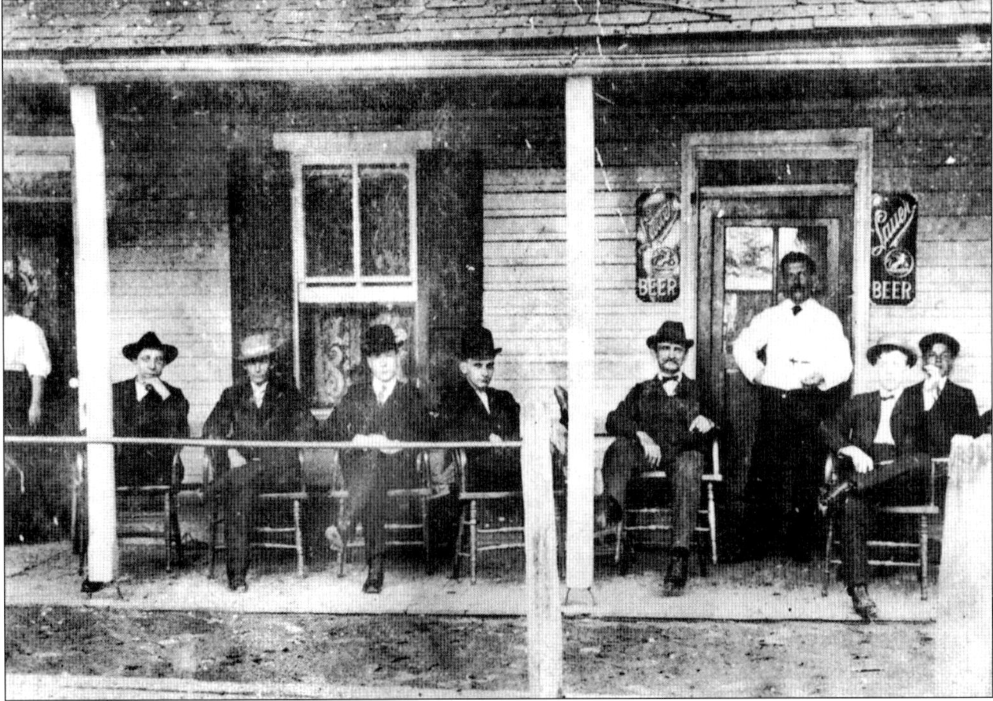

Old hotels often served as taverns. In the time period *c.* 1915, when this photograph was said to have been taken, these types of hotels were a common gathering place. Notice the Lauer beer signs. Frederick Lauer, from Pennsylvania, was one of the first brewery owners and supplied beer not only to the region but throughout Pennsylvania and other states.

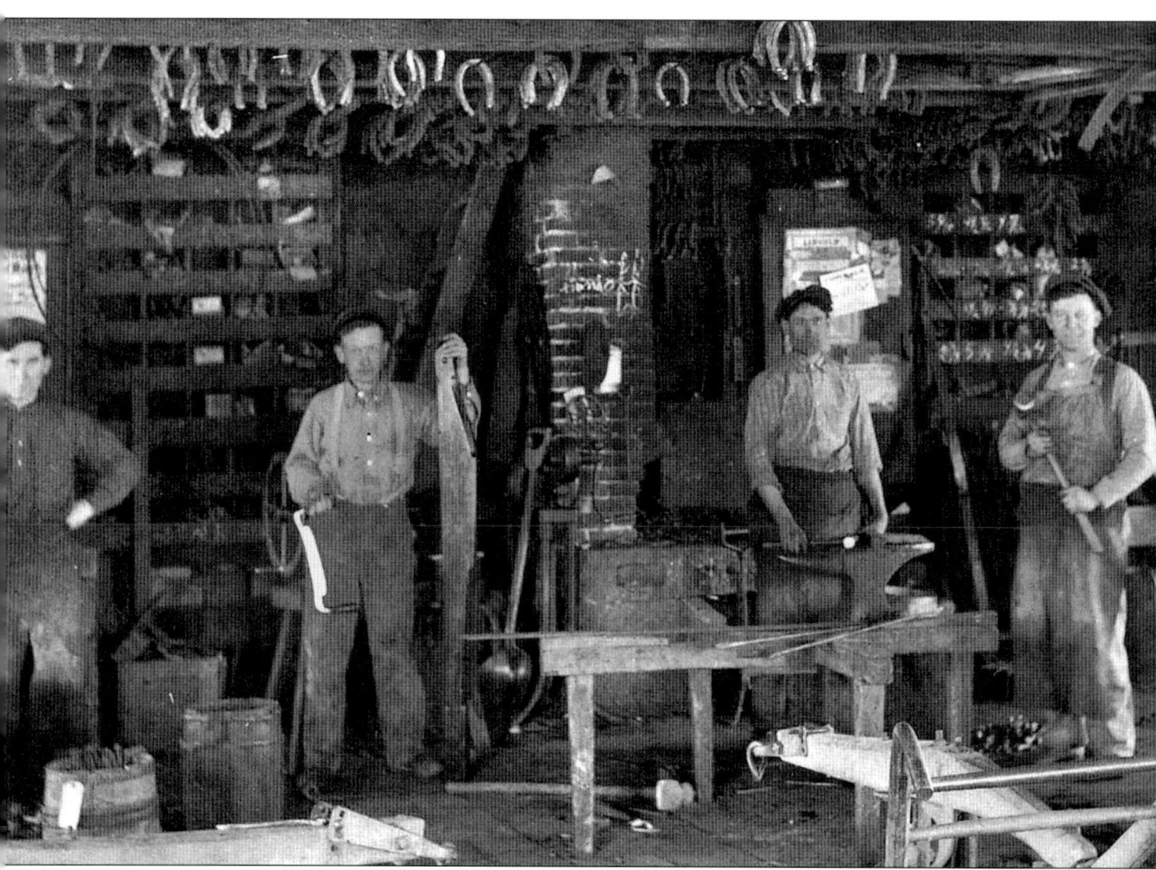

Unidentified workers are seen in front of a blacksmith shop in 1915. Notice all of the horseshoes hanging from the ceiling, as well as hanging on the barrels throughout the shop.

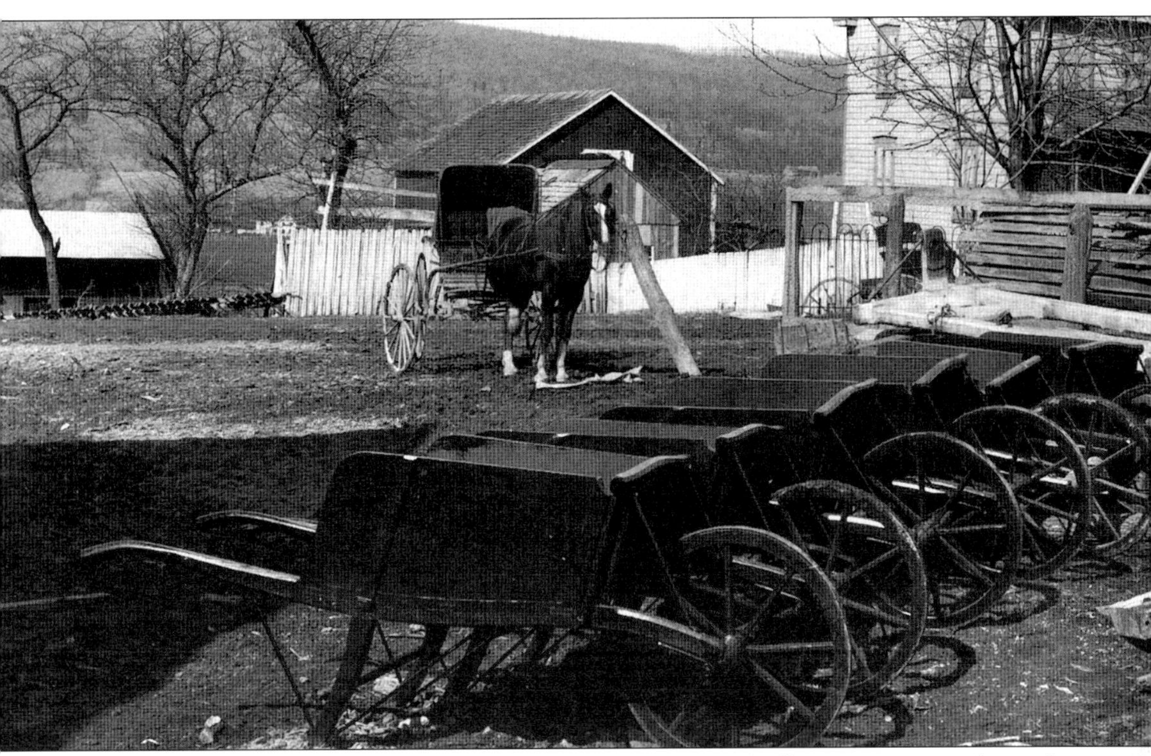

Outside of a blacksmith shop, wheelbarrows are ready for sale. These wheelbarrows were manufactured by the shop—just one of their products that was available to the community.

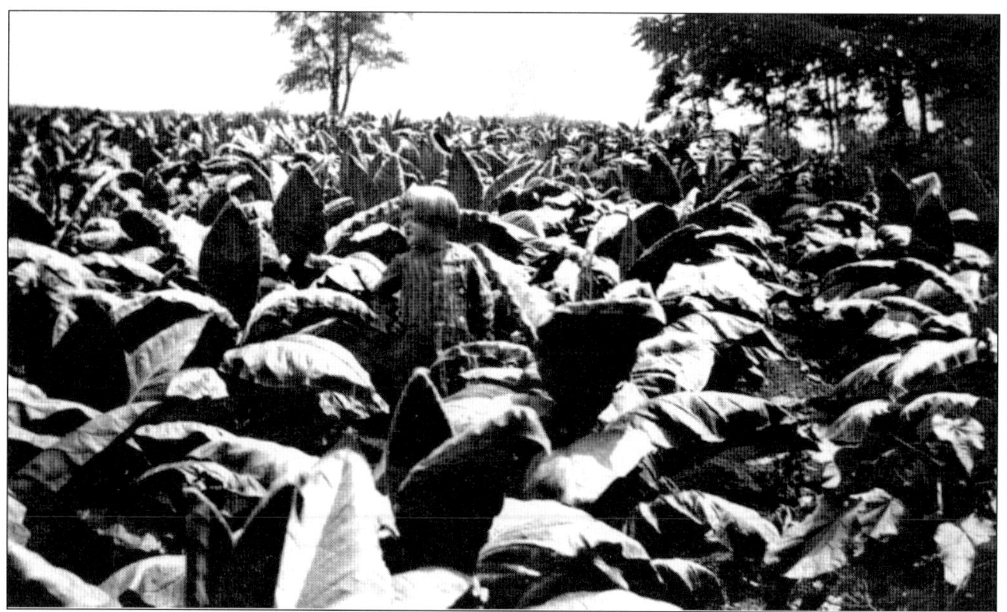

Tobacco farming was a big business in the region. Notice in the top photograph a child is among the tobacco leaves. The back of the photograph reads, "This is where Robert is looking for Ledy or Jacob." It is believed that the bottom photograph shows Jacob working in the crop.

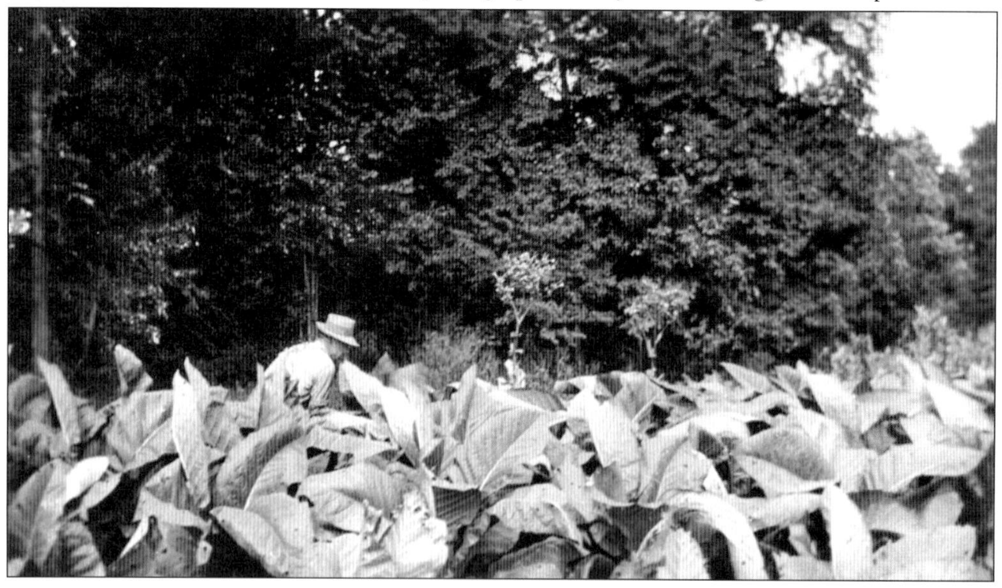

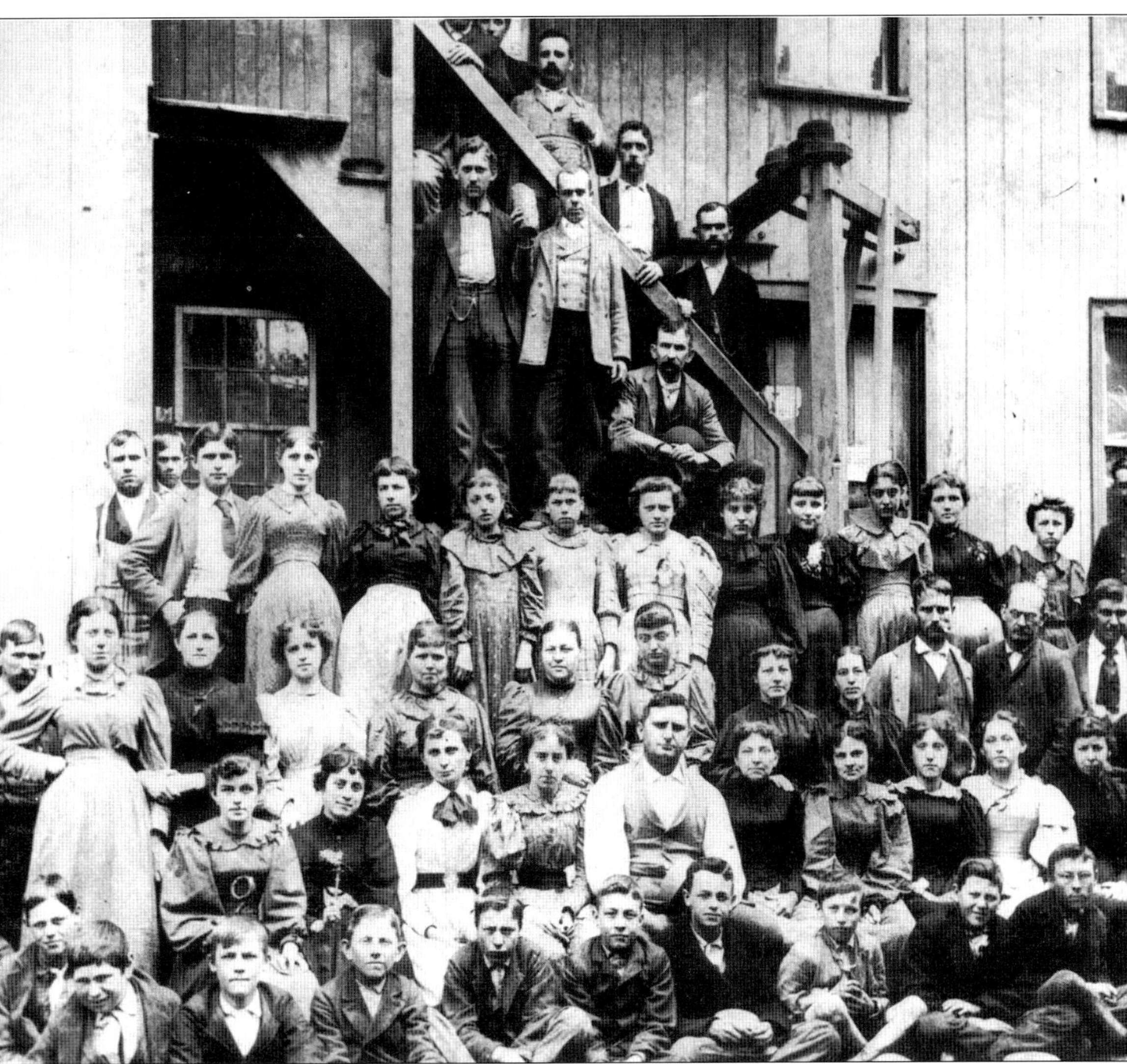

The workers of the Empire cigar factory are said to be dressed in their Sunday best for this photograph. Notice that many of the workers are actually very young children. The man with his hand on the railing standing on the steps is identified as the owner, Martin Kinport.

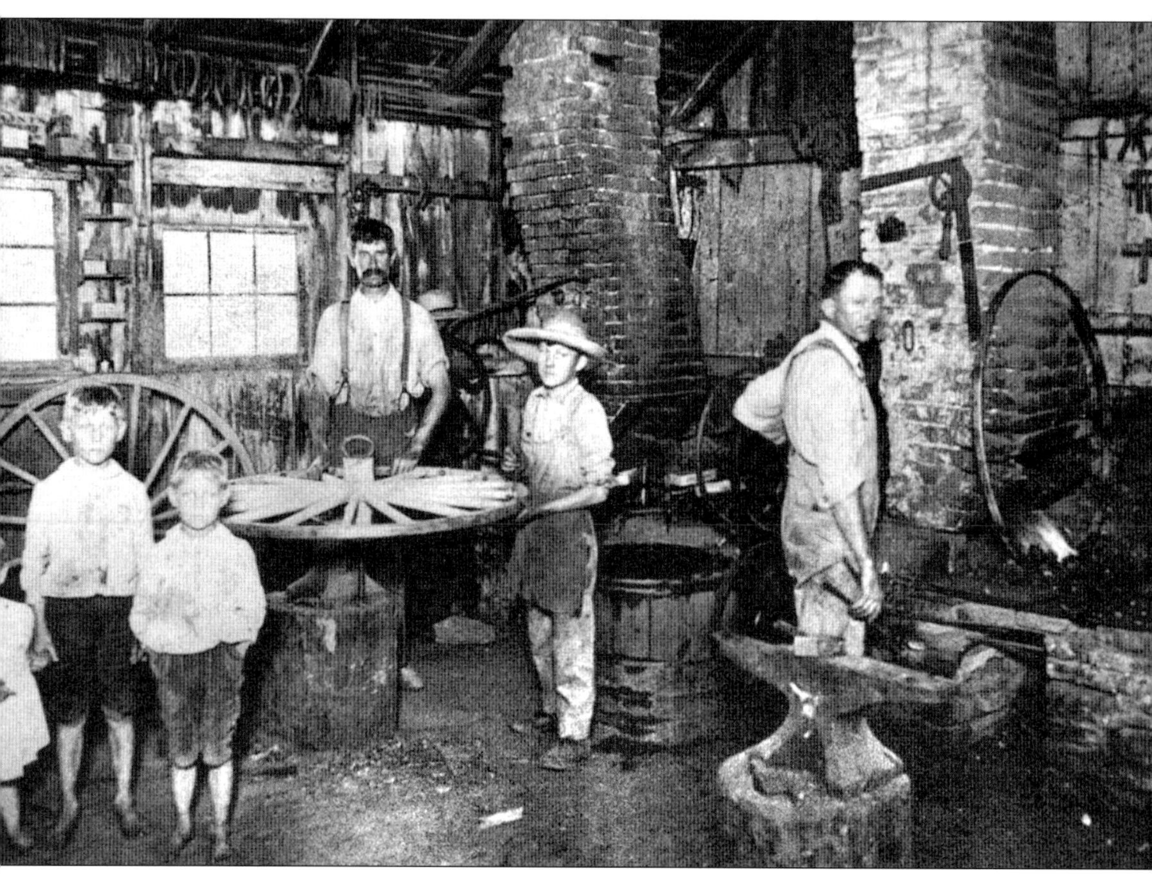

Henry Steely stands to the right of his blacksmith shop in this photograph. He was born in 1866 and passed away in 1940. This photograph was likely taken between 1900 and 1920. Notice that the children are barefoot.

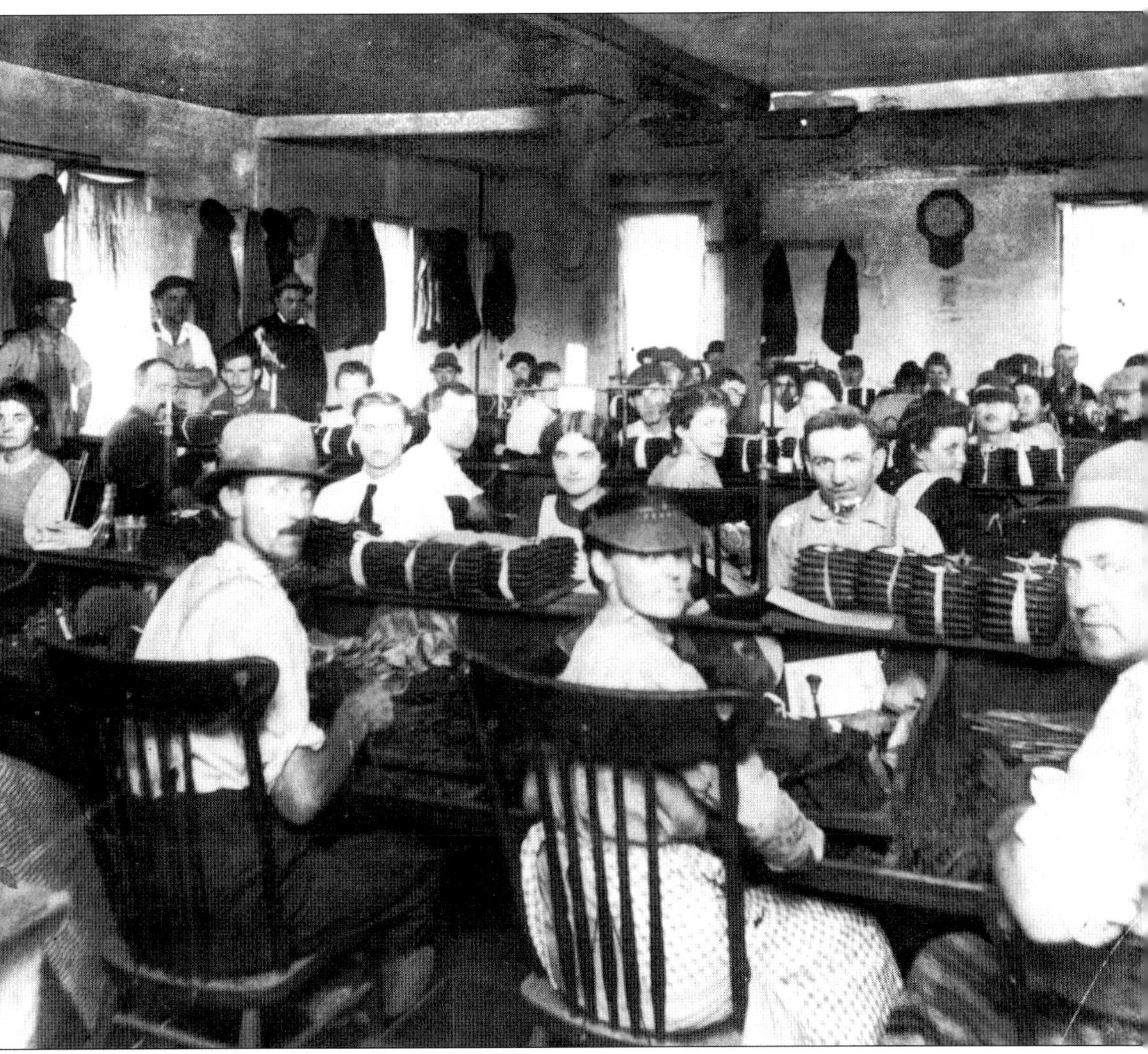

Workers in the Kinport's cigar factory are seen in this photograph from 1910. There are tobacco leaves being rolled at each station, and the finished cigars sit atop each station. The employees hung their coats and hats around the perimeter of the room. This style of hanging belongings is still often found in the authentic older farmhouses of the area and can be found in kitchens and living rooms as well.

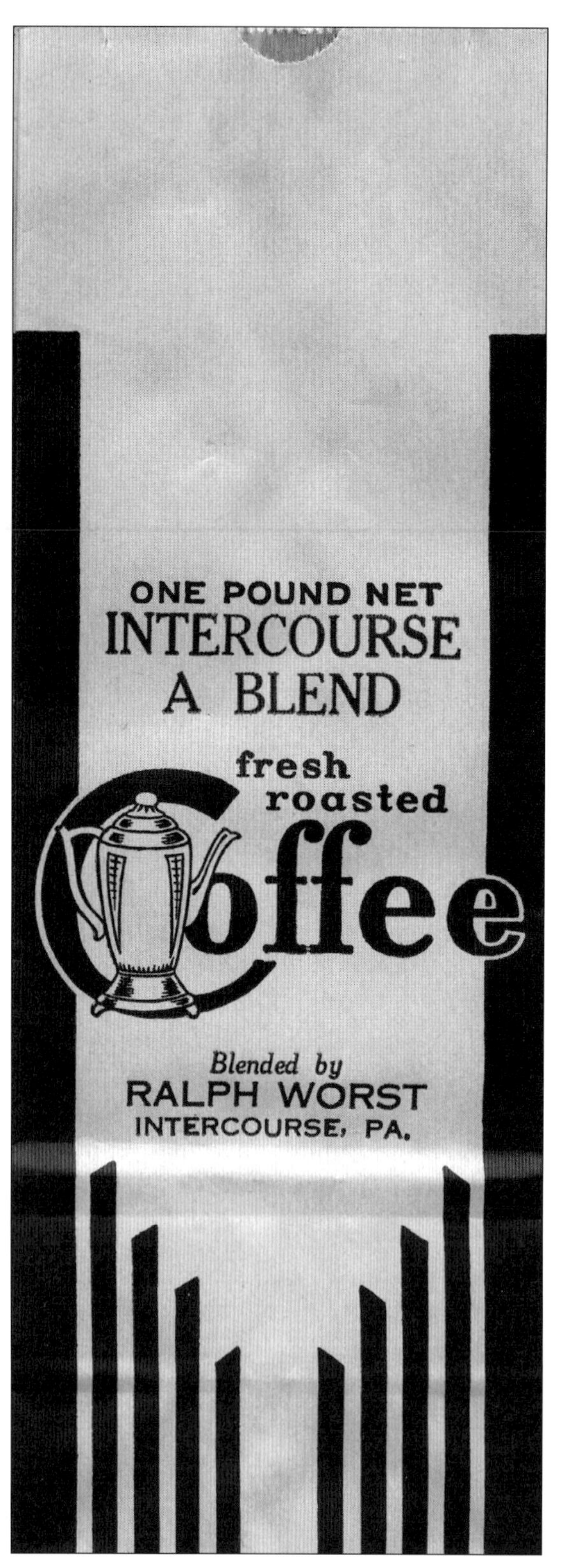

The date of this Ralph Worst coffee bag, which is in great condition, is unknown.

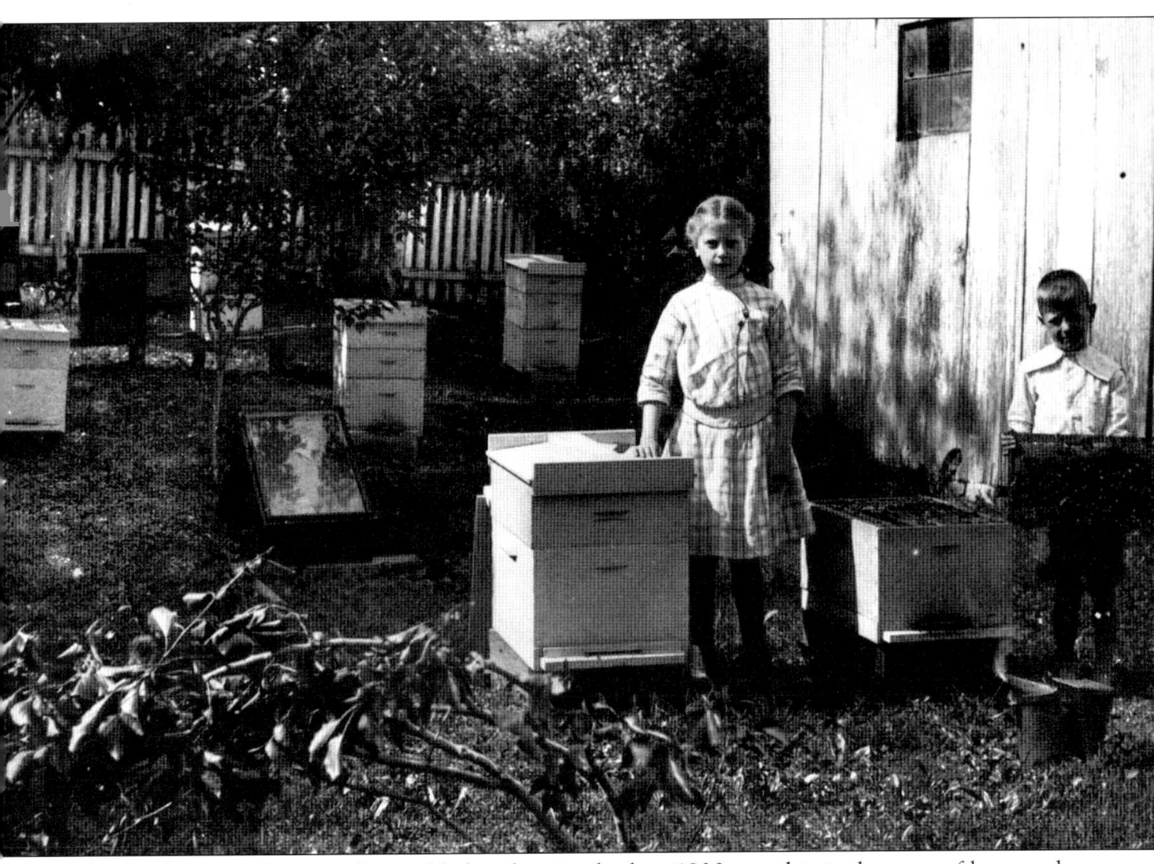

This beekeeping photograph was likely taken in the late 1800s, as this is the type of box used during that time to catch swarms. Apparently neither of the children has bee allergies, since the boy is casually holding a screen of bees. Queen bees in that time were fairly expensive compared to other costs of the time. For example, gas was often below 22¢ a gallon, where one queen bee cost between 40¢ to up to $1, depending upon the type of bee. Extracting honey was sometimes executed by using a warm knife.

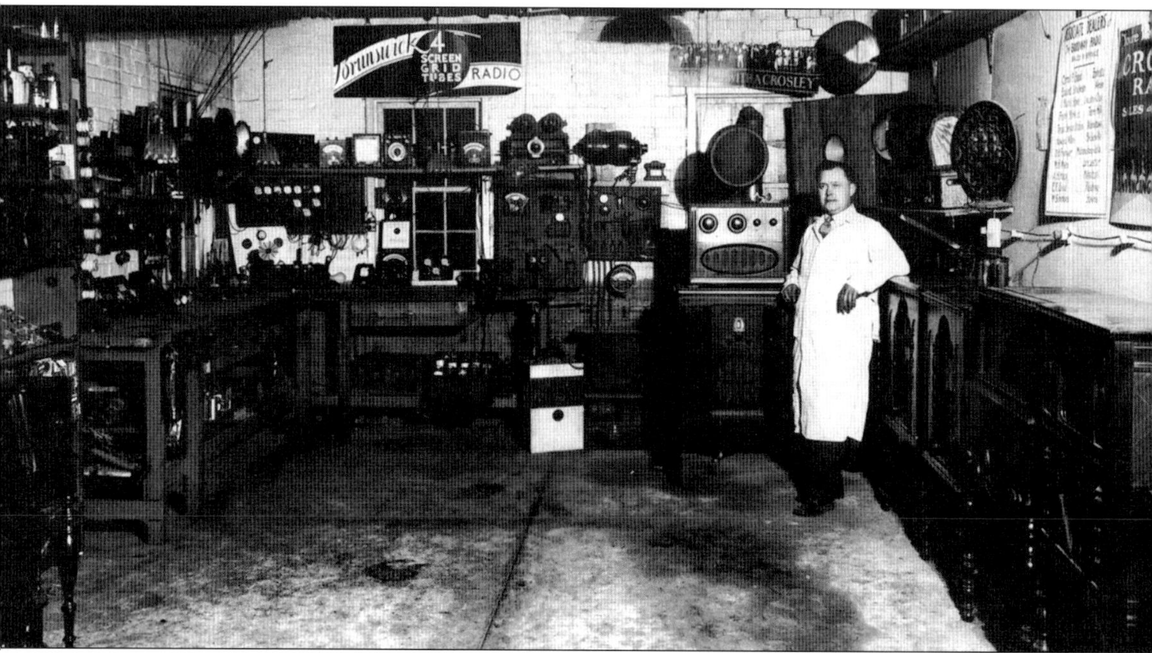

This 1930 photograph shows a business that changed often with technology but maintained the same result: music. The music store was owned by Earl C. Good and was called Good Way Sound. The business may have been located in a small warehouse or garage, as the walls and floor seem very primitive even for that era. There are many Crosley radios, as well as a sign for the radios to the right of the photograph. Most of the more fancy Crosley radios are located on the right side of the store. Remember that this was the only means of broadcasting at the time, and many people depended upon their radios for wartime updates. The Crosleys on the right likely cost between $100 and $200 each, so only well-to-do families could afford them. In time, less expensive versions were available for about $35.

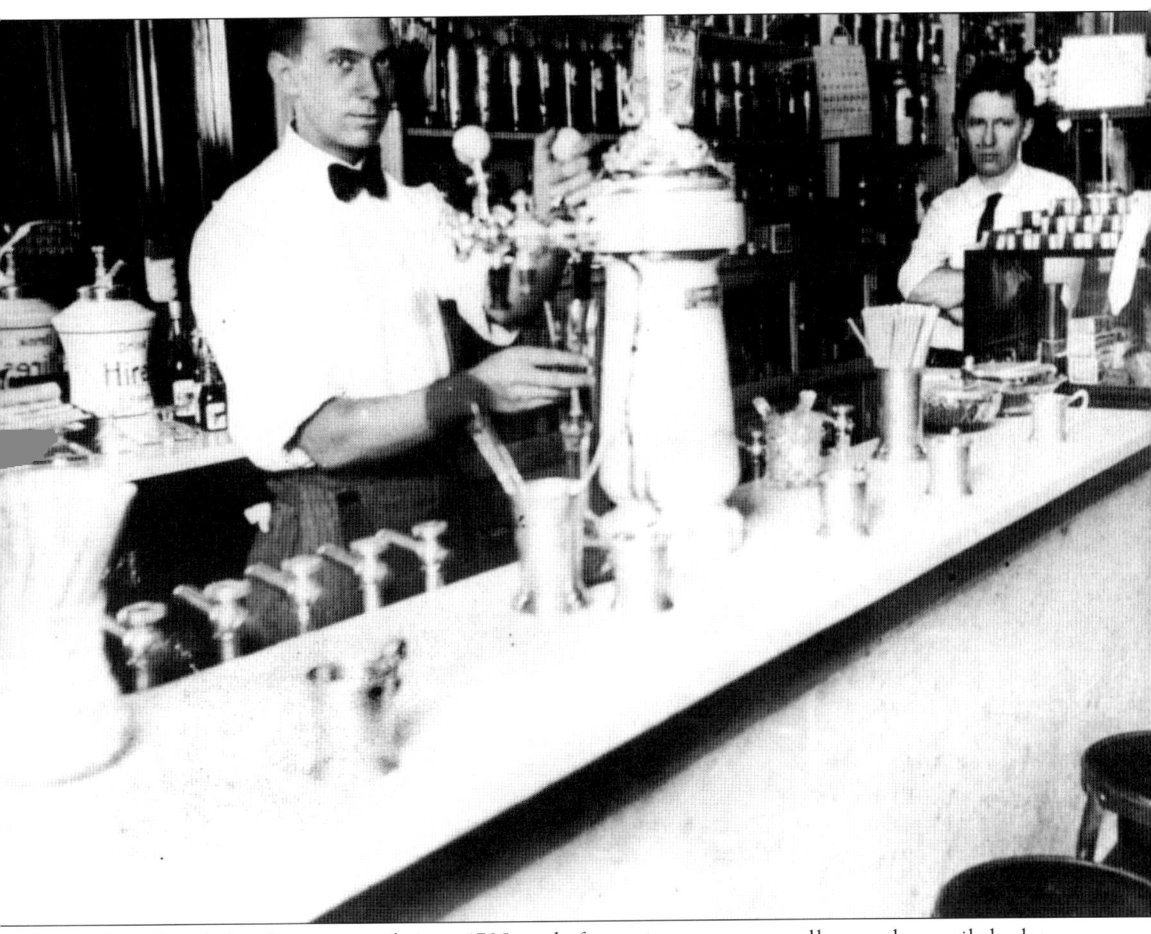

Although soda has been around since 1798, soda fountains were not really popular until the late 1880s. This photograph, taken in 1925, shows the typical home of a soda fountain, in a pharmacy. This happens to be the Royer Drug Store. Shown here are Edwin Spangler and John Weaver. The cost of a soda at this time was less than 10¢ per drink.

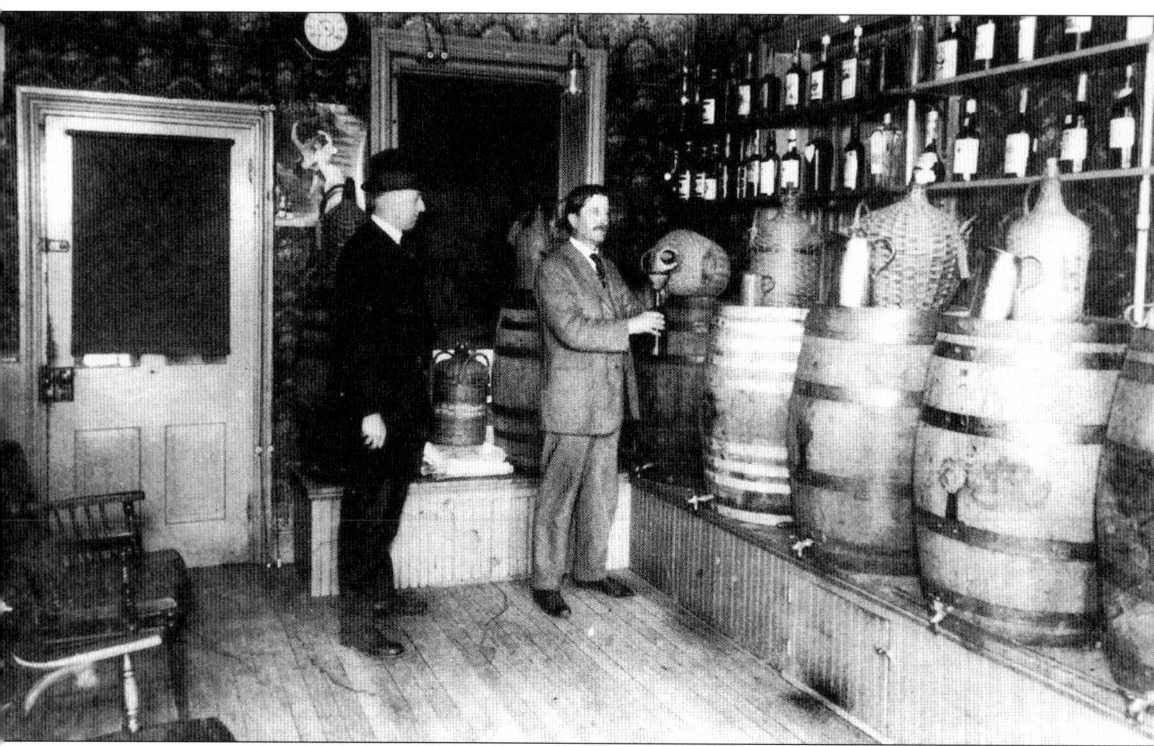

J. Yost and Robert Carter are shown in their liquor store. The establishment was probably not the only place to purchase alcohol, as most drugstores also sold medicinal whisky.

John Ocker Sr. poses in front of the Old Glory store, which he owned. General stores often looked similar regardless of where they were in the country. They provided food, hardware, sometimes mail, and often medicine. Many provided fabric as well. They were often seen in new communities where populations were growing. Some general stores even issued marriage licenses. It appears, however, that this store was strictly a grocery store. They utilized the outside of the store to showcase fresh fruit and vegetables.

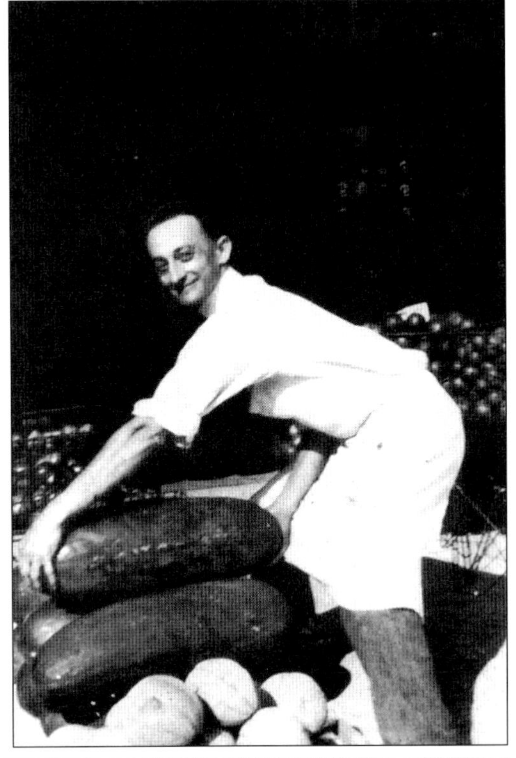

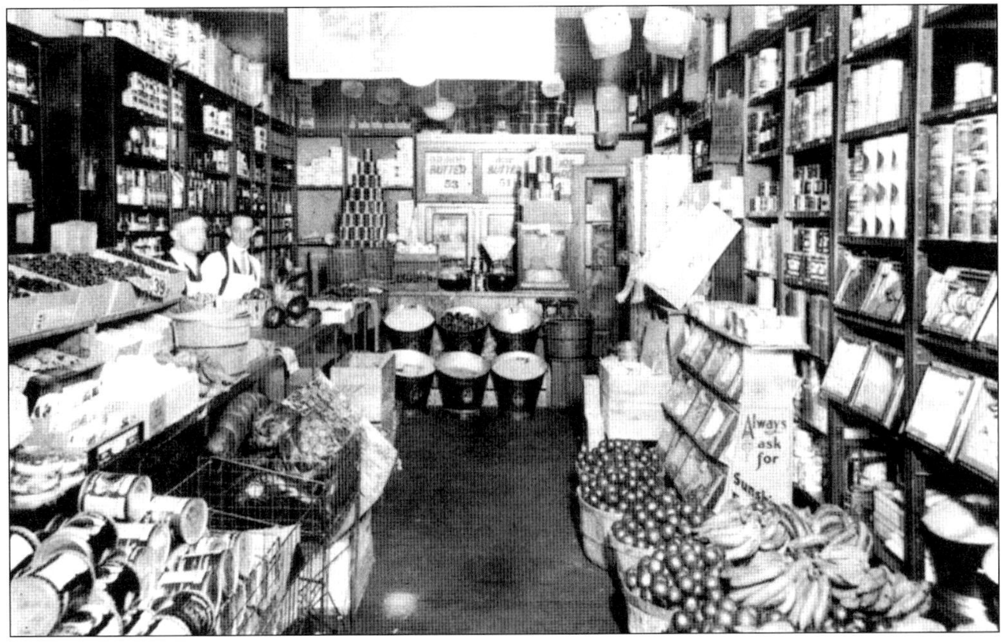

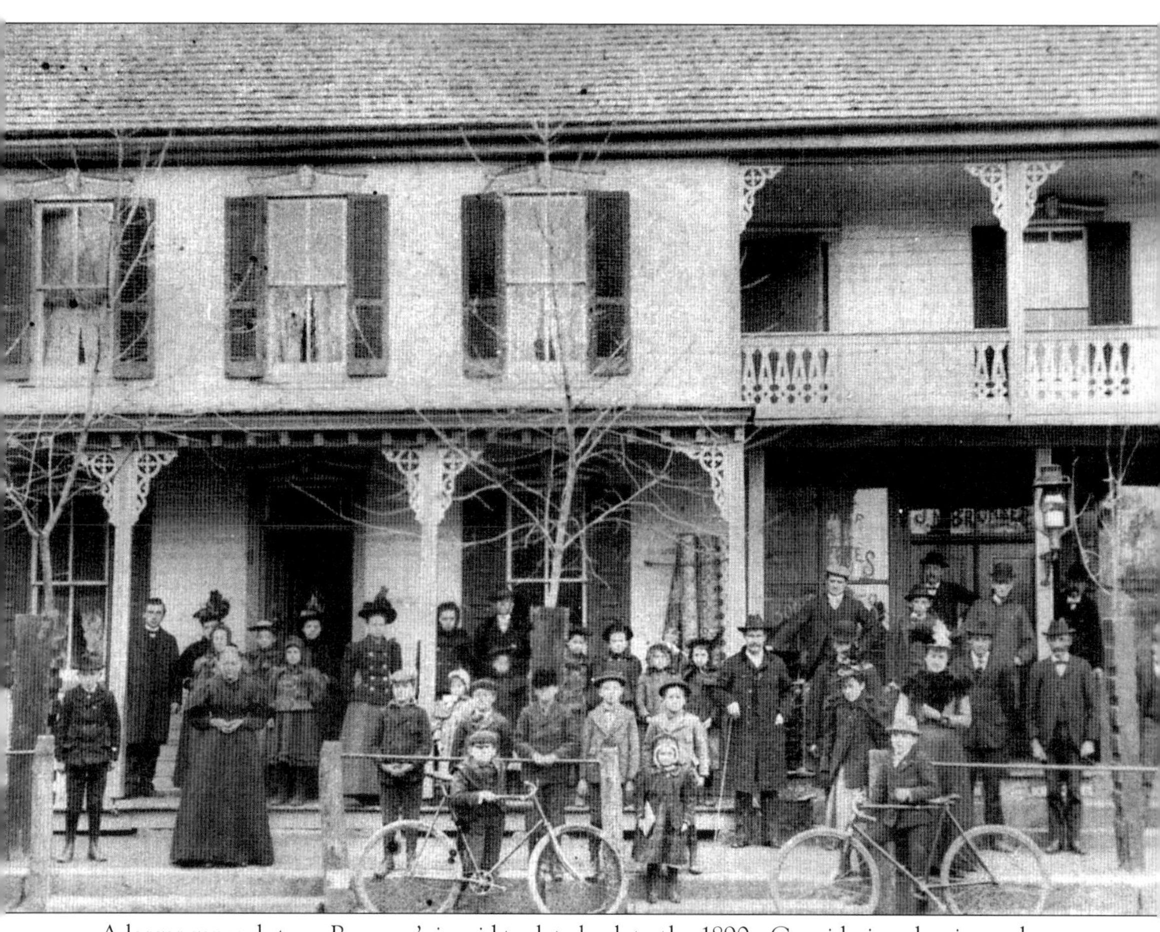

A larger general store, Brunner's is said to date back to the 1890s. Considering the size and name of the store, Brunner's General Merchandise, this store likely housed a full-service center for the community, much like a department store does today.

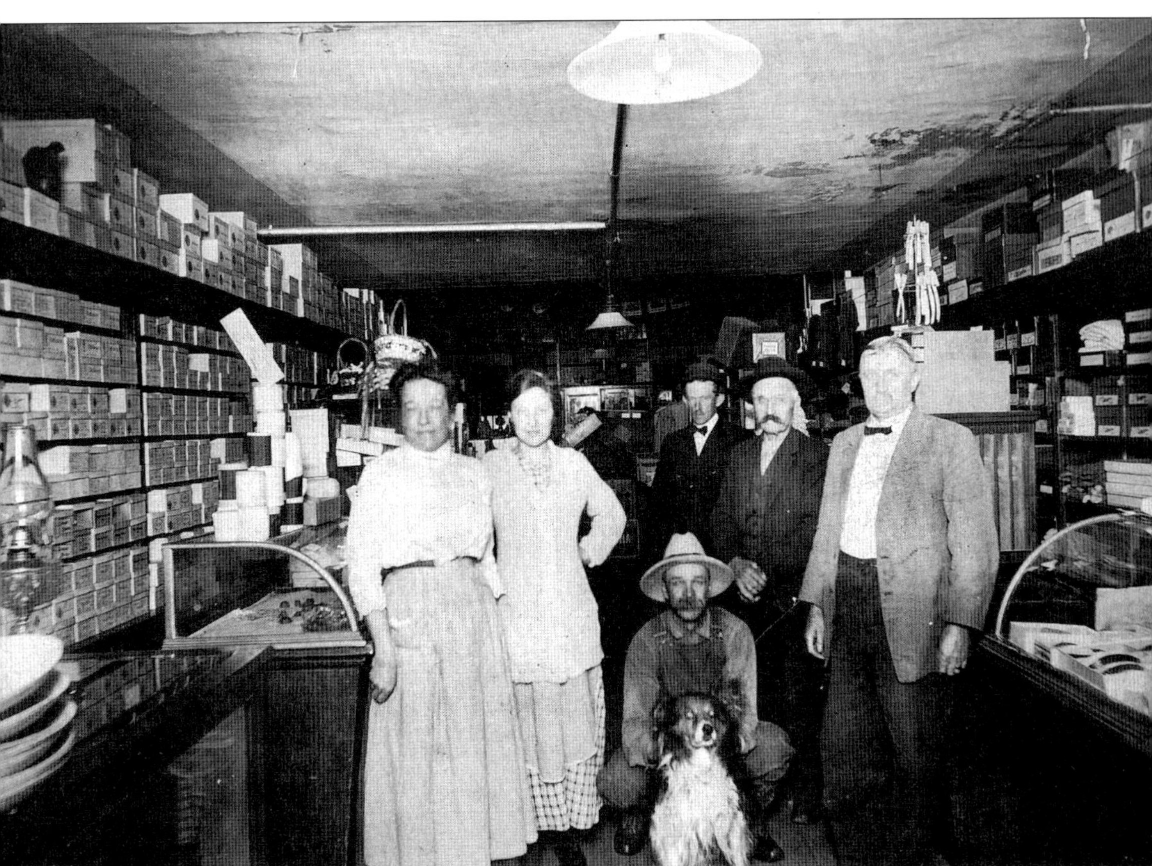

This interior view of Brunner's shows unidentified shoppers. Notice that they sell shoes, dishes, and baskets, all unrelated items in a close proximity. Also, a variety of clients or individuals seems to be portrayed, from businessmen and farmers to women who frequent the store. Animals are also allowed in.

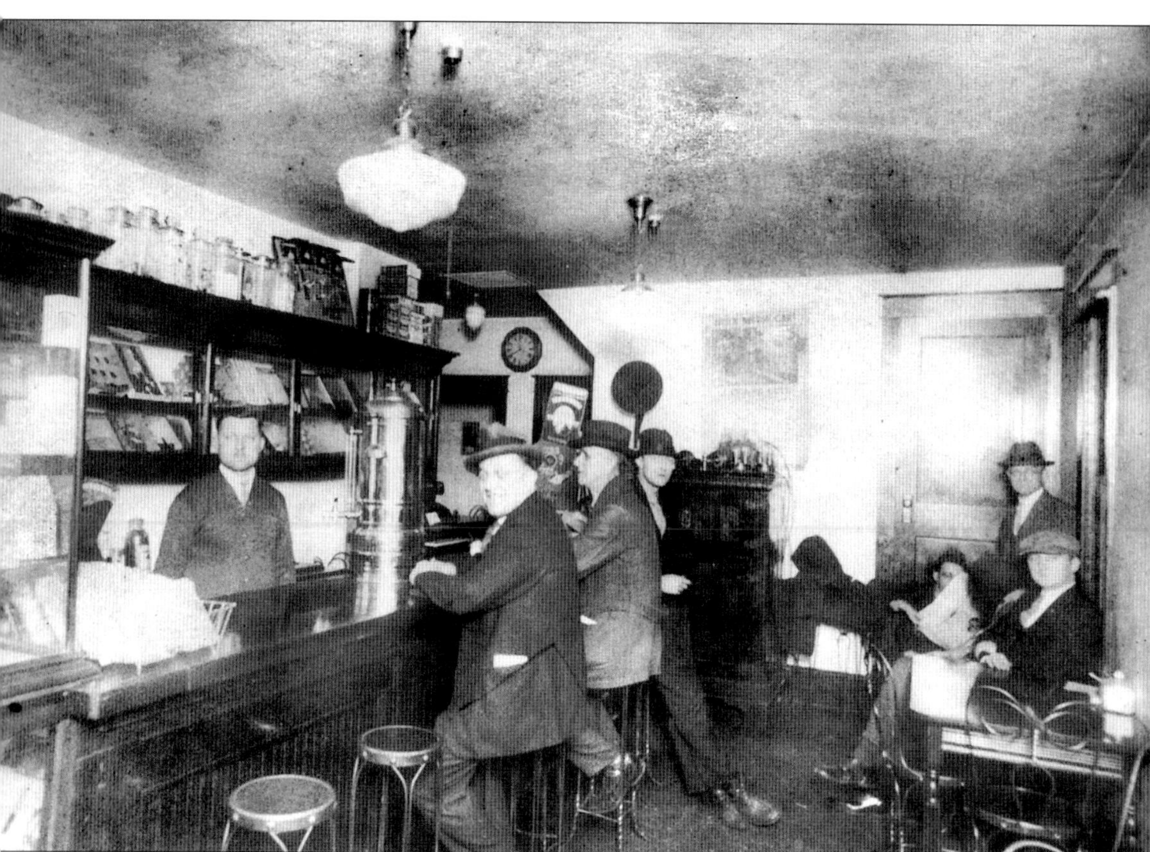

Here is a different view of the typical general store. This one is dated 1930, and the store was located on Main Street. Notice that this store also served as a restaurant. From left to right are John Fair (owner), Bill Hyman, Bill Fraser, Chester Shirk, Charles ?, Ulysses Hollinger, and Agnew Kerchner.

Application Form for

TICKET RESERVATION

PAGEANT *of* GRATITUDE

Lancaster, Penna. *June 24-25-26, 1929*

SCHEDULE OF PRICES:

Box, seating six	$30.00	Lancaster Stand	$1.50
Gratitude Stand	2.00	Susquehanna Stand	1.00
Pennsylvania Stand	1.50	Conestoga Stand	1.00

Every seat a reserved seat

Application in Person

should be made on or after Thursday, June 6, at Pageant Ticket Headquarters, located in the Union Trust Company building, 26 E. King Street.

Mail Orders

will be honored in the order received, providing the order is accompanied by *money order or check and self-addressed stamped envelope for return.* Make remittances payable to "Pageant of Gratitude." All mail orders should be addressed as follows:

T. WARREN METZGER,
c/o Groff & Wolf Co.,
26–32 N. Queen St.,
Lancaster, Pa.

Use the following form:

I enclose $......... for .... tickets at $......... each to be reserved for performance(s) checked below:

Monday, June 24 ( )

Tuesday, June 25 ( )

Wednesday, June 26 ( )

IF YOU WILL CALL FOR TICKETS PUT X HERE......

IF YOU WANT TICKETS MAILED PUT X HERE......

Name ....

Address ....

16

This is a page out of Lancaster area's 200th celebration, held in 1929. The celebration was called Pageant of Gratitude. It embraced the past inspiration, the present opportunity, and future of challenge (paraphrased from first page of the 16-page booklet) of historic Lancaster County.

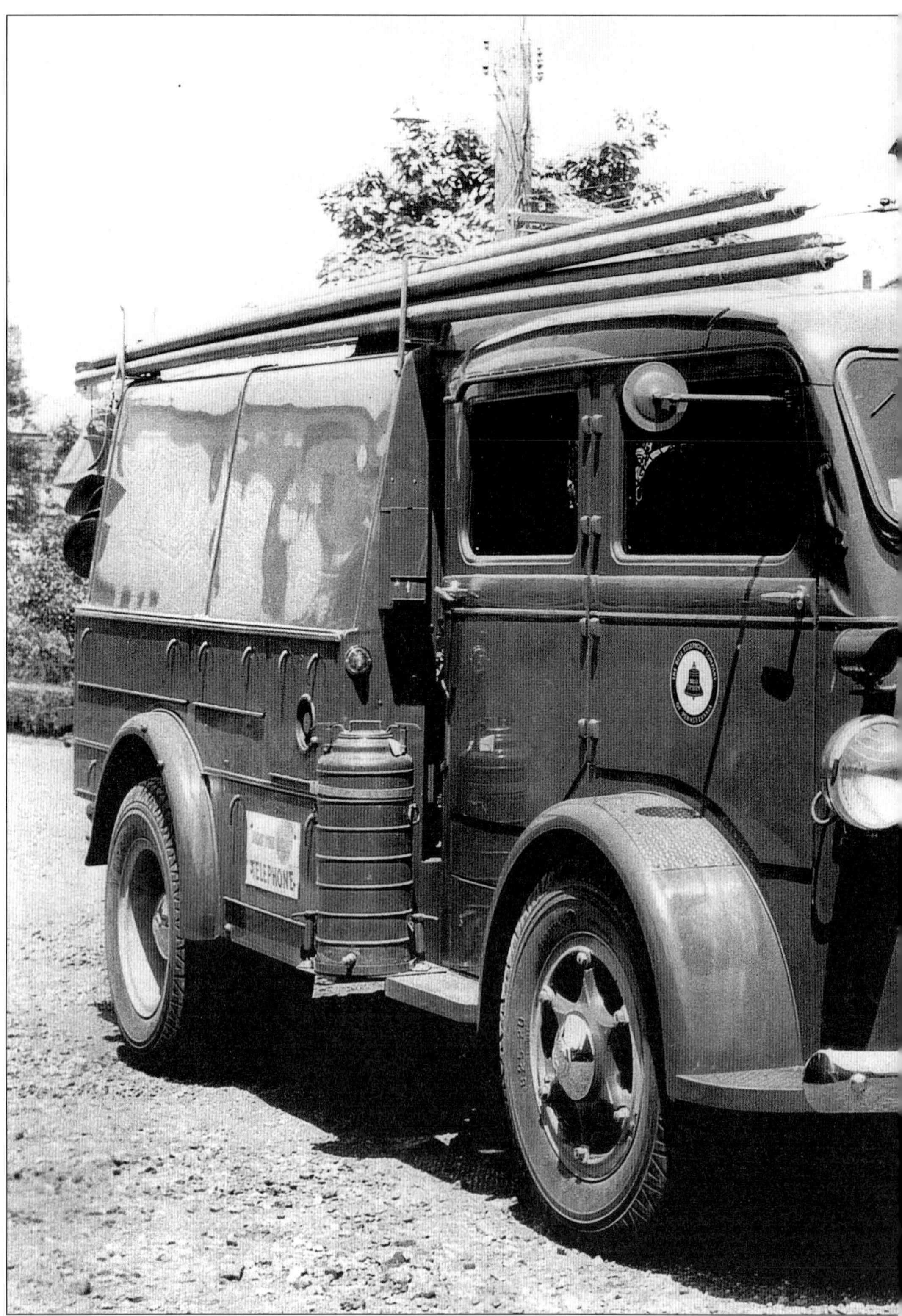
TELEPHONE

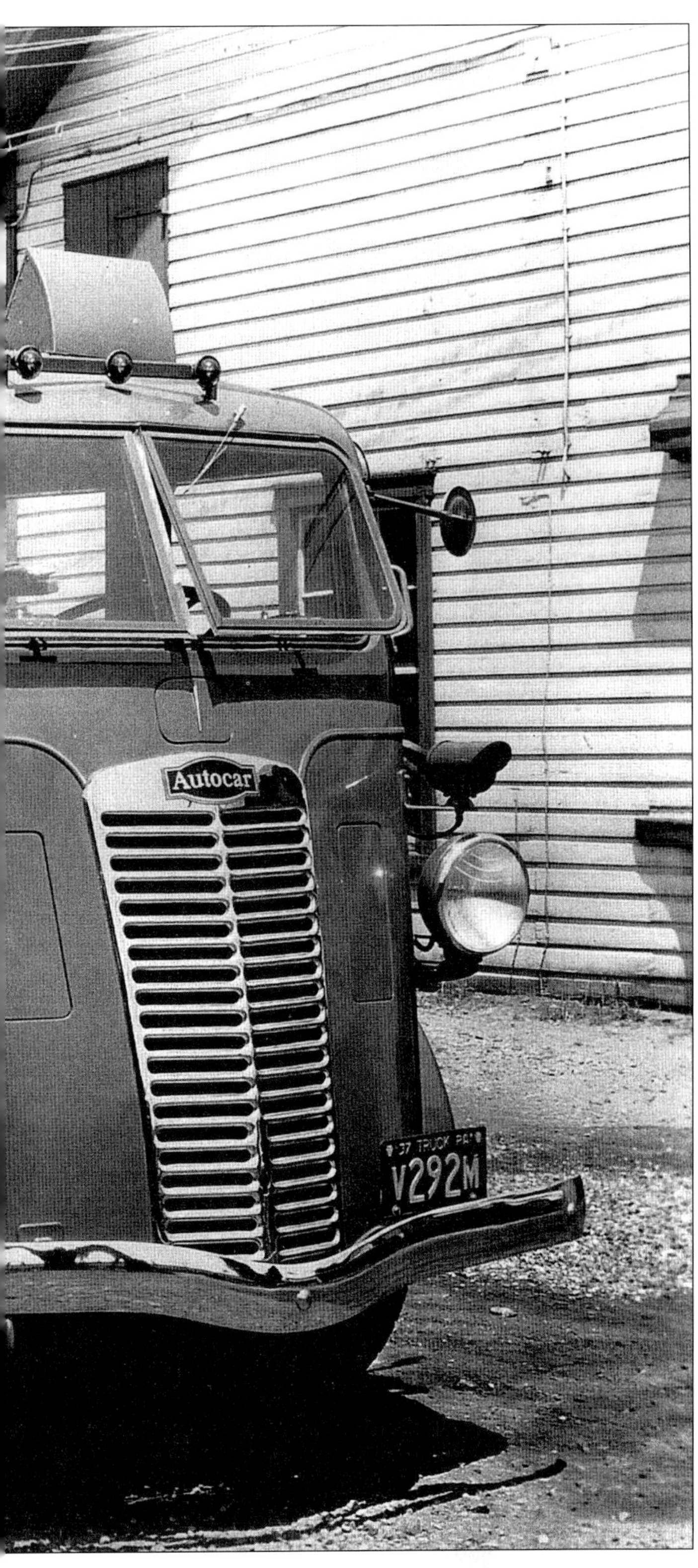

Seen here is a 1937 Bell Telephone truck. Although the telephone was developed in 1876 by Alexander Graham Bell, the Bell Telephone Company was formed a year later by Gardiner Hubbard, though Bell was affiliated. By the end of 1877, there were 3,000 telephones in service. Just 10 years after, there were over 10,000 telephones in service. The 1920s were the years of advancement for the telephone, radio, and more. In the late 1930s, as this truck showcases, the country was bouncing back from the Depression. The telephone and its conversions helped to keep some citizens working in the United States.

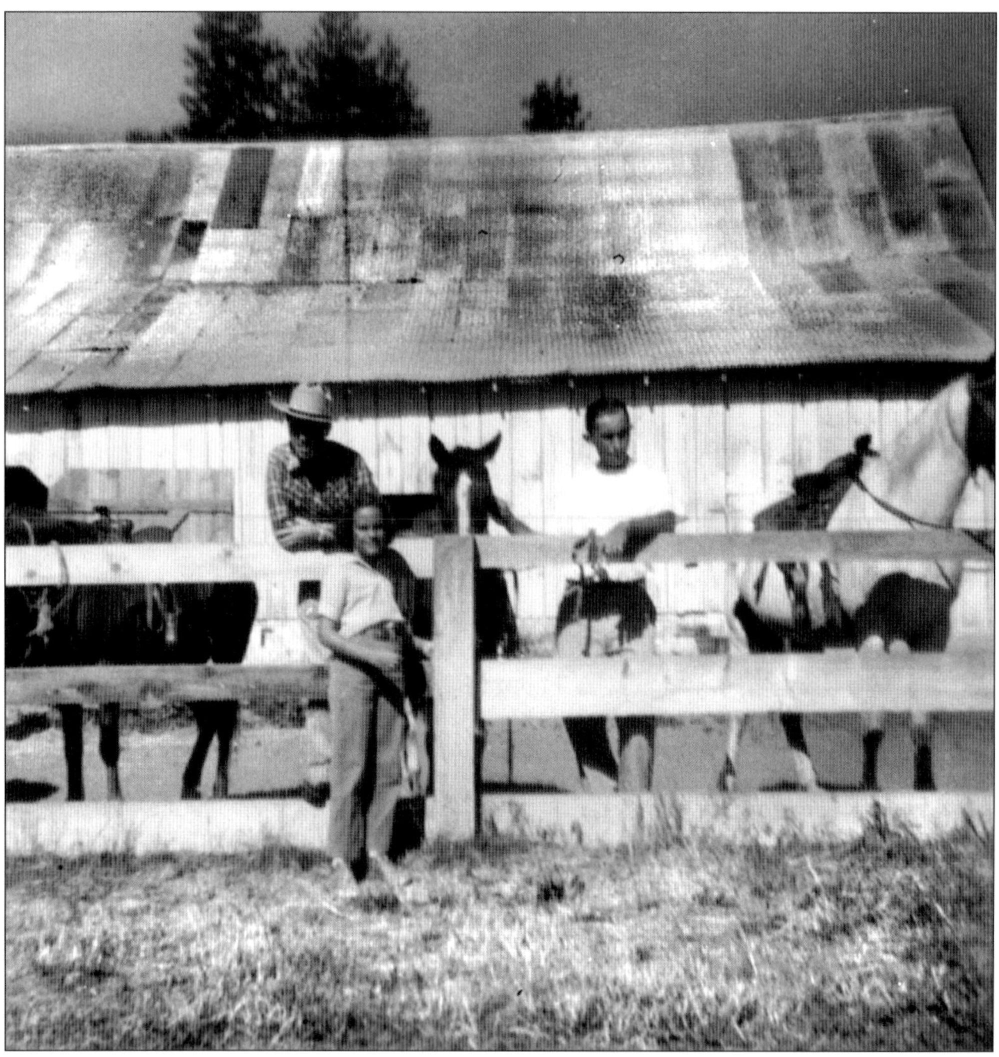

These individuals are shown at a horse farm *c.* the 1950s. Horse farming began in the 1870s as an integral aspect of community and economics. Horses were needed to pull carriages, carry out duties for farmers with crops, and haul items.

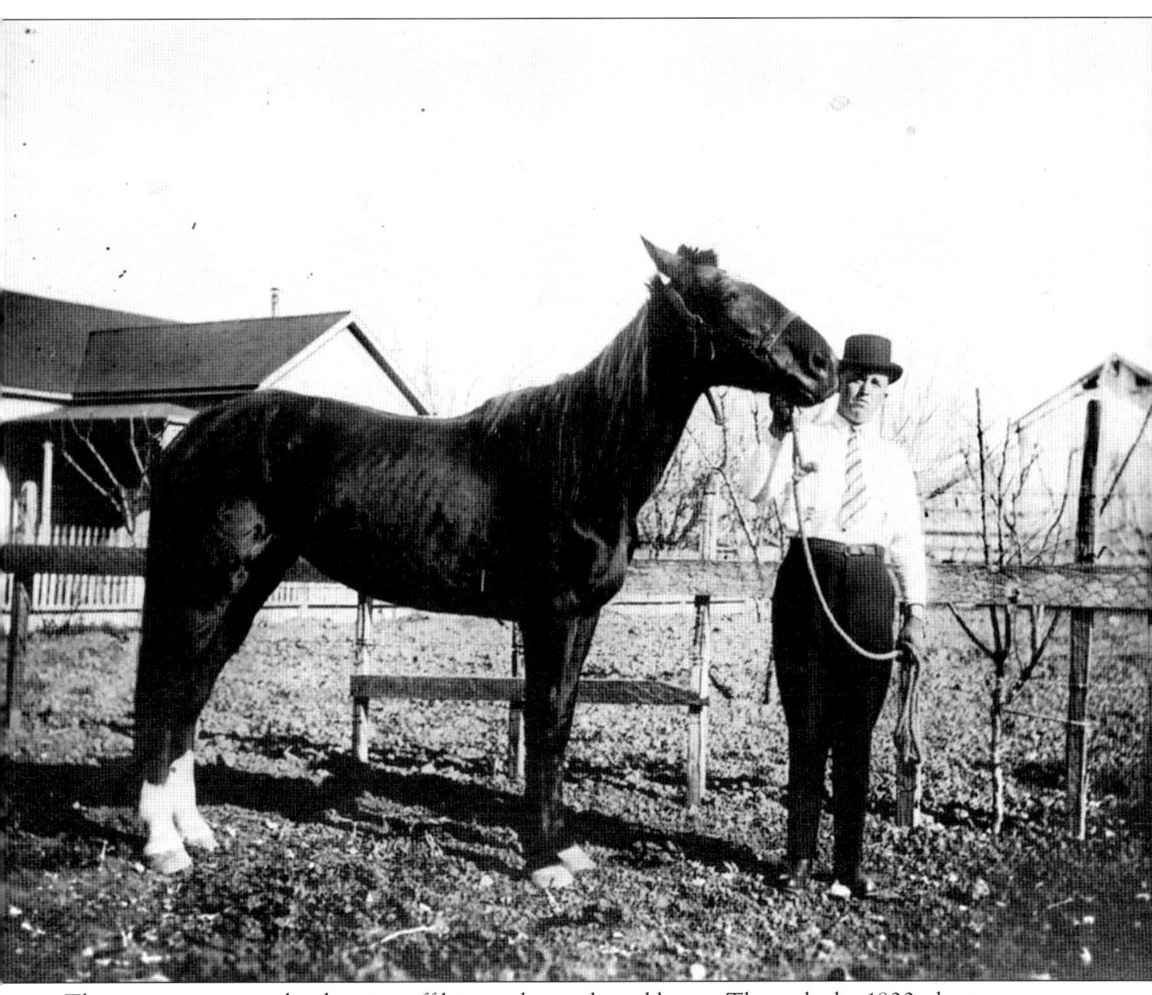

This man appears to be showing off his newly purchased horse. Through the 1800s, horses were a central aspect of life, though their place is often misunderstood in history. In this era, when visiting the country, it is not unusual to see a lone hitching post or a trough still standing even though the era during which they were used is long gone. New posts are frequently seen in this area for the Amish to hitch their horses when needed.

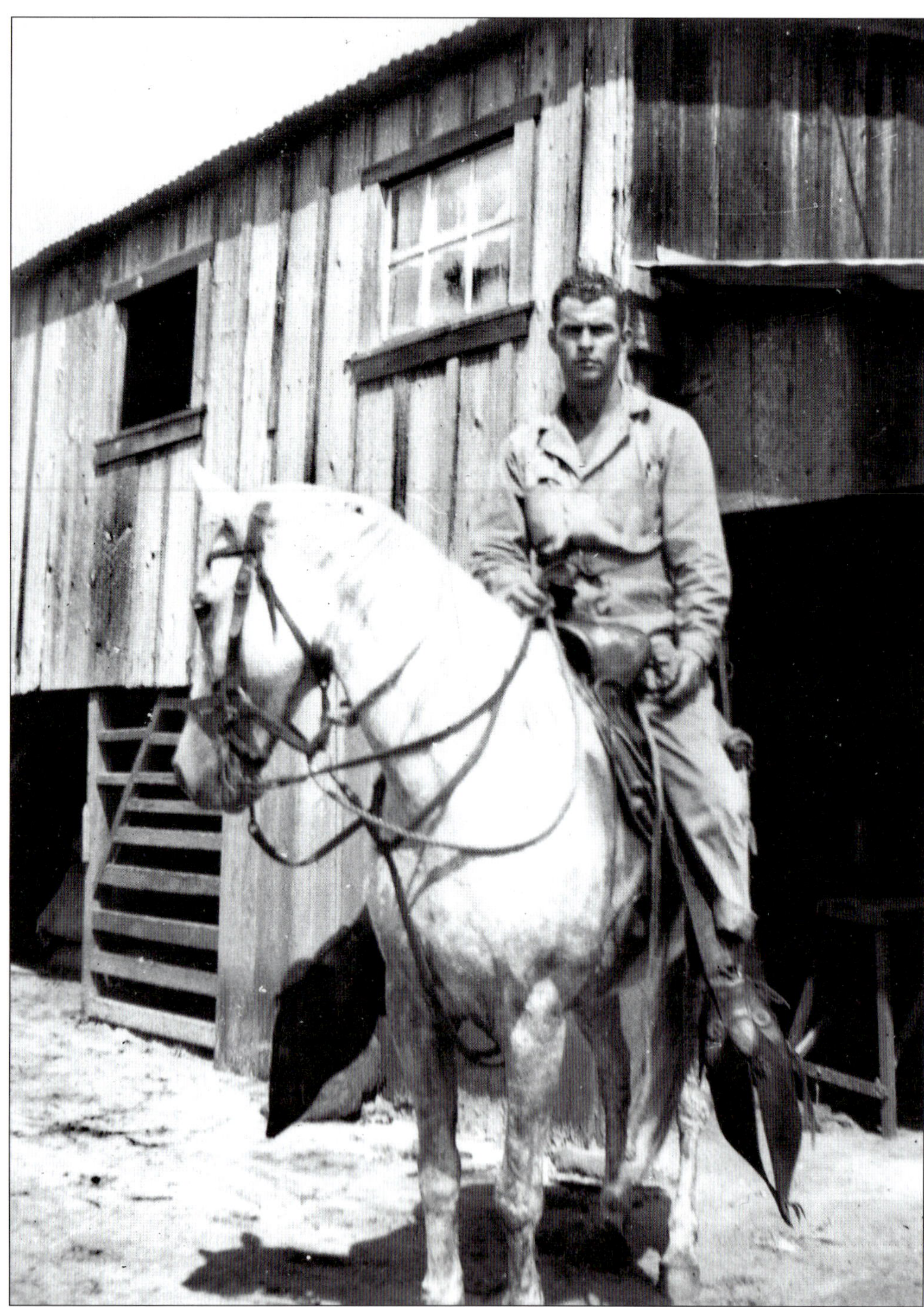

Here is another shot of a man and his horse. This man does not appear to be a farmer, as the horse is not decorated in work equipment. It was also unusual for a white horse to be a farming horse. Horses were also used in war, mainly in World War I. As many as six million horses were involved in this war. Between deaths and exports to Europe, only about 200 horses made it back to the United States; thus, horse breeding became another resulted need of the war.

Here we see an unidentified man and unidentified girl on a small horse. Notice that the man has a broom. Perhaps he is instructing and using the broom for this purpose, or she just rode up while he was cleaning the steps to the cabin to the left. Horses soon went into a transition period. After the war, technology was advancing at a rapid pace, and horses were not often used for manual labor. At this time, racing and showing horses, using horses more for sport and keeping horses as pets were much more popular.

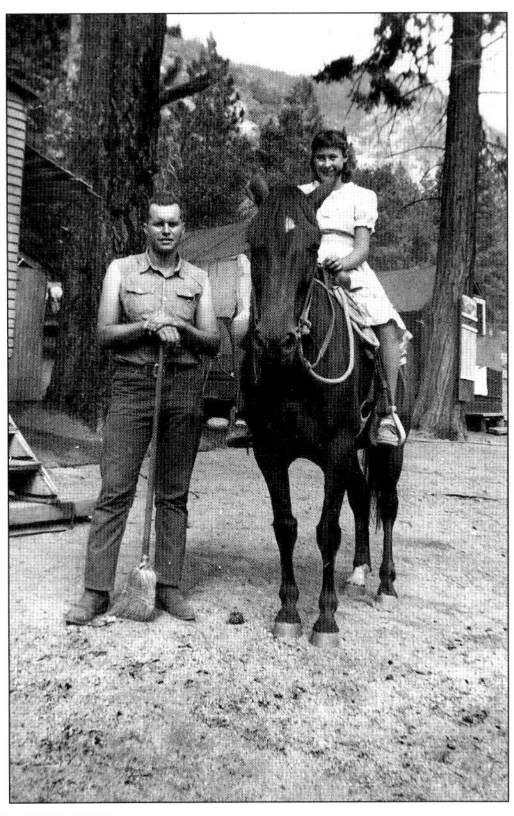

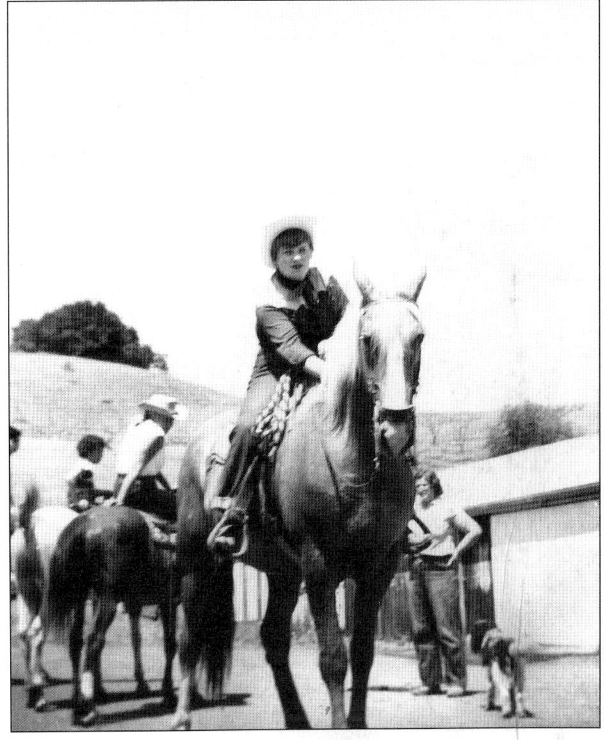

The young lady on the horse is identified simply as Barbara, and the horse is Duke. This appears to be a training lesson or a show of some sort. Today, very chic apartment or condominium houses often are constructed out of the remnants of old carriage houses. Horses were extremely important for the families and businesses of the region. Horses were the main source of labor for farmer's crops. Additionally, horses pulled carriages and hauled wagons filled with goods. They later pulled the early cabs.

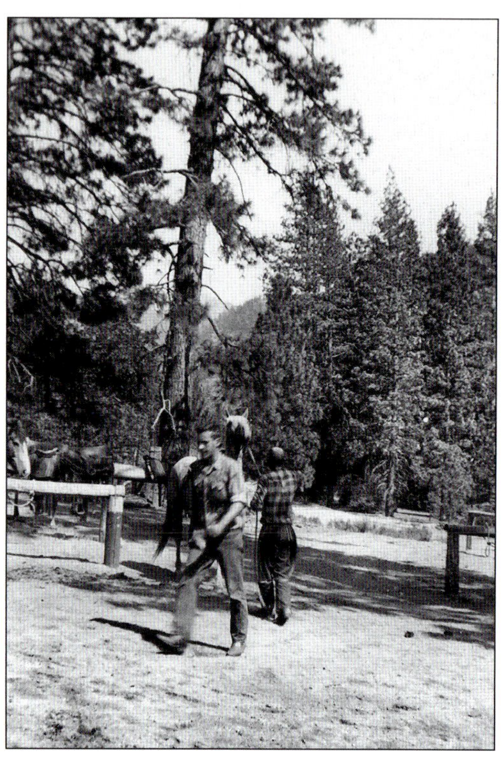

These unidentified men are at work at a horse farming establishment. Because of their presence, horses actually helped the economy, as the use of their brawn brought about a need for carriage makers, harness makers, horseshoe makers, and feed merchants. Breeding horses was a big business in the early to mid-1800s as the need for bigger, stronger horses grew from farmers and those who wanted horses to pull larger wagons and more people. Farmers soon realized that they could be one person doing the work of 30 with a few good horses.

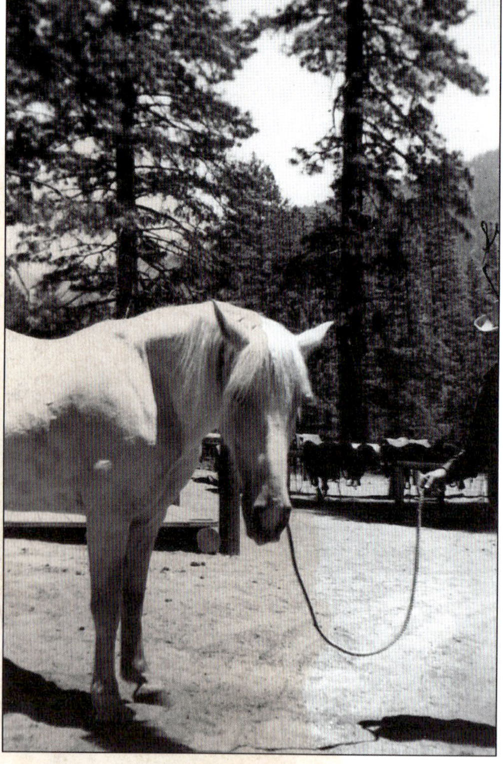

The word *suede* is written on the back of this photograph, possibly indicating that the man to the extreme right is nicknamed Suede or that he is wearing a hat of suede. In either case, this region holds a mixture of both old and new, synchronizing in harmony, not only in regard to horses, but in all of the cultures of past and present. This is the heritage of Intercourse, Leacock, Paradise and Salisbury.